Praise for
REFORM YOUR INNER MEAN GIRL

"Today, women are unhappier than ever, and we need new tools to deal with our overwhelm and our overly critical minds. Christine Arylo and Amy Ahlers have developed a transformational process that offers women important keys to greater happiness. This is deep work that is effective and accessible."

—MARCI SHIMOFF, *New York Times* bestselling author of
Happy for No Reason

"Read this book and change your life. It will explain who your Inner Mean Girl is, why she acts like she does, and how to transform her into a self-compassionate inner guide."

—KRISTIN NEFF, PHD, bestselling author of *Self Compassion*

"Christine Arylo and Amy Ahlers' deep, provocative, and fun Inner Mean Girl transformation process gives women the gift of an accessible, light-hearted experience, that shows them exactly how to wrangle their Inner Mean Girls into submission!"

—RHONDA BRITTEN, Emmy Award winner and author of *Fearless Living*

"Christine and Amy are an unmatchable team when it comes to teaching women how to stop being so hard on themselves. They are brilliant at shining the light on the shadow that has the power to disable even the most confident and successful woman."

—KRISTINE CARLSON, *New York Times* bestselling author of
Don't Sweat the Small Stuff for Women

"Amy and Christine are without a doubt the real deal when it comes to helping women to break free of the self-sabotaging voice of the inner critic. They are truly masterful!"

—ALEXIS NEELY, new economy finance expert

"The Inner Mean Girl work is essential to the development of the feminine psyche. Many books have been written about how to navigate the inner dialogue of women, so why are we still so hard on ourselves? This book holds the key to unlock that mystery. I have witnessed thousands of women's lives transformed as a result."

—SHILOH SOPHIA, artist and founder of Cosmic Cowgirls

"This book is literally medicine for the body, mind, and soul. Imagine, a book that might improve your longevity while freeing you from the beasts of negativity that inhabit your mind! Just what the doctor ordered."

—LISSA RANKIN, MD, *New York Times* bestselling author of *Mind Over Medicine*

"This book offers every woman a tremendous gift of freedom from self-judgment and unrealistic expectations, so she can be free to express her true self, live her heartfelt dreams, and be empowered to make them come true!"

—CHRISTINE HASSLER, bestselling author of *Expectation Hangover*

"Ahlers and Arylo are changing the way people relate to their inner critics, and people think and act more powerfully as a result. After over twenty-five years of teaching and practicing self empowerment, I heartily recommend their work and have witnessed the resulting transformations firsthand."

—SARK (Susan Ariel Rainbow Kennedy), bestselling author and artist

"If you have an internal 'mean girl' who has you feeling down about your situation, your past, your future, and your chance for happiness, Amy Ahlers and Christine Arylo are just the kind of people who can pull you back up. Use this book as a coach, a comforter, a BFF, and a path to a more joyful life."

—MARTHA BECK, *New York Times* bestselling author and columnist for *O, The Oprah Magazine*

AMY AHLERS & CHRISTINE ARYLO

REFORM YOUR

INNER MEAN GiRL

7 STEPS TO STOP BULLYING YOURSELF AND START LO♥ING YOURSELF

ATRIA BOOKS
New York London Toronto Sydney New Delhi

 BEYOND WORDS
Hillsboro, Oregon

ATRIA BOOKS
An Imprint of Simon & Schuster, Inc.
1230 Avenue of the Americas
New York, NY 10020

BEYOND WORDS
20827 N.W. Cornell Road, Suite 500
Hillsboro, Oregon 97124-9808
503-531-8700 / 503-531-8773 fax
www.beyondword.com

Managing editor: Lindsay S. Brown
Editors: Gretchen Stelter, Emily Han
Copyeditor: Michelle Blair
Proofreader: Kristin Thiel
Cover design: Sara Blum, Devon Smith
Interior design: Devon Smith
Composition: William H. Brunson Typography Services

First Atria Books/Beyond Words hardcover edition April 2015

For more information about special discounts for bulk purchases, please contact Simon & Schuster Special Sales at 1-866-506-1949 or business@simonandschuster.com.

The Simon & Schuster Speakers Bureau can bring authors to your live event. For more information or to book an event, contact the Simon & Schuster Speakers Bureau at 1-866-248-3049 or visit our website at www.simonspeakers.com.

Manufactured in the United States of America

10 9 8 7 6 5 4 3 2 1

Library of Congress Cataloging-in-Publication Data

Ahlers, Amy.
    Reform your inner mean girl : 7 steps to stop bullying yourself and start loving yourself /
Amy Ahlers & Christine Arylo.
        pages   cm
    1. Criticism, Personal.   2. Self-talk.   3. Self-esteem in women.   4. Self-perception.
I. Arylo, Christine, 1971–. II.   Title.
BF637.C74A45   2015
155.3'3391—dc23
                                                                        2014039917

ISBN 978-1-58270-509-5
ISBN 978-1-4767-7985-0 (ebook)

The corporate mission of Beyond Words Publishing, Inc.: *Inspire to Integrity*

For Amy's youngest daughter, Evie Rose,
Who rode the waves of this book's creation in utero—
you're a dream come true;

For Christine's goddess daughters, Lucie and Janie,
Who remind me often of both the delicateness and
the strength of our precious hearts;

And to the little girl who lives inside of you—
May she always remember that she is loved, seen, and sacred.

CONTENTS

Introduction ix

The Self-Bullying Epidemic xxi

PART I: MEET YOUR INNER MEAN GIRL

Step 1: Reveal Your Type of Inner Mean Girl 3

Step 2: Expose Your Inner Mean Girl's
Tricks and Triggers 51

Step 3: Discover What Motivates Your
Inner Mean Girl 87

Inspired
Action: Bring Your Inner Mean Girl to Life—
Make Your Inner Mean Girl Exposé 111

PART II: MEET YOUR INNER WISDOM

Step 4: Turn Up the Volume on Your Inner Wisdom 119

Step 5: Make Your Inner Wisdom Your
Most Trusted Ally 145

Inspired
Action: Create a Sacred Self-Love Altar—
Claim Sacred Space for Yourself 169

CONTENTS

PART III: MAKE SHIFT HAPPEN

Step 6: Give Up Self-Bullying for Good   175

Step 7: Assign Your Inner Mean Girl Her New Job   199

Inspired

Action: Put Your Inner Mean Girl and Inner Wisdom
to Work for You—Commit to a Breakthrough   229

Conclusion: An Invitation to Join the Self-Love Revolution   237

Acknowledgments   241

The Inner Mean Girl Hall of Fame   243

Superpower

Toolshed: Instant Inner Mean Girl Deactivators and
Inner Wisdom Strengtheners   252

Notes   262

About the Authors   264

INTRODUCTION

Mean girls. You've see them on reality TV and on the movie screen—women tearing each other down to get a man, win the contest, or get ahead. You've read about them in the tabloids, quasi-celebrity sparring matches fueled by who said what about whom. And like most women on the planet, you've likely tangled with a few yourself—mean girls from your childhood playground and classroom and mean girls in grown women's bodies who now show up in your neighborhood, the conference room or PTA meeting, or as a frenemy inside your circle of friends. We have all been on the receiving end of not-so-nice words or actions coming from another girl or woman. As a result, for sheer emotional protection, we've learned to develop survival skills, and when we can, we steer clear.

But there is one type of mean girl that no woman escapes from, one who has more power than any other. In less than a minute, she can sabotage you; make you feel like crap about yourself; trigger feelings of fear, stress, and guilt; and even diminish every success you've worked for. Who is this all-powerful mean girl? And for heaven's sake, why can't you just avoid her? Because this mean girl lives inside of you; she is your *Inner* Mean Girl™.

Just like the bully on the playground or in the conference room, there is a force within you that fills your mind with negative thoughts, pushes you to take actions that are not in your best interest, and undermines you any chance she gets. She is the one that bullies, sabotages, criticizes, and judges you; the one who puts enormous pressure on you to be perfect, do it all, and keep it all together on the outside no matter how much you are falling apart on the inside. You might recognize her by the thoughts she fills your mind with, such as:

"YOU DON'T HAVE TIME TO REST. YOU SHOULD BE DOING MORE."
"DON'T EVEN BOTHER TRYING. YOU WILL JUST FAIL."
"YOU'LL BE ALONE FOREVER. NO ONE WILL EVER REALLY LOVE YOU."
"TAKING CARE OF YOURSELF IS SELFISH. YOU HAVE TO TAKE CARE OF OTHERS FIRST."
"LOOK AT WHAT SHE'S DOING! WHY AREN'T YOU THAT SUCCESSFUL/PRETTY/TALENTED?"
"YOU ARE SUCH A FRAUD. YOU DON'T REALLY KNOW WHAT YOU ARE DOING."

Ugh, we know. Thoughts like these don't feel good. The truth is that the Inner Mean Girl, just like an outer mean girl, hurts. But we have two pieces of good news. First, you are not alone; all women have an Inner Mean Girl. Second, while you may not be able to escape or kill off this annoying inner force, you can reform her. Yes, just like you wished someone might have sent that mean girl in grade school, high school, or college away to some kind of reform school for bullies, you can take your Inner Mean Girl to reform school and transform the self-bullying and self-sabotaging parts of you and free up a force within that is even more powerful—your *Inner Wisdom*.

Your Inner Wisdom is that wise, supportive, loving, divinely con-nected force within who always acts in your best interest and always tells you the truth. She's been with you since the moment you were born, but over the years, due to lots of social conditioning and outside influences, her voice has been muffled by the rants of your Inner Mean Girl, and she's taken a backseat.

It's important for you to know that both of these forces are always at play within you, driving your choices, determining your emotional state, running the stories and thoughts in your head. At times, it can feel like a tug-of-war going on inside. And usually, especially in high-stress or high-stakes situations, your fear-inducing Inner Mean Girl wins over your calm, wise, centered Inner Wisdom. That, however, is about to change.

Up until now, you may not have had the tools you needed to distinguish between these two internal forces so that you could consciously put your Inner Wisdom in charge of your thoughts, emotions, and choices. Even if you've worked with your inner critic in the past, women tell us that when they go beyond the idea of an inner critic to finally identify and reveal their Inner Mean Girls and create actual *relationships* with them—as well as with their Inner Wisdoms—they experience breakthroughs like never before. We believe this is because for women, that critical, sabotaging, stress-creating force inside feels much more personal than a gremlin-like monster or an intellectual concept like a saboteur or a critic. When you've been attacked by an outer mean girl, you feel hurt, and the same is true when your Inner Mean Girl attacks. The only difference is that you are hurting yourself.

In the pages that follow, you will take seven powerful, proven steps to reform your Inner Mean Girl and put your Inner Wisdom in charge. We've shared this approach with over thirty thousand women around the world through our Inner Mean Girl Reform School programs, workshops, and retreats—women of different races, socioeconomic backgrounds, sizes, shapes, and ages. As it turns out, Inner Mean Girls (whom we refer to also as IMGs) begin as young as age six or seven and can wreak havoc for a lifetime if not reformed. And while we've noticed that no woman seems to escape from this hurtful and sabotaging inner force, on the flip side, we've never met a woman who didn't also have a strong, brilliant Inner Wisdom.

As women learn how to shift their minds, bodies, and hearts from being controlled and affected by their Inner Mean Girls' fear and criticism to being led and supported by their Inner Wisdoms' love and guidance, we have witnessed women start new careers, move to their dream cities, write books, lose unwanted pounds, get married, create deeper friendships, leave unhealthy relationships, increase income and financial security, achieve lifelong dreams, and gain a day-to-day sense of peace, well-being, and happiness. That is the power of reforming your Inner Mean Girl and choosing to put your Inner Wisdom in charge.

How to Use This Book

We are thrilled that we get to be your guides on what is sure to be a life-changing adventure. Our lives have both transformed significantly because of the intimate relationships we have with our Inner Mean Girls and Inner Wisdoms today. Now reformed, our IMGs play supportive roles in our lives, and our Inner Wisdoms are our go-to girls, guiding our choices, managing our thoughts, and monitoring our emotions.

The first action for you to take to get this transformation started is to read the foundational chapter, which will provide you with essential context about your Inner Mean Girl. Then in step one of this seven-step adventure, we'll introduce you to thirteen common archetypes of Inner Mean Girls. You see, not all IMGs are mean and cruel—some appear sweet, some quite optimistic, and others seem totally rational. Armed with incredible new insight, in step two, you will meet your personal IMG face-to-face and uncover her Big Fat Lies, which are the thoughts and judgments she fills your head with. In step three, you will learn what motivates your IMG and why you haven't been able, until now, to stop the self-bullying, self-sabotaging thoughts and actions. In steps four and five, you will meet your Inner Wisdom, for the first time, or, if you already are familiar with this inner force, you will deepen your relationship. We will share practical, effective ways for distinguishing between these two inner forces and how you can change your thoughts and emotions from sabotaging to supportive, from critical to compassionate, and from pressure filled to peace-full.

By the time you hit steps six and seven, you will be prepared to fire your Inner Mean Girl and hire your Inner Wisdom. While you may want to ship your IMG into exile, that tactic just doesn't work—she always finds a way back and usually comes back stronger and meaner. Instead, we will show you how to transform your IMG so she can work for you instead of against you. And you'll see that just like mean girls on the playground, all your Inner Mean Girl really needs is some love to transform from an enemy into a trusted ally.

> **ALL YOUR INNER MEAN GIRL REALLY NEEDS IS LOVE TO TRANSFORM.**

We recommend that you take each step in order—don't skip ahead. Each step builds on what comes before. In fact, we encourage you to slow down and let yourself experience the transformation each step offers. While the end result will be a new job for your Inner Mean Girl and reestablishing your Inner Wisdom as your inner CEO, throughout the book you'll find rich concepts and tools that will make your transformational experience deeper and long lasting, including:

♥ **Superpower Tools.** These are practical processes that empower you to take action when your Inner Mean Girl strikes. We call them superpower tools because they have the power to turn down the volume of your Inner Mean Girl and turn up the volume on your Inner Wisdom, quickly. Think of these as tools you can take out of your tool belt at any time to transform negative thinking and self-sabotaging choices in the moment. You can also use these superpower tools preemptively, to ward off potential future IMG attacks and help strengthen your connection to your Inner Wisdom.

♥ **Inner Wisdom Reflections.** These are reflective awareness builders that remind you to pause, take a breath, and look inside to absorb the process and find valuable insight. Your Inner Mean Girl loves to tell you to skip these reflections. She might say, "You don't have time"; "They aren't such a big deal—just keep reading"; or "I'll get back to that later" (which of course you never do). Your IMG doesn't see much value in slowing down or in reflecting inward instead of outwardly acting, because she knows that your Inner Wisdom thrives when you pause. Wisdom only comes through with conscious reflection. Love yourself enough to make the space for your Inner Wisdom. You'll learn a lot about yourself and as a result take more aligned actions that lead to more happiness and success.

♥ **Superpower Challenges.** At the end of each step, we will dare you to do an exercise that serves to bring all the information, wisdom, and tools in the step together, making the teaching personal and ensuring that you experience the transformation of the step fully. Have fun with these. This is all about receiving insight and experiencing internal shifts by taking action in your life.

♥ **Transformation Tales.** We invited some of our favorite transformational teachers to share their struggles about and secrets for how they transformed their Inner Mean Girls. In each chapter, we've included one of their stories, which we think you will find inspiring and helpful. It can be comforting to know that even people whose profession it is to guide others to live their best lives struggle with self-bullying, self-neglect, and self-sabotage.

♥ **Inspired Actions.** At the end of each section, we've created an Inspired Action that will inspire you to take creative, empowered action. Take these from a place of self-love, as in, "I choose to do this for myself," instead of from obligation, as in, "I have to do this."

Oh yes, we should probably mention that the Inner Mean Girl reformation process that you are about to go through is meant to be a mix of playfulness, humor, and powerful self-reflection to give you access to deeper places within yourself. So, for any of you with IMGs who can make you feel overly serious, discount play as a waste of time, or keep you stuck in your head, wanting information instead of actually feeling and experiencing processes, there are a few things we want to say to you and your Inner Wisdom right now.

Don't let your Inner Mean Girl convince you that playfulness makes this process trivial in any way, because we've found just the opposite to be true for every woman who has surrendered to the process and allowed that playful, creative side to come out. The journey you are about to embark upon with yourself, with us as your guides, will take you deep to places that can be hard to be in. Beneath all the criticism, judgment, and sabotage are much more vulnerable feelings, such as shame, fear, and anger, and even feelings of being unlovable and unworthy. Not happy-making stuff, right? But if you want meaningful and lasting transformation, you have to look deep within to reveal and heal these more vulnerable parts of yourself. We find that the playful approach lights up what can be a scary place to go, and the creative approach takes you out of your rational mind, where your Inner Mean Girl reigns, and gives you access to more of your intuitive mind, where your Inner Wisdom can get through. So, we invite you to:

1. Embrace the lightness and the playfulness.
2. Take the time to pause and reflect throughout the journey.
3. Take the inspired actions we ask you to take.
4. Use the tools we give you in your day-to-day life immediately, so you can start seeing the results. Just like when you work out and your abs and arms feel stronger, you are motivated to keep working out. This program strengthens your emotional and spiritual muscles in

the same way. You'll feel stronger and drop the emotional baggage that weighs you down.

5. Stay committed to yourself; don't give up midway. Be a best friend to yourself throughout this entire process. Giving to yourself is the best thing you can do for your success, your happiness, and your relationships.

If you just do these five things, you will experience transformation, and that's why you are here, right? In fact, one small but mighty tip that can help create a powerful and positive experience for you is to create an Inner Wisdom journal. Throughout the book, we'll ask you to take notes, take Inner Wisdom reflections, and complete superpower challenges. Having a sacred, personal place to capture your thoughts and progress facilitates deeper transformation. Writing things down so that you can see them makes a hand-eye-brain connection that makes your thoughts and heartfelt insights feel more real, and enables the transformation to stick more strongly.

Additionally, because we are so committed to your transformation, we put together a special Inner Wisdom Kit for you. This kit, which you can access free online, is full of meditations, videos, expert interviews, and samples from our students that will enrich the experience of your journey, especially if you want to go deeper. It's a gift from our heart to yours. To access the kit, just take a trip over to **innerwisdomkit.com** and use what's there to inspire you through this transformation.

Speaking of transformation, before you move on to the rest of the book, we thought you might like to know who you are about to go on a journey with. It seems like a good idea, doesn't it, to know who your guides are on any adventure, to make sure they know the way? We think it's always better to take a trip with someone who has gone there before, and, boy, have we both been in the grips of our Inner Mean Girls (sometimes without even knowing it). Thankfully, we lived to tell the stories, and in the process, we promised to ourselves to live Inner Wisdom–led lives, a promise which, if we had not each made it on our own before meeting each other, would have resulted in our partnership never occurring. Inner Mean Girl Reform School would not have been conceived or created, and this book would never have existed.

The Partnership That Almost Wasn't

This is the story of how we, Amy and Christine, your guides throughout this book and the cofounders of Inner Mean Girl Reform School, met . . . and almost didn't meet. It's a shining example of what happens when you allow your Inner Wisdom to lead and transform your Inner Mean Girl into a new ally.

IT'S CHRISTINE HERE. In 2009, I was on my first book tour, for *Choosing ME Before WE*, traveling around the country and appearing on TV shows to help women choose self-love inside their relationships. During that time, I had hired an assistant to help me find speaking engagements, and through an internet search one day, my assistant stumbled upon Amy, who had just created The Women Masters teleseminar series and was interviewing luminaries such as Marianne Williamson, Lisa Nichols, and SARK. This was at a time when very few people were doing teleseminars. My assistant sent me an email saying, *I think you might want to know about this woman.* So I clicked on the link to check out who this Amy lady was and what she was up to. As I read about her online programs, my Inner Mean Girl (or what we'd come to call an IMG) began to flare up. My body got all warm, and I started thinking, *You've been wanting to do these programs too, but you haven't! Why haven't you even started? You are so far behind!* Followed quickly by, *Amy is doing what you wanted to do. Now you can't do it. It's too late!*

Fortunately, I had already reformed my first Inner Mean Girl, whom I had affectionately named Mean Patty the Comparison Queen, who used the destructive bullying tool of comparison to make me feel oh so small on the inside no matter how successful I appeared to others on the outside. (We always name our

Inner Mean Girls so that we can develop relationships with them; you can't really know someone if you don't even know her name.) Mean Patty had red hair, wore a smock with an upside-down heart on it, and carried big rulers with her, which she used to compare my accomplishments to other women's successes, usually in areas where I had not yet ventured or areas where I had dreams and desires that had not yet manifested. (Her rulers were so big that she even had the audacity to compare me to women like Oprah and Barbara Walters—talk about never measuring up!) Luckily, Mean Patty had been reformed and reassigned the new job of being my talent scout, which meant her job was to go out and find women doing awesome things and bring them back to me to *inspire* instead of *torture* me.

So, I calmly reminded Mean Patty that she was now my talent scout, and her job was to find other women to inspire me. She calmed down, my emotions calmed down and my body cooled down, and I paused to ask my Inner Wisdom what action to take. My Inner Wisdom wisely guided me to open my heart and compose a soulful email to Amy. Smart move!

MEAN PATTY, CHRISTINE'S
INNER MEAN GIRL

IT'S AMY HERE. I remember what a busy time that was in my life. My inbox was constantly overflowing with thank-you emails and requests from women around the world wanting to be featured on The Women Masters series. But when I received Christine's email, it was as if it vibrated off the screen. The subject line read, *Kindred spirits connecting*. I opened the email, and there was Christine. Fortunately, I had also done some Inner Mean Girl reforming. Instead of feeling less-than because I was not yet a published author or flying around the world speaking and being on TV like Christine, I leaned into inspiration and checked in with my Inner Wisdom. My Inner Wisdom told me to invite Christine to coffee.

Now here's where this story gets even more interesting. Lo and behold, we realized as we talked about where we might meet up that we lived less than five minutes from each other in the San Francisco Bay Area (talk about synchronicity!). We were astonished at the proximity. After that first coffee, we were even more blown away by our resonance with each other's work. We vowed to form a sisterhood of sorts, where we could support each other and our work, and where I, Amy, could teach Christine more about the online world, and she could help me navigate the publicity and book publishing world.

Then one destiny-made day, as we hiked through the woods talking about my television pitch and what Christine had been speaking to women around the world about, Christine uttered the words *Inner Mean Girl*, and a virtual school, a book, and a revolution were born. Since that day, together we have touched tens of thousands of women around the world under the Inner Mean Girl Reform School banner—including you right here! None of this would have been possible had we let our Inner Mean Girls make our choices, instead of trusting our Inner Wisdoms.

Now It's Your Turn

The beauty and power of your Inner Wisdom is how listening to its guidance and following through with inspired action can create incredible opportunities and possibilities you never could have imagined. Your Inner Wisdom is a natural force within you that can guide and bless you with insight and honesty in ways that will help you live your best life. We've experienced it, and the women we've worked with have experienced it, and now you can experience it for yourself!

THE SELF-BULLYING EPIDEMIC

There is a silent epidemic plaguing women around the world of all ages. It's affecting us at record levels. It begins when we are young girls, and it's the root cause of most of the poor choices in our diets, relationships, careers, health, and finances throughout our entire lives. Unexposed, it wreaks havoc on our physical, emotional, mental, and spiritual health. Just look at these numbers:

- One in three women will die of heart disease. That means one woman per minute—and not just because she's been eating too many french fries.[1]
- Sixty percent of all doctor visits by female patients are attributed to stress.[2]
- Twice as many American women are on antidepressants compared to American men.[3]
- Women today are less happy than their counterparts in the 1970s, even though we have more freedom and equality.[4]
- Twenty million women and girls in the United States suffer from eating disorders, double the number of men.[5]

What's going on? How can we have more earning potential, career opportunities, and freedom of choice, yet be less happy, more stressed, and plagued by a rise in disease? There are many more statistics that we could list here showing lots of external factors that contribute to the pressure we feel as women to do, be, and have it all and result in the unrealistic expectations we try to live up to. Most of these factors you are probably well aware of—external influences that surround us, such as the myriad of images and stereotypes of what a successful woman should be able to accomplish or what a beautiful woman is in our society. Add to that a slew of societal norms that don't support personal sustainability or happiness but instead negatively affect our well-being, drain our health, emotions, and quality of life, and no wonder we end up with unfulfilling high-pressure jobs, crappy eating habits, lack of fitness and health, work/home imbalance, and more. No wonder so many of us feel we are never doing or accomplishing enough.

And while these external forces are certainly no good for the female psyche and sense of self-worth, there is an internal force affecting our current reality as women (as well as the girls we are raising) that is just as detrimental and toxic, if not more. This internal factor is self-bullying, and the culprit behind it is your Inner Mean Girl. Chances are you suffer from self-bullying in more ways than you know, in more places in your life than you are aware, including your love life, career, bank account, and body image. Just like a mean girl on the playground or in the conference room will push, cajole, and sabotage you from the outside, an *Inner* Mean Girl torments you from the inside out. Take a look at some of the most common signs that your IMG has been sabotaging you and check to see if you have any of these self-bullying symptoms. Do you:

♥ Get down on yourself for all the ways in which you don't measure up to the expectations you or others have for your body, career, children, finances, or relationship?
♥ Rarely feel like you've accomplished enough no matter how much you get done or how successful everyone else thinks you are?

♥ Pressure yourself to say yes to others even when you don't really have the energy and/or time to give?

♥ Obsessively think or run negative storylines or endless to-do lists through your mind?

♥ Continually do things that sabotage you—eating too much, staying in the wrong relationships or dating people that aren't nice to you, spending money you don't have on things you don't really need?

♥ Feel afraid to go for your dreams fully, so you procrastinate or settle?

These are all forms of self-bullying—and that's just the short list! And while you may not be able to see evidence of all the ways in which you internally beat yourself up, that doesn't mean the bruises and scars aren't there—and that they don't sting or hurt. If most people could hear the hurtful thoughts that go on inside your head or witness the judgments and pressure you put on yourself, they would call the authorities on you. From our work, experience, and research, we found that one of the most prevalent reasons women are unhappy, unfulfilled, and stressed out is the mental and emotional abuse suffered at their own hands, through their own self-destructive thoughts and self-sabotaging choices.

> ONE OF THE MOST PREVALENT REASONS WOMEN ARE UNHAPPY, UNFULFILLED, AND STRESSED OUT IS THE MENTAL AND EMOTIONAL ABUSE SUFFERED AT THEIR OWN HANDS.

Consider the act of picking up this book an intervention, putting a stop to this internal abuse. You've made the choice to stop bullying yourself and start loving yourself—brava! And the good news is you are not alone, it's not your fault, and there is hope.

You Are Not Alone

Most women don't want to talk about this self-bullying epidemic. Who wants to admit that while we smile and look like we are keeping it together on the outside, on the inside, feelings like shame, fear, guilt, and being unlovable are stewing? But you know as well as we do that not talking about these emotions and self-judgments doesn't make them go away. In fact, truth telling in the presence of other women is a brave, bold step toward healing. And really, there isn't any need to hide these parts of you any longer, since every woman you know is probably feeling and thinking the same things.

If you listen closely to the women you work with, the women you love, and the women standing next to you in line at the checkout or for school pickup, or even watch closely the women you admire and look up to at work or in the public eye, you'll notice they too are listening to similar internal critiques, silently beating themselves up, and putting incredible pressure on themselves.

With decades of combined coaching, teaching, and mentorship experience, and after suffering and recovering from this negative thinking affliction and self-sabotage syndrome ourselves, we've witnessed firsthand that self-bullying has nothing to do with how successful, smart, or beautiful a woman appears. In fact, some of the most outwardly successful or physically beautiful women we know, women who supposedly have it all, have Inner Mean Girls that drive them to commit acts of abuse against themselves. Just listen and look at what women who many of us look up to are so courageously and vulnerably sharing about their own Inner Mean Girls:

> Oprah admitted to the world that her focus on her weight has robbed her of joy: "I'm mad at myself. I'm embarrassed. I can't believe that after all these years, all the things I know how to do, I'm still talking about my weight."[6]

Arianna Huffington, founder of the *Huffington Post*, woke up in a pool of her own blood with a broken cheekbone and injured eye when she collapsed from overwork and exhaustion, and admitted, "They found that there was nothing medically wrong with me, but just about everything wrong with the way I was living my life."[7]

Elizabeth Gilbert, bestselling author of *Eat, Pray, Love*, declared, "The real battle for me was my own self-abuse . . . to learn how to stop and drop the knife I was holding to my own throat. I was never good enough."[8]

It's obvious that women from all walks of life, status, and achievement deal with their own versions of an Inner Mean Girl. You are not alone—we're all in this together.

The Genesis of Your Inner Mean Girl

As a woman, you certainly weren't born programmed to compare yourself, judge yourself, and feel guilty or inferior, right? It's not like when you were a baby you laid around in your bassinette comparing your thighs to the baby's next to you, or as a toddler were concerned that your naps were a waste of time. You were not born hardwired to be hard on yourself; you were born preprogrammed to love yourself, but along the way, some wires got crossed, your Inner Mean Girl got formed, and you got trapped in a cycle of thoughts, habits, and patterns that has been almost impossible to work yourself out of, until now.

Your Inner Mean Girl is part of the human experience, and she is also a part of you, so you can't kill her off even if you tried. And we don't want you to try and run from her either. We want you to run straight toward her and love her, because as it turns out, your IMG doesn't mean to hurt you; she actually wants to protect you.

Yes, you read that correctly. *Everything* your Inner Mean Girl does—all the toxic habits of comparison, judgment, driving you to perfectionism, over-giving, overdoing, underexpressing, and procrastinating—in her mind, serves one mission: protecting you. She actually loves you so much that she has devoted her life to keeping you safe and keeping you far away from any experience that could possibly cause pain or suffering. So then, how is it that if she is so committed to keeping you from pain, she is also the one who fills your head with thoughts that hurt you, compelling you into actions that sabotage and sacrifice you?

> EVERYTHING YOUR INNER MEAN GIRL DOES—ALL THE TOXIC HABITS OF COMPARISON, JUDGMENT, DRIVING YOU TO PERFECTIONISM, OVER-GIVING, OVERDOING, UNDER-EXPRESSING, AND PROCRASTINATING—IN HER MIND, SERVES ONE MISSION: PROTECTING YOU.

Well, at some point in your life, a younger you created your Inner Mean Girl because you needed protection. You had an experience when someone hurt you, in which you felt unsafe or unloved, or in which things around you felt out of control. When your excitement, self-expression, love, and innocence were met with fear, criticism, anger, guilt, shame, or blame—from a teacher, a parent, a neighbor, or anyone you counted on for recognition, love, or a sense of safety.

The younger you decided to never have that experience or those feelings again, so with all the emotional maturity you were able to muster at the time, which was not much, you created your IMG and her self-bullying ways. Your IMG made it her job to protect you from emotions and experiences you didn't want to feel. And to do her job well, just like any bully, she used the most effective tool she could find to motivate you—fear.

For years, your Inner Mean Girl has been using fear to motivate you—in ways that you may be aware of and in many more you've been oblivious to—because for a time, these toxic habits and thoughts did, indeed, protect you. She, and you, learned that employing these toxic habits—like overworking, over-giving, over-worrying, being overly busy—were actually effective. Maybe the payoff of all that IMG fear has been you being more productive, personable, outwardly successful, accepted, and most of all safe and loved. She helped you feel a sense of belonging, even if it is to a tribe that no longer serves you.

The thing about fear is that it comes in many forms, just like Inner Mean Girls do—and outer mean girls, for that matter. Not all Inner Mean Girls are mean. And not all fear feels scary. Mean girls in the hallways or at the office have their individual tactics and personas, and so do IMGs—some are straight-up mean, while others pretend to be your friends and then backstab you, and others just drag you down with them. Some come off as strong, some weak; some seem crazy, and others are just plain bitchy. But what is always true is they are *all* scared, confused, and not likely to give up control any time soon.

Your Inner Mean Girl is the face and force of fear. And depending on her personality, she can express her fear in all kinds of ways, even in ways that make her (and you) seem like you are never afraid. Fear can show up as anxiety, worry, procrastination, and doubt—those are the easy ones to spot. But fear and your IMG are also at the root of all the times that you try to control your situations, relationships, and appearance, the times when you sell yourself out, shortchange your own self-care, and feel like you failed.

Love Your Inner Mean Girl, Empower Your Inner Wisdom

The remedy to this epidemic boils down to this: love your Inner Mean Girl and empower your Inner Wisdom.

What your Inner Mean Girl most needs to stop her hurtful behavior is just a lot of love, safety, and security. She needs to know and trust that you will be able to protect and take care of yourself, that you will get what you need to feel loved and safe; otherwise, she will not give up her job. She's that loyal to you! You can't kill an IMG, but you can love her into a new job, by giving her what she—and you—need most from yourself: compassion.

Just think about any outer mean girl you have encountered in your life. Your first instinct was to protect yourself from her, right? But what if you opened your heart and saw her with compassion, saw what was going on inside of her? What would you see? You'd see that every outer mean girl is a manifestation of an Inner Mean Girl, a scared, threatened part of us that doesn't know how to get what she needs, so acts crazy and manipulative, and often cruel, to protect herself.

Keep this in mind the next time you encounter a woman who isn't being so nice to you or a child who isn't being kind your kid. You can't condone the outside bullying, just as we can no longer condone your internal bullying, but to paraphrase Gandhi's famous words, "Be the change you wish to see." We all wish for a more compassionate world in which women and girls support each other, instead of tear each other apart. But the end to *outer* mean girls has to also include an end to *Inner* Mean Girls.

The good news is that our natural state of relationships with others and with ourselves is compassion, which is your Inner Wisdom's natural state. The key for this remedy to work is to empower your Inner Wisdom to be your go-to girl for the thoughts you have and the choices you make. You can choose what thoughts you listen to and what actions you take—those fueled by your Inner Mean Girl or by your Inner Wisdom. Your

> **THE END TO *OUTER* MEAN GIRLS HAS TO ALSO INCLUDE AN END TO *INNER* MEAN GIRLS.**

Inner Wisdom is the force within you that motivates you through compassionate truth and fierce love, instead of through criticism, guilt, shame, anger, and stress. Both your Inner Mean Girl and your Inner Wisdom believe they have your best interests at heart. But your Inner Mean Girl, driven by fear, just isn't capable of making the best choices for you. You've got to take charge and hand over the power to your Inner Wisdom.

IT'S AMY HERE. I want to introduce you to my Inner Mean Girl. Her name is Negative Nelly. (Yes, you too will get to name your Inner Mean Girl.) She's been around most of my life, speaking in a whisper, but when I became a mom, she came out and descended on me like a storm in full force. It was as if when I gave birth to my first daughter, Annabella, I also gave birth to an unwanted guest—one who had the power to take over my thoughts and make me believe Big Fat Lies, like "You're doing it all wrong" and "Your baby is doomed." Her favorite thing to tell me was "You're a horrible mom." She would compare me to perfect moms whose babies were sleeping through the night on day three (do those babies even exist?). Negative Nelly made me feel anxious, overwhelmed, and completely inadequate.

NEGATIVE NELLY, AMY'S
INNER MEAN GIRL

I remember one particularly unruly Inner Mean Girl attack that paralyzed me with fear. I was exhausted with a newborn in my lap, spit up in my hair, and a dog that was begging to be walked. I hadn't showered in days, and I was beyond my limit. I questioned if I should have ever become a mom. I felt certain I was doomed to a life where I felt trapped, anxiety ridden, and depressed. It wasn't pretty. I was desperate. I knew that if something didn't change, I was bound to end up becoming a "helicopter mom," hovering around my daughter, worried and fearful, putting my own self-care and well-being last on the list.

Out of sheer desperation and exasperation, I committed to making a change, no matter what. With unwavering compassion and confidence, I told Negative Nelly that she was not allowed to make my decisions or choose my perspectives anymore, and that while I knew she was just trying to keep my baby and me safe, her fear was hurting us, not helping. I finally, really, truly, cross my heart, made a promise to tune in to my Inner Wisdom every single day, something I had tried to do on and off for years but had never been able to stick with. Now, committed, when I tuned in, I finally heard my Inner Wisdom's voice loud and clear over Negative Nelly's; my Inner Wisdom told me that all of the stress and anxiety I was experiencing as a new mom was *normal*. It was part of the process. She assured me that there was a community of mothers just waiting for me. She led me to a mom's group called Mindful Mamas that is filled with incredible women who unconditionally love and support me. This community has helped me become more of the mom I want to be.

I know that if I had left Negative Nelly in charge, if I had kept playing with the idea of instead of actually doing a daily practice in which I connected with my inner loving truth, I would have never attracted such a wise group of mamas. I would have remained isolated, stuck in my compare-and-despair game, filled with worry and fear, neglecting myself on all levels, tuned in to my IMG instead of my Inner Wisdom. It's astonishing what can happen when you reform your Inner Mean Girl and empower your Inner Wisdom!

Even though Negative Nelly still makes an appearance with each new phase of parenting (potty training, kindergarten, and, dare I say it, puberty), I know how to turn down the volume on the voice that is feeding my fears, and love instead of judge that part of me. And most important, I know how to tap into my Inner Wisdom to hear the truth.

You too have the opportunity to become stronger at cutting through the fear of your Inner Mean Girl. This way your Inner Wisdom's guidance can get through and as a result be the driving force behind the thoughts that fill your mind and ultimately direct your emotions, choices, and resulting actions. But first, there are a few things you need to know about how that brain of yours works both for you and against you. Otherwise, try as you might, you won't be successful at breaking through the habits and patterns that sabotage you or the negative stories that run through your mind. With a little bit of scientific fact and spiritual wisdom, however, we'll set you up to be more successful at attuning your mind to your self-loving, wise woman nature.

Get Your Brain on Your Side

Now, we aren't brain scientists by any means, but over years and years of coaching, leading classes, and research, we've learned a thing or two about how our brains work that has helped us and our students. What brain science has found explains so much and is aligned with what spiritual teachers have known for thousands of years. And where science and spirituality meet, we find superpower!

To begin with, did you know that your brain has more than sixty thousand thoughts in a day and that approximately 80 percent of those thoughts are negative?[9] No surprise, right, given that our culture and the media have been filling your brain with garbage? Over the years, these self-sabotaging ideas and images have created impressions on your brain, like deeply entrenched grooves. These grooves are called neural pathways, and the more established the pathway and the more often the pathway is used by your brain, the more ingrained the belief or thought becomes.

It's just like taking the same route home day in and day out. You follow the same path, groove, as if you are operating on automatic pilot, out of habit—just like your mind reruns the same negative beliefs and thoughts, and why you keep making the same self-sabotaging choices. And while you could go a different way, unless there is some major accident or reason to detour, you are not likely to deviate from the same old route—even if another route would be more beautiful. This is why it's so hard to change a toxic habit or a self-sabotaging pattern and break through to more expansive, abundant beliefs—the grooves in your brain are so deeply ingrained that your mind defaults to the pathway most traveled, most comfortable and known, especially in times of high stress or in situations where you feel vulnerable, unsure, or unfamiliar. To make a change, break limiting patterns and beliefs, you have to create new pathways.

From a spiritual perspective, the yogis have known this for years, and many yoga practices are created to break these subconscious patterns and return us to our divine truth and to that state of inner calm that any of you who have practiced yoga have felt. Yogis call these *sanskaras*, or the impressions left behind that often condition future behavior. At the highest state a yogi can achieve, she is still not free, because she has to overcome her sanskaras to truly achieve freedom. That's how difficult and stubborn these subconscious patterns can be: they are often the last thing dealt with on the yogic path.

Even if you haven't ever been on the mat, you've likely experienced a moment of absolute presence when you are not thinking about the past or fretting about or planning the future; you are just in the present, the now. This is your natural state of being, the place your Inner Wisdom resides. You want to be able to live in the present moment more often (not just on the mat or when on vacation or when life is relatively easy) and get back to that centered, clear, calm space faster in your day-to-day life. You deserve to live more often in that peaceful state, where you have a sense that everything is okay, where fear isn't running you, where you feel safe, loved, and whole, even in the midst of busy, pressure-filled lives and especially during difficult or uncertain times.

This is quite challenging, of course, due to the scientific fact that certain parts of your brain are wired to focus on what is wrong, what's not working, and what could possibly go wrong. Yes, thanks to the part of your brain called the amygdala, whose job it is to be on constant lookout for danger, you have a bit of an uphill battle on your hands. This part of our brain was super useful when we had to be on constant lookout for lions, tigers, and bears (oh my!). Its job was to be vigilant 24/7, looking for danger that could get you killed or eaten alive. If it sensed danger, its job was to send a huge bolt of fear through you, triggering your body to go into the fight-or-flight stress response and get you moving. Good job, brain!

The problem is that you no longer have to worry about fighting off big cats or bears (unless you are living out in the jungle or on safari, which most of us are not), but your brain doesn't know that. It triggers the same kind of fight-or-flight response when any kind of perceived danger emerges. Say you feel threatened or misunderstood in your relationship with your parent or partner, or you feel unseen or undervalued at work, or you feel vulnerable about dating or the shape of your body—your brain reacts just as if you were being attacked or prepares in case there could be an attack. You see you've gained a few pounds or are late on a bill—and you feel like your life is in danger. Fear shoots through your body, launching you into an all-out stress response, driving you to take impulsive, self-sabotaging actions that if you were sane, calm, and in connection with your Inner Wisdom, you would pause and think twice about.

When a pathway in your brain gets activated by outside stimuli, it causes information to travel through and across synapses, which then creates a reaction that you may or may not be conscious of, and these reactions establish the behaviors, patterns, and beliefs—the grooves—that create your reality.

This is also why oftentimes your reactions are out of proportion to the situation. Let's say your partner, relative, or friend says something to you that, while maybe not the best choice of words, sets you off completely and you either go banshee and lose it on that person or you get obsessed and cannot stop thinking about it. Your brain has sensed danger and sent your body into fight-or-flight. It's like that saying in relationships: "The fight about the toothpaste is never about the toothpaste . . ." The toothpaste is the activator of a neural pathway.

And have you ever noticed that sometimes you will even imagine something terrible is happening and you react as if it's real? Your spouse is going to leave you. Your coworker or boss is out to get you. You're going to lose all your money. You end up wasting a whole lot of energy worrying and thinking about something that hasn't happened. It's like a dress rehearsal of the worst-case scenario. As a result, you have less energy and time to do what is truly important and fulfilling for you.

Are you getting the sense of how powerful your neural pathways are? Why it can be so challenging to change those ingrained grooves?

Now, don't get discouraged. Because we have some really good news for you!

Scientists and Yogis Agree: You Have the Power to Change Your Mind

Did you know that your brain is plastic? Yep. It's true. Okay, well, not made of that plastic stuff people drink bottled water out of, but plastic in the sense that you can literally shape and shift your brain to create new neural pathways. You have the power to make new grooves that serve you, even in times of stress.

Not so long ago, scientists believed that our brains were fixed and static, that we couldn't change our thought patterns, but they finally clued in to something that spiritual teachers have known for thousands of years: we have the power to change our thoughts, patterns, and behaviors, to rewire ourselves. Which means *you* can choose how you respond to the impulses and triggers.

A well-known story about an early NASA experiment states that they placed convex goggles on astronaut candidates that turned everything they saw upside down. Now why on earth would they do this? Well, this was back in the days before simulation technology, so it was the only way they could simulate what it would be like to be weightless in space. They had the astronauts wear the convex goggles for long spans of time, completely disorienting them, so they could test the effects of spatial disorientation on their bodily systems. Would they become nauseous? Would their blood pressure skyrocket? Could they actually stand it?

What occurred after about three to four weeks of this experiment astonished the team. The astronaut's brains actually started to turn everything they saw right-side up while they *were still wearing the goggles.* So after three to four weeks, each of their brains had formed enough new neural connections to correct their vision. The brain wanted to reorient the astronaut so it built new pathways. This correlates with what yogic masters in the Kundalini yoga tradition have taught for centuries, that in forty days, you can change a habit if you focus on a specific desired change.

What does this all mean for you? It means that you have the power to release toxic habits, give up negative thinking, and change self-sabotaging patterns into self-loving, supportive ones. Your brain doesn't control you; you have the power to direct your mind and your choices. You have the power not just to uncover your Inner Mean Girl but also to change how you react to her, how she reacts, and what she focuses on. Which is exactly what we have put together for you in these seven steps.

What excites us so much about this is that, as women, we are at a choice point, as if standing at a crossroads where we have the opportunity to choose collectively and individually how we live our lives, measure our success, and motivate ourselves to achieve our dreams and take care of who and what we love. We can either continue to choose to accept the current cultural realities for women and girls as the norm, which means we continue to pressure ourselves to live up to unrealistic expectations, or we can choose to change the societal ideals so they support us to create sustainable lifestyles, where we enjoy external success and internal happiness and health.

In every moment of every day, we stand at the choice point of what thoughts fill our minds, what emotions fill our bodies, and what actions fuel our lives—we have a choice as to whether we tune in to and follow the guidance of our Inner Mean Girls or our Inner Wisdoms. We can choose to stay silent and hide the ways in which we bully, sabotage, judge, and shortchange ourselves, or we can choose to be courageous and vulnerable and speak up and stand up, together—for ourselves and for generations to come. We wouldn't think twice about standing up for a child or a woman we loved if she was being bullied, diminished, or ostracized, so how about we choose to apply that same level of fierce love to ourselves?

> EVERY DAY, WE STAND AT THE CHOICE POINT OF WHAT THOUGHTS FILL OUR MINDS, WHAT EMOTIONS FILL OUR BODIES, AND WHAT ACTIONS FUEL OUR LIVES.

Make a Commitment to Yourself!

We imagine that you want change—or you wouldn't be here with us on this journey—and you know now how change happens, and how it sticks, or doesn't. While it would be nice to be able to take a quick pill to give up your toxic habits, shift just doesn't work that way. The good news is we are going to arm you with both scientific facts and spiritual principles to understand the process your brain, body, heart, and spirit go through as you embark on creating the best, happiest life for yourself. We'll also give you incredible superpower tools that you can use in the moment and as preventative care to control what voice broadcasts through your mind and informs your actions—your Inner Mean Girl or Inner Wisdom.

Before we can do that with you, we need you to set the foundation for your success in this transformational journey by committing to yourself. So, let's pause for a moment to lock in your devotion to yourself and also open up the door to the support and sisterhood available to you. With this book in your hand, imagine standing with us, shoulder to shoulder, along with all the other millions of women around the world who have bullied themselves—as little girls, teenagers, and adults—and say *enough*! It's time to love ourselves and stop tormenting ourselves. Go ahead and place a hand on your heart in solidarity and commit to be as compassionate, kind, patient, caring, supportive, and accepting to yourself as you would be to someone you love. Say these words out loud or to yourself, a promise to you:

I commit to being as compassionate, kind, patient, caring, supportive, and accepting to myself as I would be to someone I love.

You don't need to know the how yet, and you for sure don't have to do it "perfectly" (that'd be an IMG setup). For now we invite you to commit to completing the journey you are about to undertake with us—all seven steps, no matter what. Life may get busy, or things may come up, yet remember in this moment that you have decided to make yourself a priority.

We also invite you to embrace our Inner Mean Girl Reform School Credo as a way to approach this transformation and a way to approach life. It has served us and the women we serve well, and now we offer it to you.

And now, it's time for step one of your Inner Mean Girl transformation journey!

THE INNER MEAN GIRL
REFORM SCHOOL CREDO

1. All Mean Girls—inner and outer—need and deserve love. All your Inner Mean Girl really wants is to be loved, to feel safe, and to belong.

2. Everyone has an Inner Wisdom that is the source of truth, unconditional love, and compassion. While the path isn't always easy, she always guides you to your best life.

3. We are all worthy of compassion. Compassion isn't earned; it's your birthright, and it starts by giving love to yourself.

4. Your external reality can only change when you first change your internal reality. When you take responsibility for your inner world, the outer world will respond.

5. In every moment of every day, you have a choice as to which inner voice you believe, broadcast, and follow. You can choose to listen to the loving voice of your Inner Wisdom or the fear-filled voice of your Inner Mean Girl.

6. Playfulness and creativity are two of the most powerful transformation tools you have. They make even the scary things fun and accessible, providing you access to deeper levels of insight and personal awareness.

7. When women come together, shift happens. An isolated woman is powerless to the fear of her Inner Mean Girl, but a woman surrounded by other women willing to speak the truth is invincible.

PART I

MEET YOUR
INNER
MEAN
GiRL

STEP 1

REVEAL YOUR TYPE OF INNER MEAN GIRL

The first step in all Inner Mean Girl (IMG) transformations is absolute, honest awareness at multiple levels—emotional, spiritual, physical, and mental. This is a very personal affair. Getting to know your Inner Mean Girl isn't just a mental exercise in which you can read a few paragraphs and then proclaim, "Okay, yes, I have an Inner Mean Girl, I get it." It's not like you can check off a box and be done in five minutes. Like in any relationship, there are steps to be taken and multiple layers to observe in order to truly get to know the other party well. You need to become intimate with this part of yourself. Of course, your IMG would prefer your relationship stay impersonal and intellectual, so she can stay hidden and keep her job. But that's not why you are here with us.

You are here to increase your awareness of and power over this inner force—and awareness is where the power is. *Awareness* is the number one enemy of the Inner Mean Girl, because once you see her for what she really is—a part of yourself that needs to be loved—the power balance begins to shift in your favor. Awareness is the key to your freedom for two simple reasons:

1. You cannot change what you cannot see.
2. You cannot change what you feel victimized by.

Without a heightened level of awareness, nothing can truly change. You have to be able to see something to shift it. If you remain clueless about how your IMG operates and what her underlying motivations are, you just keep struggling with the same self-defeating patterns, no matter how much you talk or think about them or how hard you try to make different choices. Without awareness of who she is and what she is up to, the same judgmental, sabotaging, and bullying thoughts will keep finding their way back into your brain, deepening those old neural pathways, no matter how many affirmations you say.

Which is why it's time to get quite intimate with your Inner Mean Girl. To gain so much awareness of this inner force that you'll be able to identify, understand, observe, and even sense and feel her working within you, so you have the power to make conscious choices about your thoughts, feelings, and actions. To truly stop the judgmental thoughts and self-defeating choices, you have to go deeper within to expose the parts of yourself that you may not have wanted to look closely at before. Or that you may have looked at and worked with previously but in ways that have not given you the freedom and inner peace you'd like. Many women stop short of diving deep, so their transformations don't stick. The self-sabotage and negative self-talk continues, no matter how many workshops they take because they aren't going deep enough to get to the true source.

If we know anything about these self-sabotaging parts of ourselves after meeting so many Inner Mean Girls, it is that avoiding looking doesn't make them any less present. Fear, shame, blame, judgment, and all that shadowy stuff will still be there, running under the surface. In fact, ignoring these parts of yourself or just skimming the surface just makes your IMG more powerful. And while it may seem scary or hard at first, once you get in there and start looking around, what you find is not as horrible as you think. There is transformational gold in these deep places inside of you—and that transformation always starts with more awareness.

Be an Observer, Not a Victim, of Your Inner Mean Girl

Together let's get to the bottom of exactly who your Inner Mean Girl is, why she is here, what triggers her, and what weapons she uses to fill your mind with judgmental and sabotaging thoughts (which we call Big Fat Lies), and let's have some fun doing it. We want you to think of yourself as an investigative reporter writing an exposé on one of the most interesting people of the year—this person just happens to be your Inner Mean Girl. And like any good journalist, before you sit down for a candid one-on-one interview, you have to do background research so you're prepared.

In this first step, your mission is to move from being a *victim* of your Inner Mean Girl to an *observer* of her, using the power of awareness. While you may already be aware of many of your self-sabotaging habits—like criticizing yourself, saying yes when you should say no, overworking, procrastinating, putting yourself last—there are still ways in which you are being victimized and controlled by these habits, or you wouldn't be here. We understand. It can feel like no matter how hard you try, you just keep repeating these negative patterns. And it can feel like "this is just how things are" or "this is just who I am," neither of which are true.

When anxiety, fear, overwhelm, or stress is happening *to* you, you often feel helpless to change it, at least for any length of time. But when you can separate yourself from these experiences and emotions to see that your Inner Mean Girl is actually the one running your thoughts, feelings, and actions because she's freaked out and trying to protect you, the self-bullying spell breaks and you start to see things totally differently. By observing what she's driving you to do and think, you can gain insight and awareness into what is really occurring—instead of being a victim to the fear and self-judgment driven thoughts and feelings. Armed with this new level of awareness and understanding of your IMG, you can

5

then begin to shift the toxic habits into loving, empowering, compassionate thoughts, choices, and habits.

Remember, your original nature is self-loving, not self-bullying. As you call out your Inner Mean Girl, you will begin to see that the self-sabotage, self-hatred, and self-bullying really belong to her, not to you.

We'll never forget the moment when Kate, one of our early students, realized she was not actually her Inner Mean Girl. For years she had been plagued with feeling inferior and thinking that in the end, no matter how perfect she made everything, she was going to end up all alone.

From morning till night, no matter how much she did, her mind still found more things that had to be taken care of—finishing orders for her clients, finding the love of her life (who she was convinced might never come), spending more time with her friends (who she was sure were going to bail on her at any minute), picking the lint off her couch lint ball by lint ball (not kidding!). Kate had become a victim of her Inner Mean Girl's toxic habits of obsessive perfectionism, overthinking, and running worst-case scenarios.

> YOUR ORIGINAL NATURE IS SELF-LOVE, NOT SELF-BULLYING.

Before she met and created a relationship with her Inner Mean Girl, Kate just assumed these anxiety-filled thoughts were her own. She had resigned herself to believing that this obsessive, often fearful person was just who she was and how she was destined to be forever. Now, before you paint a picture of Kate as some neurotic mess, let us tell you that Kate is a beautiful and strong woman, with a fair amount of self-esteem, who had the courage to start her own business designing clothing in her early twenties. But her IMG was turning Kate into a woman driven to obsessive levels of perfectionism, with a continuous low hum of anxiety running through her that could spike to overwhelming amounts in minutes. During these times when her IMG got triggered, Kate's confidence plummeted, she began avoiding her friends, she couldn't stop doing, and most of all she ceased to enjoy the life she had worked so hard to create for herself.

When Kate took the first step of exposing her Inner Mean Girl, she saw a persnickety perfectionist and an obsessive-compulsive Doing Addict (one of the thirteen types of IMGs we'll describe in the next few pages) who was masking deeper places of loneliness and insecurity inside. This first step, awareness of this inner part, was a game changer for Kate. It was the beginning of a process that would allow her to see herself more deeply and clearly than ever before, and to have the courage to look straight into the underlying feelings and fears that her IMG, whom she later named Regina, had been working so hard to keep hidden—using toxic habits like negative thinking, obsessive perfectionism, isolation, and pessimism. Once her Inner Mean Girl was fully revealed, Kate could see herself separate from those thoughts and self-sabotaging habits, and she was able to connect to her voice of truth—her Inner Wisdom—and begin making more aligned, healthy choices that supported Kate in being who she wanted to be and creating the kind of life she really desired. With this new awareness, Kate gained the power to leave behind a romantic relationship that had run its course, to become more social with people she loved to be around, and to take her business to a new level.

Now it's your turn to expose the Inner Mean Girl lurking in the shadows and wreaking havoc on your life.

The Thirteen Types of Inner Mean Girls

In our Inner Mean Girl Reform School program, we've worked with women of all ages from around the world and have uncovered thirteen distinct types of Inner Mean Girls. We call these the Inner Mean Girl Archetypes. Archetypes are personas that your IMG takes on, each with its own set of weapons (tools and tricks she uses to sabotage and bully you), toxic habits (the destructive patterns she keeps you trapped in), and favorite Big Fat Lies (the words she fills your head with to control you).

You will use these archetypes as the starting point to reveal and see your specific Inner Mean Girl.

As a bonus, you will also begin to notice the Inner Mean Girls your family, friends, and coworkers have, which can be infinitely helpful when dealing with misunderstandings and conflict in your relationships, giving you more compassion for yourself and others. You may even begin to see how the Inner Mean Girls of women you know can very quickly become outer mean girls, which is a great help in not getting embroiled in relationship dramas that can drag you down, drain your energy, and take you off your center.

Another thing to know is that while these are common archetypes, your relationship with your Inner Mean Girl is personal and has to be dealt with using both honesty and compassion. We call this loving truth. On this adventure, and in every area of your life, it helps to be completely honest with yourself, even when it stings. Your IMG is not going to like you probing these deeper places of yourself, and looking this deeply may feel uncomfortable, so just expect that some stuff may come up instead of being surprised when it does.

Our mission is to coax your Inner Mean Girl out of the shadows of your subconscious and into the light where you can see and relate to her. Some of these IMG archetypes are pretty hilarious when you recognize what these nefarious inner forces try to get away with and the crazy antics and tools they employ to protect you. No one can say that your Inner Mean Girl isn't creative and resourceful, that's for sure. Over the years we've found that if you continually come back to your sense of humor during this internal investigation and approach this deep work with a sense of playfulness and compassion (remember, you've been doing the best you could up until this point based on what you've had to work with!), you'll not only experience transformation but you'll also have more fun in the process.

Following is a full description of the thirteen Inner Mean Girl Archetypes. Notice that some archetypes are obviously mean, while some are more elusive in how they show up, because they may appear to be less mean or critical, but they are just as manipulative and self-sabotaging.

Read each of the archetypes and notice which ones resonate with you. Mark each one you can relate to. Don't get freaked out if several of these archetypes seem familiar—we all have pieces of each archetype, and many women do have multiple Inner Mean Girls. We'll talk about that later. For now, just become familiar with each one and take notice of which ones feel most present in your life today.

THE ACHiEVEMENT JUNKIE

Imagine an insane mountain climber who, even after she has climbed to the top of the mountain, never stops to take in the view or celebrate. Instead, she immediately looks for the next mountain to climb. The Achievement Junkie never celebrates milestones. She drives you hard to get to a goal you will never reach because the finish line just keeps moving. The Achievement Junkie makes it her job to keep you addicted to pursuing goals, so she fools you into believing that there is a magical destination that will prove you have finally arrived, so you can rest and stop working so hard. But of course that day never comes. You never feel like you have accomplished enough because you never see, remember, or acknowledge how much you have actually achieved. There is no harm in being an achiever; it's the junkie part that hurts you.

WEAPONS

The Big-Ass Moving High Bar. The Achievement Junkie goads you to set superhigh bars for yourself, driving you to put forth enormous effort, and stress. Then, just as you are about to clear the high bar and claim success, she flicks the bar up, and you miss the mark. No matter that you just achieved more than most; you feel like you fell short. So, of course, you pick up your pole, set a new unrealistic goal, and exhaust yourself trying to get there.

The "When I Get There" Binoculars. These warped future-focused lenses show only what you have yet to achieve in order to reach success or be happy—in your career, relationship, weight, finances, etc. Lusting after the day you get "there," you remain perpetually unsatisfied, because there is no "there"! So the junkie never gets her fix, and you never enjoy, relax, or receive the fruits of your labor.

TOXIC HABITS

Basing self-worth and happiness on external outcomes and recognition

Being chronically dissatisfied

Discounting and not acknowledging milestones or achievements

Overfocusing on the future

Overworking and over-efforting

Pressuring yourself to always be further ahead

Seeking external validation

Setting unrealistic expectations

BIG FAT LIES

"*WHEN* YOU GET THERE, *THEN* YOU'LL BE HAPPY."

"THERE ISN'T TIME TO CELEBRATE OR REST."

"YOU'RE NOT *THERE* YET."

"YOU MUST WORK HARD AND DRIVE YOURSELF HARD TO SUCCEED."

"YOU ARE NOT WORKING HARD ENOUGH."

THE COMPARISON QUEEN

The Comparison Queen has made it her job to assess how well your life is going and how well you are doing by comparing where you are now to where she thinks you should be, could be, or used to be. She never asks you questions like "What would make you happy?" She is much more concerned about how you stack up against other people, usually in specific areas of your life—your financial status, relationship status, career status, or your body shape and fitness level. Her energy is directed to constantly sensing how you are measuring up. And when you don't, or if she perceives you are lagging behind other people, she pulls out her big weapons, the mirrors of comparison—one that makes you feel inferior to others and the other superior to others. But they both have a devastating impact, you feel like crap about yourself or isolated and disconnected from others.

WEAPONS

The Inferiority Mirror. The Comparison Queen uses this mirror to reflect how everyone else is better than you—more beautiful, successful, organized, you name it, making you feel like you are falling behind and not measuring up. The mirror also reflects the "better" previous or fantasy versions of yourself. The result? You compare yourself to who you used to be or who you think you should be and determine the woman today is not as beautiful, successful, or good.

The Superiority Mirror. This mirror fills your mind with superior thoughts about yourself compared to other people. It reflects an elevated self-image that makes you feel better about yourself by making others less than and you better than. This mirror is tricky because it gives you a high that makes you feel good, but the long-term cost is isolation and loneliness.

TOXIC HABITS

Basing your worth and happiness on other people's expressions or accomplishments

Comparing yourself to others

Judging others

Judging yourself

Measuring yourself against an idealized or previous version of yourself

Rejecting yourself

Trying to be someone other than your true self

BIG FAT LIES

"YOU SHOULD BE FURTHER ALONG."

"SO-AND-SO IS MUCH PRETTIER/SMARTER/MORE SUCCESSFUL THAN YOU."

"YOU'RE FALLING BEHIND."

"YOU JUST AREN'T AS PRETTY/YOUNG/THIN AS YOU USED TO BE."

"YOU'RE WAY BETTER THAN HER."

THE DOING ADDiCT

Like an Energizer Bunny gone mad, the Doing Addict is your inner taskmaster and slave driver. She's made it her job to make sure you don't relax or play until your work is done or the to-do list is checked off (which it never is). She makes you feel like a slacker if you're not busy doing something. She can't sit still, so neither can you. Simply being and doing "nothing" makes her uncomfortable, so she likes to keep your mind running and thinking like a ticker tape with the endless number of things you need to do, should have done, have yet to think about. The only time she lets you rest is if you get sick or have some life catastrophe; it's the only way she can justify slowing down. She is a kissing cousin to the Achievement Junkie, but she differs in that she doesn't care about attaining big goals. Her sole focus is keeping you busy doing anything.

WEAPONS

The Big-Ass To-Do List. This list is never ending, it never gets shorter, and there is no prioritization—everything must get done NOW! TODAY! And BY YOU! Your Doing Addict climbs into your bed and head at night, rattling off all you didn't do and must remember to do tomorrow, making sleep futile. When you wake, the list awaits, creating stress before you ever get out of bed. It never includes what's most important to you, so your dreams, joy, and self-care get put on hold.

The Guilt and Glorification Gun. This gun either shoots guilt at you to make you feel bad about what you are not doing or glorification because you are doing such a great job staying busy.

So you feel guilty when you do anything that doesn't directly correlate to productivity. And your self-worth becomes tied to how much you do and how busy you appear.

TOXIC HABITS

Attemping to accomplish more than humanly possible in a day/week/month

Basing self-worth on how much you get done

Feeling like a victim/martyr to your obligations

Making everything a priority

Thinking obsessively

Overdoing, doing more than really necessary

Resting and slowing down only when sick

Using busyness as an excuse

BIG FAT LIES

"YOU CAN'T REST. YOU HAVE TO KEEP PUSHING THROUGH."
"RESTING ISN'T PRODUCTIVE. STOP BEING LAZY."
"YOU SHOULD BE ABLE TO GET MORE DONE."
"YOU CAN'T PLAY OR RELAX UNTIL ALL YOUR WORK IS DONE."
"YOU HAVE TOO MUCH TO DO. YOU CAN'T
<INSERT SELF-LOVING ACT>."

THE DRAMA QUEEN

The Drama Queen thrives on chaos and loves to keep your life in a state of turmoil, feeding off the adrenaline. The Drama Queen isn't there to help or fix; she never wants the drama to end. She doesn't care if the drama is yours or someone else's; she thrives on gossip and loves to spend hours talking, processing, and pontificating about your and other people's problems. It's like living in your own reality TV show. She can also become paranoid and make you feel like people are out to get you. She'll build elaborate dialogues in your mind about the unkind things other people are saying about you, convincing you that people are conspiring against you. To protect you, she drives you to collude with others against whomever she's identified as a threat. And while it feels like you are connecting with others in solidarity of this drama, in reality you are separating yourself and hurting people. Your Inner Mean Girl becomes an outer mean girl.

WEAPONS

The Drama Maker. The Drama Queen does not like there to be peace and quiet for any length of time; it makes her feel nervous that she'll be out of a job, so she has a special penchant for taking things in your life that really don't need to be a big deal and blowing them up to epic proportions. If life is too calm, she will seek out drama or intensity, in your life or someone else's.

The Gossip Generator. The Drama Queen loves to keep you gabbing and embroiled in talking negatively about others. *Gossip* by our definition is: "saying anything about a person—either a person you know personally or a person you don't—that you would not repeat if that person were present." She wastes a lot of your energy, time, and mental space on gossip and talking about other people's lives instead of your own.

TOXIC HABITS

Being addicted to intensity

Constantly talking about your problems

Creating drama to get attention or create false connection

Creating a problem where there doesn't need to be one

Making up elaborate stories in your mind

Obsessively thinking that people are talking about you or colluding against you

Participating in or starting gossip

Stirring the pot and urging others to collude with you

BIG FAT LIES

"THEY ARE ALL TALKING ABOUT YOU."
"THEY KNOW YOU ARE A FRAUD."
"THAT PERSON HAS IT IN FOR YOU AND IS GOING TO TAKE YOU DOWN."
"YOU CAN'T TRUST ANYONE."
"LIFE IS FULL OF CHAOS. THAT'S JUST HOW IT IS."
"DID YOU HEAR ABOUT . . . ?!"

THE FiXER AND RESCUER

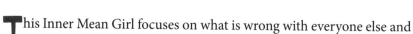

This Inner Mean Girl focuses on what is wrong with everyone else and then gets you to spend all your energy and time helping other people. She makes you ignore your needs, problems, and challenges in the name of helping others, and she convinces you that what you are doing is the noble thing, the only choice you could make. It's your duty to help. Right?!

In reality, what's happening is that she's trying to keep you from focusing on the person who needs your help the most: you. Her job is to keep you from taking an honest look at your own life. She also makes you believe you have the power to change someone else and convinces you that you know what is right for others—talk about an ego. She loves to over-empathize with people as a way to connect, and your life and mind become consumed by other people's lives—distracting you from your own life.

WEAPONS

The Trouble Finder. The Fixer and Rescuer feeds on other people's problems, woes, tragedies, and challenges—they make her, and you, feel useful, needed, and special. She uses this special internal homing device to scan for people in trouble. Once she locates someone in "need," she compels you to give away your energy, time, and money, claiming it's in the name of love, when often it's meddling and over-giving.

The Trouble Maker. When she can't find something or someone for you to fix, she will turn a small swell into a big storm, just so she (and you) can feel useful. This weapon gives her the ability to make little things feel really big and urgent. As a result of this fabricated trouble, which can seem quite real, people become over-reliant on you, conveniently giving her job security.

TOXIC HABITS

Avoiding your own problems by focusing on others' issues

Taking over responsibility for other people's problems and lives

Creating big problems out of small situations

Meddling

Over-caring—sacrificing self to care for others

Over-empathizing—feeling other people's pain for them

Over-giving—enabling others by giving too much

BIG FAT LIES

"THEY NEED YOU."

"YOU ARE THE ONLY ONE WHO CAN HELP."

"IF YOU LOVED THEM, YOU WOULD HELP THEM."

"IF YOU DON'T HELP THEM, NO ONE WILL."

"IF YOU JUST <INSERT ACTION>, THEY WILL CHANGE."

THE GOOD GiRL

Meet your inner people pleaser. She's desperately afraid that no one will like her if she doesn't do what people expect of her, say the right thing, or sacrifice herself. Her job is to make sure you behave according to the Good Girl rules (which of course are really Big Fat Lies), including: "Good girls give to others before taking care of themselves"; "Good girls don't rock the boat"; "Good girls never say anything controversial or that could be offensive"; and "Good girls always say yes to helping others, even when their cup is empty and they have nothing left to give."

She makes you believe that doing things for others from obligation, guilt, and loyalty to the detriment of yourself is normal. She makes you do things because "it's the right thing to do" even if it's not right for you, always putting others first. She doesn't know how to keep healthy boundaries and will tell you to give everything away—your time, money, and energy.

WEAPONS

The Good Girl Mask. The Good Girl looks innocent, sweet, and good on the outside. But it's all a façade to make everyone believe that you are a good girl: caring; loving; giving; always doing what is right; never thinking about herself, only other people. The Good Girl IMG doesn't want anyone to see what is really behind that mask, be that feelings of anger or a wild woman rebel. She keeps you smiling even when you are seething underneath.

The People Pleasing Meter. The Good Girl is addicted to pleasing others, so she is constantly scanning for what other people need, driving you to make choices based on what will serve others, not you. She drives you to please others but rarely allows you to think about what would please you or to act in a self-serving way without feeling guilty as a result.

TOXIC HABITS

Acting and giving from guilt and obligation

Allowing people to take advantage of you

Over-giving to others, creating a deficit of time, money, or energy for yourself

Over-caring for others and undercaring for yourself

Saying yes when you want to/ need to say no

Self-repression, holding back your true thoughts, feelings, and expression

Setting loose and unhealthy boundaries

BIG FAT LIES
"YOU HAVE TO DO THE *RIGHT* THING."
"IF YOU SAY NO, PEOPLE WON'T LIKE YOU."
"OTHERS SHOULD COME FIRST."
"TAKING CARE OF YOURSELF IS SELFISH."
"YOU CAN'T SAY THAT/DO THAT!"

THE HEAD TRIPPER

The only thing that holds credence with this Inner Mean Girl is rational thought and practicality. If she can't see it, or it can't be proven scientifically or in physical reality, she doesn't believe it. She won't let you trust your instincts. Her job is to discount your intuition and anything that feels too "touchy-feely" or "woo-woo." She doesn't believe in serendipity, coincidence, or providence. She is all about the intellect, the mind, and what can be proven. She also prides herself on your ability to not cry, to be unshakable, and to keep your emotions under wraps.

She has also made it her job to assess all risk in your life and not let you take any unnecessary chances. If it were up to her, you'd live a "safe" life where nothing changed. The Head Tripper is a master at using your mind against you. As a result, she is not just rational but she is also a dream stealer.

WEAPONS

The Wet Blanket. She carries around a big wet blanket to extinguish any dream you might have that could possibly stretch you out of your comfort zone. Feeling passionate about a new possibility? She'll douse that fire with all the reasons why you shouldn't try it. Have an idea you'd like to explore? She'll smother it with the rational reasons it will never work. She can also use this spirit-dampening tool to hide your desires from you so that when asked questions like "What do you want?" or "What are your dreams?" all you can offer are a blank stare and the response "I don't know."

The Feeling and Intuition Pooh-Pooh-er. To keep you distrusting your intuitive sensations, when you have a feeling or an intuition, or something unexplainable occurs, she zaps you with doubt or skepticism, to discount or dispel any belief, trust, or faith that may have emerged.

TOXIC HABITS

Avoiding taking risks and making change without total certainty

Thinking cynically

Discounting serendipity and spirituality

Needing to be seen as responsible

Overanalyzing and running worst-case scenarios

Obsessively searching for answers from other people or on the internet

Overvaluing rational thought and the mind over the heart, feelings, and intuition

Short-circuiting your dreams because they aren't "realistic"

BIG FAT LIES

"BE REALISTIC."

"SHOWING YOUR FEELINGS IS A SIGN OF WEAKNESS."

"YOU HAVE TO BE A RESPONSIBLE ADULT; YOU CAN'T TAKE CHANCES."

"<INSERT YOUR DREAM> WILL NEVER WORK."

"THAT WAS JUST A RANDOM COINCIDENCE. MAGIC ISN'T REAL."

THE INViNCIBLE SUPERWOMAN

This Inner Mean Girl expects you to be Atlas: she puts the weight of the world on your shoulders and doesn't let you set it down—because you should be able to handle it all. Her job is to keep you looking strong, never showing weakness. She over-schedules and over-commits you and then watches you melt (behind closed doors, of course) because of the pressure—or until you get resentful of all the things people expect of you, even though you are the one who agreed to them. Her motivation is simple—to avoid looking weak or feeling vulnerable, so she pushes support away so people don't think you can't do it on your own. Inside, you are under so much pressure that what you really need is a good cry (to release the stress), to quit your superwoman job, and to learn that keeping up the façade of strength is costing you your happiness—and your health.

WEAPONS

The Superwoman Cape. She loves to put on her modern-day superwoman cape, making you believe you should be able to hold up your family, job, health, and home without sweating it, even though you are a mere mortal with limitations, which makes you human, not weak, a fact she is not impressed with. Wearing the cape, you are trapped in the role of "Master of the Universe," which means you have to keep working, controlling, and taking care of everything—no time for joy, play, or rest.

The "I Am Fine" Bullhorn. She's got a bullhorn that broadcasts the slogan "Everything is fine. I am fine. I've got it handled." This racket gets played over and over, radiating out into the world. People assume you have it all under control because you look like you are fine and are never in need of help, so people rarely offer it. And even if they did, she'd just make you reply, "I am fine. I've got it handled."

TOXIC HABITS

Being the strong one for everyone else and not having anyone to support you

Keeping up the false appearance that everything is okay

Not accepting support from others

Overestimating what you can accomplish

Pushing hard to make stuff happen

Pressuring yourself to do more, be more, and have more

Starving yourself from joy and then binging on pleasure

Treating your body like a work-horse and disregarding your physical needs

BIG FAT LIES

"YOU CAN HANDLE THIS. JUST KEEP PUSHING THROUGH."
"DON'T BE WEAK. BE STRONG."
"YOU ARE THE ONLY ONE WHO CAN DO THIS."
"IT WILL TAKE WAY MORE TIME TO SHOW SOMEONE ELSE HOW TO DO THIS, SO JUST DO IT YOURSELF."
"THERE IS NO ONE WHO CAN SUPPORT YOU. YOU HAVE TO DO THIS ON YOUR OWN."

THE MARTYR (AKA THE SPIRITUAL GURU, STARVING ARTIST, OR SUPERACTIVIST)

This Inner Mean Girl has made it her job to use your spirituality, creativity, or social mission as a way to pretend you don't need things on the physical plane or as a way to convince you that you are above being and feeling successful. She makes you feel better about yourself by keeping you suffering for your cause, art, or spiritual pursuit, almost as a way to prove yourself worthy. She can also convince you that having money is a bad thing—even though you'd really like some more of it. She has a great knack for making you feel superior to others when you face difficulty in personal relationships or when the state of your life is kind of in the toilet. As a result, you become more disconnected from the people you are putting yourself above. If any success or abundance comes your way, she'll tell you you're a sellout, and you'll feel disloyal to your artistic or spiritual tribe.

WEAPONS

The Self-Sacrifice Tape Measure. She loves to measure you based on how much you are sacrificing yourself for your cause, art, or spiritual pursuit. She makes you think the more you sacrifice—time, money, health, opportunities, relationships—the better you are doing. She even measures you against how much others sacrifice, to make you feel better about your lack of success or happiness.

The Spiritual Bully Bat. The Martyr bullies you and others with spiritual language to keep you from admitting the truth. She says, "Just trust," when you need to wake up to the truth, or says, "The Universe is your source," while you write a check that will bounce. She turns this tool on others, accusing them of not being spiritual or dedicated enough to their art or cause, saying if they just "trusted" enough or got into "vibrational alignment," it'd all work out. This weapon is tricky because the Martyr uses sound spiritual law against you.

TOXIC HABITS

Discounting your physical needs in the name of a greater cause

Feeling superior to or separate from "ordinary" people who just don't get it

Judging that having money is evil or wrong

Over-identifying with being an artist, healer, activist, or a spiritual being

Using spiritual principles or false hope to avoid reality

BIG FAT LIES

"YOU DON'T NEED MONEY."

"YOU HAVE TO SUFFER FOR YOUR CAUSE/ART/MISSION."

"IF YOU MAKE TOO MUCH MONEY, YOU WON'T BE AS CONNECTED WITH THE PEOPLE YOU SERVE."

"SUCCESSFUL PEOPLE ARE GREEDY/BAD/NOT AS GOOD."

"IF YOU BECOME SUCCESSFUL, YOU WILL CHANGE OR LOSE YOUR FRIENDS."

THE OVERLY OPTIMISTIC, PARTYING CHEERLEADER

Meet the life of the party, the one with a smile always on her face, the one who tells you that everything will work out for you, even if you are about to dive headfirst into a self-sabotaging choice. This Inner Mean Girl makes it her job to make you feel good and happy in the moment, consequences be damned. She is all about instant gratification and tells you to charge it, eat it, do it, try it, if she thinks it will feel good in the short term. She'll cheer you right off a cliff just to avoid feeling dark or hard emotions, and she hates feeling disappointed or like she is being denied of some kind of pleasure. Moderation is not in her vocabulary—she prefers excess and consuming whatever she is indulging in: food, shopping, watching TV, etc. She keeps you pumped up and positive all the time, even when that's not for your highest good.

WEAPONS

Pollyanna Glasses. These glasses make sure all you see is the positive possibility, the opportunity, and the good that could occur, blocking out any possible disappointments, warning signals, challenges, or pitfalls. They only focus on the optimistic viewpoint, which makes you believe it will all work out fabulously. However, you miss the whole picture and get blindsided later down the path, which doesn't end as rosy as you had hoped.

The Party Permission Slip. When you are stressed or freaked out, this IMG knows all you need is someone to give you permission to open up the floodgates to indulge in anything and everything that will take off the pressure. She's happy to oblige. The name of the party is gluttony—spend money, consume food, drink the entire bottle, watch ten episodes in one day. It's all good . . . until the party is over, and you are left with the financial, emotional, and physical hangover.

TOXIC HABITS

Avoiding honestly assessing risks and potential consequences

Being overly optimistic without discernment

Denying reality

Numbing out with TV, sex, food, anything that feels good in the moment

Overspending

Over-consuming anything, including food and drink

Thinking wishfully that isn't grounded in reality

Trying to avoid hard and heavy feelings

BIG FAT LIES

"JUST PUT IT ON THE CREDIT CARD. YOU CAN PAY IT OFF LATER."
"GO TO THE PARTY. YOU CAN FINISH ALL THAT WORK LATER."
"LET YOURSELF HAVE THAT BAG OF COOKIES (OR THIRD GLASS OF WINE). YOU'LL EAT HEALTHY TOMORROW."
"YOU DESERVE THIS. YOU'VE BEEN WORKING SO HARD!"
"JUST WORRY ABOUT THAT TOMORROW."

THE PERFECTIONIST

This highly critical and often harsh, picky, or sharp Inner Mean Girl is like the most judgmental parent you could ever imagine. Her job is to wag her finger at you, blame you, and run around your life, house, relationship, body, and career pointing out everything you are doing wrong, that could be done better, or that doesn't measure up to her ridiculously high perfectionist standards, which you never meet (who could?). For her, nothing you do is enough unless it is perfect, which of course nothing can be, so nothing is ever quite enough, including you.

Having a party? She'll have you cleaning the house for hours beforehand and then walking around all night putting things in order instead of enjoying yourself. She is—and so you become—obsessive, working overtime, and worrying about details no one else ever notices or even cares about. And if she can't find something to criticize you for, she'll drive you to pick on and criticize others.

WEAPONS

The Mighty Magnifying Glass of Perfection. She has the power to zoom in on everything you are not, making you feel like you failed. Asked to bring cupcakes to your kid's school, but you bought instead of baked? She's there shaming you: "You should have been able to make these cupcakes yourself. You're a bad mother." Someone offer you a compliment for your effort or results? She will deflect the love and respond by noting what you could have done better.

The Ridiculous Expectation Setter. This IMG expects you to know everything right now, even if you are just a beginner. She gives you no space to learn or improve. She will make you feel inferior because you haven't mastered this skill. She'll also keep you so focused on making things perfect that you procrastinate on getting your ideas, projects, and dreams into the world because "they aren't perfect yet." So you and your work stay stuck.

TOXIC HABITS

Criticizing yourself harshly

Criticizing others

Expecting yourself to be masterful immediately

Holding and judging yourself and others to unrealistic expectations

Overthinking and overfocusing on details that don't matter

Pointing out what isn't perfect

Procrastinating

Striving for perfection to the detriment of completing projects

BIG FAT LIES

"YOU'RE NOT ENOUGH; YOU ARE NOT GOOD ENOUGH."

"IT'S WORTHLESS IF IT'S NOT PERFECT."

"YOU SHOULD HAVE THIS FIGURED OUT BY NOW. WHAT'S WRONG WITH YOU?"

"YOU AREN'T DOING IT RIGHT."

"IT WILL NEVER BE PERFECT SO JUST FORGET ABOUT IT."

"YOU CAN'T SHARE THIS OR PUT THIS OUT INTO THE WORLD UNTIL IT'S PERFECT."

THE REJECTION QUEEN

The Rejection Queen's job is to protect you from getting hurt and feeling unloved, but her methods have the opposite effect—you feel more rejected, distant, and lonely. She shows up in three ways. First, she can make you feel rejected, convincing you that you are unlovable, doomed to be alone, and that people don't want to hang out with/talk to/partner with you. She figures if she makes you feel rejected, you won't be rejected by others. She keeps you playing small, not taking risks, and keeps you from reaching out to others for support. Second, she cajoles you to trust the wrong people, setting you up to get betrayed or rejected, just to prove it isn't safe to let people in. Her third tactic is to keep you in relationships that are unhealthy or past their expiration date because to her it's better to keep the love you have, even if it's codependent, toxic, or conditional, rather than face being alone.

WEAPONS

The "You Are Unloved" Mirror. This reflects the story of how unloved, unlikable, and alone you are, so all you see are the ways you are lonely, not invited, or don't belong. The mirror supports the story that you can't trust love, or others, keeping you from reaching out or stepping out because you'll be rejected.

Shields of Protection. She builds walls, towers, and force fields around your heart to keep anyone from getting too close, so you don't get hurt. But ultimately these shields keep you from the intimacy and connection you crave. These shields keep other people at bay, so you only have surface-level relationships or ones based on comfort and convenience. These shields keep you safe from the one thing she fears: vulnerability. But what they do is keep you lonely and without the supportive relationships you actually need to flourish.

TOXIC HABITS

Being overly independent and self-sufficient as a way to block intimacy and vulnerability

Creating mistrusting beliefs about love and people

Doing everything on your own to avoid possible rejection or disappointment

Isolating yourself

Settling for less than you desire to avoid possible rejection

Staying in unhealthy or mediocre relationships

Story making that you don't belong

Stewing in feelings of being unloved, unlovable, and lonely

BIG FAT LIES

"YOU DON'T BELONG."
"YOU'RE UNLOVABLE."
"YOU ARE DAMAGED GOODS."
"SHE/HE IS THE ONLY ONE WHO WILL EVER LOVE YOU."
"YOU'LL BE ALONE FOREVER."
"IT'S NOT SAFE TO LET LOVE IN. LOVE HURTS."

THE WORRYWART

This Inner Mean Girl can show up with many different faces, depending on her mood, but her job is always the same: to keep you living in a heightened state of fear and anxiety. She is a professional worrier and runner of worst-case scenarios. She has a special talent for finding evidence that shows you that you can't trust everything to work out, so you have to be alert and on guard at all times. When things are going well, she looks for things to fret about. When the slightest chance of something going awry shows up, she takes it as a sign that catastrophe is about to strike. She creates crazy stories in your mind and works you up into a frenzy so you run around and make choices from freak-out mode. When things are not going great for you, she moves into doom-and-gloom mode. She prefers suffering to happiness, believing that even if things are good, they could go bad at any moment.

WEAPONS

The Doom Maker. Just like a rainmaker, the Worrywart uses the doom maker to create a personal rain cloud over your head, pouring down darkness and negativity. So no matter what you try to do to find the sunlight, she just keeps raining the doom on top of you, drowning you in feelings of misery and defeat, making you feel like life is just so hard.

The Story Maker. The Worrywart uses this to imagine stories to make you fearful. Things starting to go your way? Feeling like there is light at the end of the tunnel? That is the exact moment she tells the story *The Other Shoe Is Bound to Drop: Things Can't Keep Going So Well.* Feeling a little uneasy about something?

She'll whip up an internal frenzy with the story *Everything Is Falling Apart!*. Like nightmares, these stories keep you up at night, worrying about all the bad things that could possibly happen.

TOXIC HABITS

Creating catastrophic situations and stories inside your mind

Future tripping

Hanging on to the past

Looking for evidence of all the ways your life is hard

Obsessively thinking about worst-case scenarios and hypothetical situations

Over-worrying and acting from that worry

Overfocusing on and talking about what doesn't work in your life

Seeing the glass half empty even when good things happen

BIG FAT LIES

"IF YOU AREN'T WORRYING OR ON ALERT, SOMETHING BAD WILL HAPPEN."

"THINGS NEVER WORK OUT FOR YOU."

"DON'T GET TOO COMFORTABLE BEING HAPPY."

"YOU'RE DOOMED TO LIVE THIS WAY FOREVER."

"LIFE IS HARD. GET USED TO IT."

"THE OTHER SHOE IS BOUND TO DROP."

Inner Wisdom Reflection:
Which Inner Mean Girls Are
Running Your Life?

Now that you've had a chance to become familiar with all thirteen archetypes of Inner Mean Girls, it's time to identify your specific Inner Mean Girl(s). Most women can relate to many of these archetypes, and at first, it can feel like, "Oh man, I'm screwed—I have them all!" But don't fret—that's just your Inner Mean Girl getting fearful that you are about to expose her. Most of us can relate to almost all these archetypes because at times we have experienced each of them. As humans we all experience worry (the Worrywart), let gluttony make a bad choice for us (the Overly Optimistic, Partying Cheerleader), and sometimes feel like the world is on our shoulders (the Invincible Superwoman).

The question we want you to pause and answer is: which of these archetypes resonate with you at the deepest level right now in your life? These are the ones that feel almost like they are a part of you and your internal operating system on a daily basis. Go back and look at the ones you marked or that hit you the most as you were reading them. Reread the descriptions and notice how your body feels. Do these descriptions feel familiar, as if your body is saying, "Uh-huh. I know that game." Can you remember a few instances when these toxic habits or Big Fat Lies showed up? Which ones felt most like you just exposed something about yourself as you read them? These primary ones are what we are interested in revealing and working with.

Your next step is to complete the superpower challenge that follows to reveal exactly what Inner Mean Girls are hiding deep within you. As you take this next step, remember that this journey is all about you:

how much you give determines how much you receive. We know you're already good at giving to others. Now it's time to give to you. Your IMG may try to convince you that you don't have time to take this assessment, but we also know that you are committed to yourself, so take action. Plus, these kinds of self-reflective assessments are always so fun and revealing!

Superpower Challenge: Take the Inner Mean Girl Assessment

This assessment is not a pop quiz. There are no right or wrong answers. And there are no grades. No one else will see your results, so do yourself the favor of answering honestly. This is not the time to answer from an aspirational, hopeful place; it's time to be real. Don't approach this like one of those magazine quizzes you cheat on so you get more points in the category you want (yes, we've done it too). This is an opportunity for you to narrow down what you are personally dealing with inside. Pull back the curtain and reveal who's there.

The Inner Mean Girl Assessment

On a scale of 1 to 10, rate the truth of each statement below with 1 being not true at all, because you never feel or act this way; 5 being true sometimes, because it's a feeling or thought that is familiar, though it isn't your everyday state; and 10 being true most of the time, because this is a normal state of being or thinking for you. Don't think too much about your rating—go with your first instinct and move quickly.

THE INNER MEAN GIRL ASSESSMENT	Rate 1–10
1. I compare myself to other people in ways that make me feel bad about myself.	
2. Things never work out for me. That's just how life is.	
3. I work so hard all the time, to the point where I exhaust myself.	
4. I don't rest or relax unless I get sick or a catastrophe happens. I don't have time for resting.	
5. I have a hard time saying no and setting boundaries. I say yes to helping other people or taking on more even when my plate is overflowing.	
6. I have relationships that are unhealthy, toxic, and draining.	
7. I connect with people by feeling their pain.	
8. I believe it is wiser to listen to my rational mind more than my intuition.	
9. I believe that people who are artists, are spiritually inclined, or do work for the good of society don't have a lot of financial success.	
10. Even when I am disappointed or hurt, I make myself feel happy and look on the bright side.	
11. I feel like other people talk about me and are out to get me or tear me down.	
12. I wish that I could be more like other people who seem more successful, beautiful, thin, etc.	
13. I make choices based on what others will think. Doing the "right thing" in their eyes is a guidepost for my choices.	
14. I feel lonely and isolated.	

THE INNER MEAN GIRL ASSESSMENT	Rate 1–10
15. I get obsessive about things being perfect.	
16. I'd rather have a safe life than an adventurous life.	
17. I often feel anxious, fearful, and filled with worry.	
18. I think I should be further along in my life than I am.	
19. I feel guilty, uncomfortable, or like a slacker or loser if I'm not doing something "productive."	
20. I overindulge in things (like food, spending, alcohol, etc.) that feel good in the moment but that I later regret.	
21. I have a hard time celebrating milestones or my achievements. I just move on to the next thing.	
22. Even if I'm new to something, I expect myself to be masterful at it.	
23. I feel like I am a bad friend, mom, daughter, wife, etc. if I don't give a lot to other people, even if that means not taking care of myself.	
24. I feel like it's my job to help and fix people I care about.	
25. I'd like to delegate to others, but most people can't do as good a job as I can, so it's easier to do things myself.	
26. Chaos and drama seem to follow me wherever I go. I am always putting out fires.	
27. I feel like having more money will get in the way of my creative expression or spiritual growth.	
28. I feel overwhelmed often, but I never let anyone know. I just suck it up.	

THE INNER MEAN GIRL ASSESSMENT	Rate 1–10
29. If something can't be proven scientifically, I believe it's probably not true.	
30. I am the kind of person who is always helping others, to the point that my life is focused more on others than myself.	
31. I feel like no matter how much I do or how well I've done, I could have done it better.	
32. I feel like when I reach my goal or attain a certain level of success, then I'll finally be truly happy, perpetually putting my happiness in the future.	
33. It can be hard for me to fall asleep at night because all the things I have to do keep running through my mind.	
34. I feel like I should be able to take care of myself without needing a lot of love and support from others.	
35. I feel like I have to be strong and take care of a lot because being vulnerable or admitting I can't do something is weak.	
36. I don't need much on the physical plane in terms of money. It's just not that important to me.	
37. I think being sad or disappointed is a waste of time.	
38. I feel like the other shoe could drop at any moment.	
39. I gossip and talk about people. I don't like to admit it, but I do.	

The next step is to tally your scores for each of the Inner Mean Girl Archetypes. Add up your ratings for the corresponding statements for each archetype. Note that we had to scramble up the questions and the archetypes so that your Inner Mean Girl, who is pretty darn savvy, couldn't figure out the system and sabotage your ability to see her for who she really is. We've given you brief descriptions here for each archetype, or you can look back to their full descriptions starting back on page 10.

Add up scores for questions 3, 21, and 32.

This is your Achievement Junkie score: ___.

The Achievement Junkie is the pushy, relentless force that drives you hard to get to a goal you will never reach because the finish line just keeps moving. Her job is to keep you addicted to pursuing goals, by fooling you into believing that there is a magical destination that will indicate you have finally arrived, where you can rest, stop working so hard, and be enough. She makes you exhaust yourself and robs you of receiving the success and happiness from all your hard work. (See page 10 for full description.)

Add up scores for questions 1, 12, and 18.

This is your Comparison Queen score: ___.

The Comparison Queen is your inner judge who assesses the success of your life by comparing you to other people or to where she thinks you should be, or used to be, which in her eyes is never enough. She makes you feel like an inadequate failure or like you are falling behind and not measuring up. She can also compare your best to everyone else's worst so that you feel superior. (See page 12 for full description.)

Add up scores for questions 4, 19, and 33.

This is your Doing Addict score: ___.

The Doing Addict is an inner taskmaster and slave driver who makes sure you are always busy doing something. She makes sure you don't rest, relax, or play until your work is done or the items on the to-do list are checked off (which they never are). She makes your mind run constantly with all the to dos, making you stressed out, frenzied, always reacting to the outside world's demands. (See page 14 for full description.)

Add up scores for questions 11, 26, and 39.

This is your Drama Queen score: ____.

The Drama Queen is the turmoil creator who thrives on chaos and loves to keep your life in a state of drama, which she views as excitement. Her job is to keep you from having to deal with your true emotions by whipping up all-consuming drama in your life or feeding off gossip and other people's chaos. She makes you use all your energy on the "drama" happening so that you don't have focus on the truth of your life. (See page 16 for full description.)

Add up scores for questions 7, 24, and 30.

This is your Fixer and Rescuer score: ____.

The Fixer and Rescuer is the inner helper who loves to focus on what is wrong with everyone else and then gets you to spend all your energy and time helping others. She convinces you that what you are doing is the only choice you could make. She makes you sacrifice yourself in the name of helping others. (See page 18 for full description.)

Add up scores for questions 5, 13, and 23.

This is your Good Girl score: ____.

The Good Girl is an inner people pleaser who is desperately afraid that no one will like her or love her if she doesn't do what people expect of her or if she doesn't give to others before she takes care of herself. She makes you give more time, money, and energy than you have to give, and she stifles your true feelings and emotions. (See page 20 for full description.)

Add up scores for questions 8, 16, and 29.

This is your Head Tripper score: ___.

The Head Tripper is the rational, practical skeptic, whose job it is to discount your intuition and anything that feels too "touchy-feely" or "woo-woo." She prides herself on your ability to not cry, to be unshakable, and to keep your emotions under wraps. She makes you feel weak for having emotions, and she makes you give up on your dreams because they aren't "realistic." (See page 22 for full description.)

Add up scores for questions 25, 28, and 35.

This is your Invincible Superwoman score: ___.

The Invincible Superwoman puts the weight of the world on your shoulders and doesn't let you set it down, no matter how heavy it gets—because she thinks you should be able to handle it. Her job is to keep you feeling and looking strong, never showing any weakness. She makes you do everything on your own and take on way more responsibility than humanly possible. (See page 24 for full description.)

Add up scores for questions 9, 27, and 36.

This is your Martyr score: ___.

The Martyr is an inner spiritual guru, starving artist, or superactivist who has made it her job to use your spirituality, creativity, or social mission as a way to pretend you don't need things on the earthly plane—including money, recognition, and success. She keeps you suffering for your cause, your art, or your spiritual pursuit, as a way to prove yourself worthy or better than others. (See page 26 for full description.)

Add up scores for questions 10, 20, and 37.

This is your Overly Optimistic, Partying Cheerleader score: ___.

The Overly Optimistic, Partying Cheerleader is the one who tells you that everything will work out for you, even if you are about to dive head-first into a self-sabotaging choice. Her job is to make you feel good and happy in the moment, consequences be damned—it's all about instant gratification. She cajoles you into making choices you later regret. (See page 28 for full description.)

Add up scores for questions 15, 22, and 31.

This is your Perfectionist score: ___.

The Perfectionist is the highly critical and often harsh, picky, or sharp critical inner authority figure whose job is to point out everything you're doing wrong or that doesn't measure up to her perfectionist standards. She makes you procrastinate, give more energy and time to a project than is necessary, and obsess over the smallest details that don't matter. (See page 30 for full description.)

Add up scores for questions 6, 14, and 34.

This is your Rejection Queen score: ___.

The Rejection Queen is the one who is deathly afraid of being rejected, unloved, and alone. Her job is to convince you that you are unlovable and doomed to be alone and that people don't really want you around, showing you just how unsafe it is to let people in. And she's great at choosing unhealthy relationships for you, to prove her theories. She makes you feel lonely and left out, like you don't belong, and like it's just safer to be on your own. (See page 32 for full description.)

Add up scores for questions 2, 17, and 38.

This is your Worrywart score: ___.

The Worrywart is the professional worrier and runner of worst-case scenarios, who loves to fill your mind with all the bad things that could happen. Her job is to keep you living in a heightened state of fear and anxiety. She makes you feel unsafe, unsure, and uncertain, filling your head with crazy thoughts so you are constantly anxious, upset, or scared. (See page 34 for full description.)

Next let's look at which Inner Mean Girl Archetypes you scored highest. Circle the archetype or archetypes that have the highest sums. Circle no more than three. You may have high scores for several archetypes, or one or two might be the obvious winners. Either situation is okay.

As a general frame of reference, any archetype you scored 21 or higher on is an archetype you want to continue to explore in the next two chapters. Remember, the first step is awareness, so don't freak out—there are more steps to come! For now, celebrate that you have narrowed your list down and are closer to seeing who your Inner Mean Girl is, how she operates, and what she is costing you.

Take the Inner Mean Girl Assessment Online

If you'd like to have us tally up the results for you and send them to you, you can take the Inner Mean Girl Assessment online. Hop right on over to **innermeangirlquiz.com** and take the assessment, and we will email you the results along with a few tricks and tips for dealing with specific types of Inner Mean Girls.

What if You Have a Few Archetypes with Similar Scores?

It's totally normal to have archetypes score within a few points of each other. Over the course of our research and work with women around the world, we've found that most women relate strongly to multiple Inner Mean Girl Archetypes, but they tend to experience their primary IMG (or IMGs, as the case may be) in two distinct ways:

1. **The Gang of Inner Mean Girls.** You have multiple individual Inner Mean Girls, not just one, who are related but distinct individuals. As you start to identify your Inner Mean Girls in the steps that follow, they will feel like and reveal themselves as separate beings unto themselves. They may feel connected, as they often work together, but you will relate to them separately. Usually, there also tends to be a leader of the pack, which is the Inner Mean Girl who is wielding the most power.

IT'S CHRISTINE HERE, and I have a gang of Inner Mean Girls, for sure. While I can relate to at least seven of the archetypes, I really have five primary Inner Mean Girls (thankfully all now reformed) who travel together as a pack. They can show up individually to wreak havoc in my life or gang up on me and work me over in pairs, trios, and sometimes even all five at once. Before they were transformed and given new jobs, I imagined them like a rough-and-tumble posse wearing leather jackets with their names emblazoned on the back, carrying their individual weapons like swords. And like all gangs, there was a leader who was present most often and who seemed to cut me the deepest. When I first pulled back the curtain to see the gang of Inner Mean Girls, it was my Comparison Queen who was the ringleader, and she was the force that often rallied the others. When I think back, I can see that at different times, other ones were the leaders. My Doing Addict and my Rejection Queen were co–ring leaders in my twenties, keeping me crazy busy and my mind full of Big Fat Lies and misunderstandings about love so that I wouldn't have to leave my former relationship or feel the emotions I had stuffed for many years.

2. **The Inner Mean Girl with Multiple Personalities.** You can also have just one Inner Mean Girl who takes on different archetypes, wielding their Big Fat Lies and weapons depending on what's most effective at the time. She has multiple personalities because she can change her energy depending on what is triggering you. One day she may make you feel worried and scared like the Worrywart, but the next day she is just plain mean as she takes on the role of Comparison Queen. Regardless of which archetype she uses, you still experience her as one force within you. As you reveal and learn more about your Inner Mean Girl over the next couple of chapters, this will become clearer.

IT'S AMY HERE, and you've met my Inner Mean Girl, whom I call Negative Nelly. She can spin her head like Linda Blair in *The Exorcist* and transform from a Worrywart into a Partying Cheerleader in mere seconds. But no matter what Inner Mean Girl archetype she is taking on—and she has about four that she uses most—it feels like different facets of the same force within me. Her voice and energy might change, and the Big Fat Lies she uses as weapons on me differ depending on whom she is channeling, but she still feels like the same, singular Inner Mean Girl. Knowing the different archetypes she takes on helps me to know how to deal with her best, because what might work to calm the Worrywart will fall flat when trying to get the Partying Cheerleader to feel the darker and harder emotions she's avoiding at all costs.

Now, if your Inner Mean Girl has got your mind racing trying to figure out whether you have a gang or a single IMG, just slow down. You have only just completed step one. We have two more steps to go in uncovering your IMG fully, so we are going to throw lots of light on this inner force you will come to know and love. Remember, awareness is the first step. And you are now more aware of your personal IMGs, so give yourself a high-five.

TRANSFORMATION TALE: My Sneaky Inner Mean Girls
by world-renowned Vedic astrologer and bestselling author Carol Allen

When I first met Amy and Christine and they taught me about their work, I thought I didn't have an Inner Mean Girl. Oh, don't get me wrong—it was not all gumdrops and Christmas mornings going on in this thick skull of mine. That I knew. I was all too aware I had an Inner Confused Girl, who had a tough time making decisions, and an Inner Ditzy Girl, who was constantly losing my keys. And don't get me started about my Inner Crazy Cat Lady, who almost made my husband a sweet (cat-hair-covered) memory . . .

So it's not that I'm all Inner Smug and Superior Girl. I'm just not especially mean to myself, criticizing myself all day long, telling myself I can't achieve what I want or that I'm not good enough, that I should be doing more, having more, looking better, and all that other heartbreaking, poisonous self-talk so many people—men and women—torment themselves with.

In fact, I'm kinda the opposite. I'm pretty amazed at how well my life has turned out and am super grateful for my gifts and talents and my willingness to work hard and commit to my goals. And once my skin finally cleared up (about six months ago) and I grew past five foot two (something doctors didn't think would happen), I've been pretty at peace with my looks.

But as someone who has talked with women about their lives full-time since my twenties, I knew the incredible value Amy and Christine are providing and how necessary it is. I just didn't see how it applied to me. That is until they explained that Inner Mean Girls can disguise themselves in all kinds of seemingly benign ways and still cause all kinds of serious trouble. And that's when I realized how major my own Inner Mean Girls are.

Oh yeah, I have Spiritual Susie who is so at peace with the Universe, she trusts too easily—getting into business deals without contracts and running on assumptions that people will always do what they're supposed to do. I won't bore you with what that's cost me over the years, but I have two broken teeth (from grinding them in my sleep due to stress) and once spent a year with a stomachache from the pressure that girl put on me. (All the while she told me I was "just learning what I needed to learn" and "burning off karma." Sigh.)

Then there's I'll Take Care of It Irene, my inner Fixer, who loves to support everyone and everything (see Crazy Cat Lady reference above) while asking for little from anyone, even when people offer or it's their job to help me. She's seen to it that I overwork and undercharge, and miss out on much of the fun of life.

But then there's the baddest, meanest Inner Mean Girl of all—I'd argue as damaging as any Critical Carrie or Perfectionist Patty anywhere—and that's Cheerleader Chandra. This Inner Demon Girl has spent decades running my life, causing me oh-so-much disappointment and unmet expectations, all while prancing about like the Inner Fairy Princess everyone should be so lucky to have. This she-devil believes in my dreams and capacities a little *too* much, telling me not only that "I can do it!" but that I can do it in superhuman record time, while making no mistakes and needing no help. And that, oh yeah, the world will worship me and fall at my feet for every little thing I do, and the Brink's truck will pull up to my door laden with cash just as soon as I do it.

When Amy and Christine explained to me that my inner cheerleader was actually an IMG flinging her pompoms and doing handsprings all over my exhausted, drained, and genuinely-shocked-at-how-long-things-take-and-what-do-you-mean-I'm-not-the-queen-of-everything life, it all made perfect sense. And it was such a relief!

With this new awareness, and Amy and Christine's methods, I benched darling Chandra and gave her a new job. She's now in charge of the cats (telling them all day long how much they are like no other calico/orange tabby/tortoiseshell in the world, because we all know how rare those are!), and they just love her—while ignoring her encouragement to actually do anything.

And I am much more realistic, relaxed, and happy without having to listen to her ridiculous, rosy plans and projections for me.

Thank God for Amy and Christine. (How lucky am I that I actually get to be friends with them? Uh-oh—maybe I do have a Smug and Superior Girl in there, after all!)

Now, if they could just tell me where I put my keys . . .

STEP 2

EXPOSE YOUR INNER MEAN GIRL'S TRICKS AND TRIGGERS

Now that you've had the opportunity to reveal which Inner Mean Girl Archetypes are hijacking your life, you are ready to take the next step—to see exactly what sets your IMG off and how she messes with your relationships, career, money, health, happiness, and more. Identifying your primary archetypes was just the starting point, because just like you, your IMG is a true original. Inner Mean Girls are as distinctive as fingerprints. While we can all relate to similar archetypes, engage in the same toxic habits, and say the same types of mean and unsupportive things to ourselves, no two IMGs are exactly alike.

Step two is all about you becoming keenly aware of your individual Inner Mean Girl's tricks and triggers—how she operates, what activates her, where she shows up the most, and most important for you, how to tell when you are on the brink or in the midst of an Inner Mean Girl attack. Inner Mean Girl attacks are those times when your IMG takes control of your body, mind, heart, and ultimately, your emotions and decisions—those moments when your body goes from feeling peaceful to being full of turmoil, when your mind swells with unsupportive mental chatter you can't turn off, and when you, despite your best intentions, can't help but engage in toxic habits and make self-sabotaging choices. The work you're about to do will even allow you to practice preventative care to stop IMG attacks before they begin.

STEP 2

Your job now is to put your investigative journalist hat on and get curious about what sets off your Inner Mean Girl (or Girls, as the case may be). This new level of awareness and insight will give you the power to begin preempting, preventing, and stopping IMGs in their tracks so you don't go too far down the road of negative thinking and self-sabotage. We'll be here to lead you through this investigation, making sure you uncover four of the most enlightening pieces of information you can reveal about your Inner Mean Girl:

1. What triggers your Inner Mean Girl
2. What core Big Fat Lies she beats you up with
3. What she bullies, manipulates, and drives you to do
4. What she costs you

If you investigate these places inside of you and stay honest with yourself, by the end of this step, you will begin to experience what it is like to have more power over your Inner Mean Girl(s), to be more of an observer of and less of a victim to your emotions, habits, and thoughts, and to be more inclined to make choices that support you, not sabotage you. Do the foundational investigative work here, and as we progress through the other steps, your transformation will be more successful. Piece by piece you'll become much more aware of what's running underneath all that negative self talk and sabotage.

Important reminder: investigative reporting requires you to dig deep into places that maybe you've not wanted to or not previously been ready to unearth and reveal. That's why this is called an enlightening process; you are shining light into dark places. Surprisingly, over and over women tell us how comical (and inspiring) it is when they see the absurdity of their Inner Mean Girls' tricks and triggers. When we can laugh at ourselves while seeing the truth behind our behavioral patterns, major shifts can happen with ease and even joy. But before you start digging, there's something we need to share with you about IMGs.

A New Perspective:
Inner Mean Girl Appearances Are Good News

Yes, you read that correctly, Inner Mean Girl appearances are good news. No, we haven't gone mad. But we do have a powerful perspective to share with you. When your IMG appears, that means you are growing and risking, stretching yourself to new heights, opening up your heart to more love and your life to more possibility, and that's good news.

When our students and clients tell us about an Inner Mean Girl attack, we always smile. Not because we love to see them suffer (that really would be mean!), but because we know the truth—they are growing. They are *breaking down* to *break through*. So instead of throwing a pity party or jumping right in to solve a problem, first we celebrate: "Wahoo, your Inner Mean Girl is on the scene. Break on down to break through, baby. Good growth is on the way!" Now, we get that this enthusiasm can feel a little annoying (or even a lot annoying) when you are in the midst of feeling like crap about yourself. But this burst of celebration has a powerful effect on your Inner Mean Girl and on your brain—the good energy can disarm her and as a result stop your mind from taking you down the pathway to suffering. Your IMG expects you to resist her, which just increases her power and makes her dig her heels in even deeper, further ingraining the old neural pathways you want to reroute.

But when you greet your Inner Mean Girl with good energy, it's like zapping her with a stun gun of love. She gets thrown off-kilter, the brain pattern gets interrupted, and now we can move in for transformation and breakthrough. Instead of resisting the Inner Mean Girl attack, we will prepare you to notice her faster, so the attacks can become more like flare-ups and not devastating disasters, allowing you to recover faster, move more quickly, make better choices, and have more good growth.

The breakdown-to-breakthrough process and the notion of good growth isn't just a bunch of fluff or positive spin. Science shows us

STEP 2

that before you can break through old habits and rewire your neural pathways, your brain and body have to go through a state of instability and flux to reorder.[1] It's the chaotic rearranging, breaking down the old, and constructing the new, that allows you to arrive at new states of consciousness and mind-sets from which you can respond and react differently to external and internal stimuli. This scientific phenomenon is called Chaos Theory, and it is believed to impact everything—including you. Here's a very simplified version of how it works. Think of boiling water. The water starts at a still state, and then when heat is applied, the water begins to bubble like crazy—chaos. If left to boil, the water eventually takes on a new form—steam. Without the chaos, the water could not have changed form. Your ingrained thoughts, habits, and patterns are the same.

What's also awesome about this Chaos Theory stuff is that spiritual teachers have forever been saying the same thing, pointing out that personal transformation often happens after some sort of triggering event that breaks apart the old, stable structures we hold so dear and then sends us into chaos. If you've ever lost a job, ended a relationship, gone through a financial or health crisis, been in a challenging situation at work or with family, you know what we are talking about. If our Inner Wisdoms are in charge in these situations, we do as the spiritual teachers tell us: we surrender, knowing that major breakthroughs are underway, and even if it's hard, we keep the faith that there is a light at the end of the tunnel. Through this process, eventually we do end up in a reorganized, more enlightened state of being. It's just like a caterpillar that turns into a butterfly and changes form completely. Lots of chaos that we never see happens in the cocoon, including the caterpillar completely liquefying to transform into its new, beautiful, freer state. We humans go through the same metamorphosis.

So you can trust that when you're breaking down or in the midst of an Inner Mean Girl attack, it is a clear sign that you are in the midst of an opportunity for growth, and if you stay awake and aware, a breakthrough is ahead—as long as you don't give up and turn back or try to resist or control it. You just have to keep moving and being with the uncomfortable, hard feelings. Embrace the chaos, realize what is occurring, and let your Inner Wisdom (more on her soon) guide you through the breakdown.

A New Level of Awareness: Expect Your Inner Mean Girl's Arrival

Do yourself a favor from this day forward, and just start counting on your Inner Mean Girl to show up when you step outside your comfort zone. Stop being surprised or expecting something to be different. Of course when you step outside what's familiar, what feels safe, or what is how you have always operated, your Inner Mean Girl is going to get triggered. The worst thing you can do is pretend like you aren't afraid or uncertain, like your IMG hasn't been triggered and the attack isn't happening— stuffing your feelings down, keeping busy, or avoiding the situation just makes your life worse and your IMG more determined.

If you don't acknowledge that your Inner Mean Girl has been triggered, you become a victim to the experience and the negative effects—all you can see and feel is the fear, anxiety, depression, rejection, procrastination, anger, etc. These emotions take over, gain power and energy, and before you know it, what started as an IMG flare-up becomes a full-fledged Inner Mean Girl attack, which can be much more challenging to work yourself out of.

But if you know to expect her, learn what triggers your Inner Mean Girl, celebrate her appearance, and reframe the situation as good growth instead of freaking out about it, the next time you find yourself in the midst of an IMG flare-up, you can prevent a full-fledged attack and up-level your life (take your life to the next level) in some pretty awesome ways. When you get triggered, we want you to get curious and celebrate and open to the growth instead of getting critical and controlling and shutting down.

A great example of how this can work for you comes from one of our Inner Mean Girl Reform School students, Jane. An accomplished high school English teacher with a solid track record of success by anyone's standards (except her Inner Mean Girls', of course), Jane found herself one day in a bad place—under siege, smack in the middle of a full-blown Inner Mean Girl attack. She came to one of our community calls in a panic, feeling tense in her body, with tear-stained cheeks, and with Big Fat Lies racing in her head. She said she felt scared and sure she was destined to fail in every area of her life.

> **WHEN YOU GET TRIGGERED, WE WANT YOU TO GET CURIOUS AND CELEBRATE.**

We called out the Inner Mean Girl attack, celebrated and got excited for Jane, and then we got curious and asked Jane to do the same so we could see what was really going on. We asked Jane, "Where are you outside your comfort zone? Where are you growing and risking? In what ways do you feel exposed and vulnerable? What is the breakthrough that wants to occur?" Turns out Jane had finally started working on her novel. Aha! She hadn't connected the dots between her feelings, her fears, and her Inner Mean Girl. We could see what had happened. Her Inner Mean Girl—and Jane herself—was freaked out about going for this lifelong big dream, stepping out of her comfort zone as an English teacher to become a published author, and exposing herself to potential criticism, rejection, and failure. What if she wrote this book and no one would publish it? What if it got published and no one read it? Or perhaps worse, what if it was a bestseller and she experienced success beyond her wildest dreams? (Inner Mean Girls can sometimes be more terrified of success!)

We got her Inner Mean Girl to simmer down by bringing awareness to the situation, which gave Jane the opportunity to see why she was afraid. Jane realized that she could expect that her IMG was going to show up and try to tell her everything in her life was going to hell in a hand basket when embarking on that novel because she wanted to keep Jane from all the possible dangers that went along with stepping outside of her comfort zone, going for a big dream and making herself vulnerable (more on that in step three). With this new awareness, and with the help of her Inner Wisdom's loving truth, Jane was able to get herself out of the Inner Mean Girl attack and get some distance so she could observe and, as a result, soothe herself and her IMG. She began trusting the breakdown-to-breakthrough process.

Superpower Tool: The Good Growth Reframe

Think of an area in your life that you are struggling with right now, where your Inner Mean Girl might be flaring up or waging a full-on attack. It could be a place where you are feeling uncertain, confused, or stuck, maybe a relationship or situation in which you are struggling, or if nothing pops up, remember a situation in your past that caused you to stretch and stress. Using the four steps that follow, journal out a new story for yourself using one of our favorite superpower tools that we call the Good Growth Reframe.

1. **Call it out.** Stop and admit that you are in the breakdown process; say to yourself and write it out in your journal: *A breakdown is occurring. My Inner Mean Girl is flared up and triggered.* Naming the breakdown (instead of resisting or ignoring the intense energy) takes your IMG out of the shadow and into the light so you can deal with her.

2. **Celebrate.** Instead of making yourself feel bad or wrong for getting triggered or having a hard time, stop your IMG and the neural

pathway with a burst of exuberant celebration. Acknowledge what is happening as good, with words like: *Awesome, I must be growing!* or *Fabulous, I am having a breakdown to break through!* Even if you don't feel like celebrating in the moment (which most of the time you won't), fake it to throw your IMG off guard, and then move on to steps three and four to find your way into an authentic acknowledgment of your growth.

3. **Get curious.** Get interested in how you are stepping outside your comfort zone, without any self-judgment that things should be different than they are. Ask yourself specifically, "How am I growing or risking?" Really look at what is making you feel so vulnerable or exposed and write it out. By getting curious, you take back your power, stop being a victim to the IMG attack, short circuit self-judgment, and fear, and open up the space for a breakthrough.

4. **Claim the breakthrough.** Consciously choose that this breakdown and chaos are clear signs that you're up-leveling (moving to a new level). You are in the midst of the breakdown-to-breakthrough phenomenon. Reframe the struggle and the challenge by pausing, seeing and feeling the good growth potential, and answering the inquiry *What is the good growth potential here?* Then, instead of resisting the change and judging yourself, surrender to the breakdown and step into the breakthrough!

Keep these four Good Growth Reframe steps handy for the next time you get triggered and use them as one of your new superpower tools, and you'll be surprised by how much more empowered you feel during times of high stress and uncertainty. Infused with new enthusiasm, your life will begin to feel more joyful and peaceful.

What Drives Your Inner Mean Girl to Attack?

Now that we've reframed Inner Mean Girl attacks, it's time to get deeper into our IMG investigation, so we can prevent as many of those attacks as possible. Giving yourself permission to be curious with yourself instead of critical and judgmental will change your life. Curiosity opens the space for compassion and insight, whereas criticism closes everything down. So, what do you say? Grab your journal and a pen, and let's dive deeper and shine the light on your Inner Mean Girl and her specific tricks and triggers.

Investigation Area 1:
What triggers your Inner Mean Girl?

One of the keys to preventing an Inner Mean Girl attack is to know when to expect her to show up so you can beat her to the punch. By becoming more aware of what triggers you and your IMG, you gain the power to stop full-blown Inner Mean Girl attacks, just like Jane. Plus, we'll show you how to practice preventative care—actions you can take to prevent Inner Mean Girl attacks or flare-ups from occurring in the first place. Just like you brush and floss your teeth to keep cavities away, there are preventative measures you can take to keep IMGs at bay. It's essential to have the skills to practice both emergency care (during Inner Mean Girl attacks) and preventative care.

> CURIOSITY OPENS THE SPACE FOR COMPASSION AND INSIGHT, WHEREAS CRITICISM CLOSES EVERYTHING DOWN.

Following are ten of the most common triggers for Inner Mean Girls. While we can all resonate with most of these trigger points, we want you to read through all of them and look for and identify the places your IMG is most present currently. Likely you'll see some that used to trigger you and, while you still may have a flare-up occasionally, aren't such a big deal anymore. Look for the trigger points that are most active now or in your very recent past experiences.

The Ten Most Common Inner Mean Girl Trigger Points

1. **Body Image.** This is one of the most common areas for Inner Mean Girls to thrive. After all, our IMGs have been given a steady diet of airbrushed, Photoshopped images for years. So we're wondering, when you look in the mirror (or at magazines or other women), or bathing suit season arrives, or you're with your beloved in the bedroom, does your Inner Mean Girl start spouting her Big Fat Lies?

2. **Certain People.** When you're around relatives or certain types of people, does your Inner Mean Girl get triggered? Is there a person or people in your life who bring out your IMG big time? If yes, do yourself a favor and just name this person(s) now—no one is watching. Getting real and telling the truth about this, especially when the people are your family, can bring a cathartic release.

3. **When Things Aren't Going Well.** Does your Inner Mean Girl go into a failure spiral when one thing goes a bit haywire? Almost like she is just standing by, waiting for one small thing to happen to prove that you are doomed? Is it a struggle to be cool in a crisis? Do you feel like you are on red alert often? Do you tend to sweat the small stuff a lot because it all feels like big stuff to you? This might be one of your major trigger points.

4. **When Things Are Going Well.** Really take a look here, as success can often be scarier for Inner Mean Girls than failure. Are you constantly worried the other shoe is going to drop? Feeling a sense of "too good to be true"? The moment you experience something that

makes you happy, do your IMGs swoop in like vultures to make you feel like it's all going to end?

5. **Relationships and Love.** Does your Inner Mean Girl show up and torment you in regard to your relationships with friends, romantic partners, family, or coworkers? Does she love to rear her ugly head when you move to new levels of intimacy or when a relationship starts to change or end? Or perhaps you sabotage relationships before people can get too close. You isolate yourself or limit yourself to just a few friends, not trusting too many people. Or you become everyone's friend or overstay in relationships because you don't want to lose love. When your IMG gets triggered here, you feel things like fear, stress, judgment, resentment, or anger about the people you are in relationships with or about the state of your love life or lack thereof.

6. **Money.** This category can be easy pickin's for an Inner Mean Girl, especially since money lends itself to measurement, comparison, and straight up fear. Maybe your IMG shows up big time when you're paying your bills (or trying to) or when your friend gets a new car or house. Maybe you feel like everyone else has what you never will or that you just can't figure money out. Is your IMG constantly judging you about your money management skills (or lack thereof) or telling you Big Fat Lies, like "You'll never have enough"? If so, then this may be your trigger point.

7. **Career.** Is your career and professional life fuel for Inner Mean Girl attacks? Does she beat you up about your career choices, bully you into constant fear that you'll lose a job, or keep you staying in a job you don't like? Maybe your IMG tells you you're a fraud or imposter when you receive a promotion or a big bonus. Perhaps this is the area your IMG loves to berate you in, slowing you down, derailing

your dreams and happiness, keeping you settling and playing small. Or she can also show up as a slave driver, urging you to work hard all the time, constantly making you push ahead for the next promotion, next achievement, always focusing your attention on what you haven't yet done or become (and of course how much everyone else has!).

8. **Spirituality.** Does your Inner Mean Girl love to tell you that you should be more evolved, more spiritual, more together? When she thrives in this area, she loves to point out how much progress you have *not* made. She tells you Big Fat Lies, like "You are regressing. You've already learned this. Why is this coming up again?" Or she keeps you from spiritual endeavors and freaks you out about becoming too spiritual, too "woo-woo," or too religious and tells you Big Fat Lies, like "If you become too spiritual, you will starve." She may become an outer mean girl and make you poke fun at people she deems weird and "out there."

9. **Being Seen.** Is your Inner Mean Girl so strong that you never let yourself be seen, not fully anyway? Do you hide and play small because she has filled your head with all kinds of Big Fat Lies about how you are not enough and how unsafe it is to shine your light or be your real self? If this is happening, even when you want to be seen, you settle and hold back, and you know it.

10. **Parenting.** One of the things we most often hear moms say is that one of the biggest triggers for their Inner Mean Girl is anything and everything to do with their kids. Is your child falling behind? You're a horrible mom. Is your kid excelling and being the teacher's pet? You're pushing your kid too much. Your IMG tells you everything from "You don't spend enough time with your kids" to "You're spoiling them rotten." You just can't win. Or your IMG can also show up

as the übermom, stripping you of your identity and purpose outside of your family, making you believe you have to sacrifice yourself to be a good mom. Is this where your IMG packs the punch?

IT'S AMY HERE, and I just have to say that these trigger points can be brutal. A lot of this can be avoided once you realize and admit your triggers and if you just do some preventative care by getting the support you need on the four essential levels: spiritual, emotional, physical, and intellectual. Commit this to memory: support prevents sabotage. Your Inner Mean Girl will tell you needing support is weak, or she will make you feel guilty for receiving it, like you should have to do something in order to receive support. Your Inner Wisdom knows that getting support is one of the wisest acts you can take. She knows that every person deserves support—you don't have to earn it or pay someone back one hundred times more.

> ## SUPPORT PREVENTS SABOTAGE.

Like many moms, parenting is one of my trigger points. With my first daughter, I didn't practice Inner Mean Girl preventative care, so for the first year of Annabella's life, Negative Nelly made me feel like I was failing as a mom and kept me in a constant state of worry. Between the intense sleep deprevation and my IMG, I was a mess!

When I was preparing to give birth to my second baby, Evie, I got wise. Knowing this was a trigger area for me, I set up my support systems before she was born. I knew that I was likely to have an Inner Mean Girl attack when my baby arrived, and I loved myself enough to make sure I had the support I needed. Instead of avoiding the truth or judging myself for needing support and therefore being weak or needy, I embraced that motherhood is one of the areas my IMG can flare up, and practiced preventative care to keep the flare-ups from becoming full-blown attacks. I joined a new-moms' group so I could interact with moms who had newborns for emotional and mental support, made an agreement with my husband about giving me ten minutes first thing in the morning to do my daily practice and set my intentions (you'll learn more about how to do this in step six) for my spiritual support, and found an amazing prenatal yoga class that led into a baby and mommy yoga class for my physical support. Also, knowing myself to be a major extrovert, I found these preventative measures set me up to feel empowered, instead of giving my power over to my Inner Mean Girl. She may have gotten to me the first time, but I was not about to let her beat me to the punch for the second round!

Inner Wisdom Reflection: What Support Do You Need to Prevent IMG Attacks?

So, what do you think? What are your Inner Mean Girl's main triggers? Go back through the list of trigger points and mark the three that most currently propel you into self-bullying, self-sabotage, and all those nasty IMG toxic habits. These are the areas we want you to increase your awareness in and get more support for yourself. Let's pause here, and we will show you how to practice preventative care and ward off Inner Mean Girl attacks by getting the support you need. Grab your journal and write out your personal IMG Preventative Care Plan, one for each main trigger point.

▼ **Name the support you desire and need—spiritually, emotionally, physically, and intellectually.** For each trigger point, examine these four types of support and tap into what you need. *Spiritual support* nourishes you at a deep heart and soul level and helps you feel connected to yourself and to something bigger than you. *Emotional support* helps you deal with the ups and downs of life, and it can hold you in your weaknesses and challenges and can celebrate you in your successes. *Physical support* is the material stuff you need to have your body, safety, and basic human needs met and that keeps your physical health in a good place. *Intellectual support* is the wisdom and knowledge you need to navigate life and be successful and can give you information you don't have access to on your own. Make a complete list of all that you desire and need for support, not holding back or needing to know how you will receive it, and remembering that you don't have to achieve it all at once.

▼ **Start setting up and receiving your support.** Pick one action you can and will take in the next week for each trigger point, something that is doable and that you can be successful at without a lot of pressure. This will create momentum and will also open up the space for your Inner Wisdom to start finding support for you in ways you just can't see yet. Remember, you Inner Mean Girl loves to procrastinate. Don't let her sucker you! Take simple but mighty action to get support.

▼ **Share your plan with one person you trust and ask for his or her support in staying accountable to yourself.** Tell this person that you have promised yourself to receive support in all the ways you identified and then share the actions you promised to take. Ask if this person will check in with you about this. Remember, asking for support is wise, not weak. (When you share with others and ask for accountability, you are so much more likely to follow through for yourself.)

Investigation Area 2: What Big Fat Lies does your Inner Mean Girl bully and beat you up with?

As you dive deeper into getting to know your Inner Mean Girl, we want you to get more familiar with her voice and the sabotaging things she says to you. The more distinct her voice, the more you will be able to tell when she is present and trying to bring you down. As we talked about in step one, each of the IMG archetypes uses very distinct words we call Big Fat Lies, because that is what they are: lies. Even if they have some element of truth, which most don't, the way your Inner Mean Girl says things to you is unnecessarily hurtful, manipulative, and fearful.

There are some common Big Fat Lies we've observed among women, many of which you read about when you learned about the Inner Mean Girl Archetypes, such as:

"YOU ARE NOT ENOUGH."
"YOU'RE A FAILURE."
"SHE'S SO MUCH BETTER THAN YOU."
"IT DOESN'T COUNT UNLESS IT'S PERFECT."
"YOU'LL BE HAPPY WHEN YOU ‹INSERT FUTURE GOAL›."
"YOU CAN'T REST UNTIL YOU FINISH ALL YOUR WORK."
"YOU DON'T HAVE TIME FOR ‹INSERT SELF-CARE ACT›. THERE'S TOO MUCH TO DO."
"YOU ARE UNLOVED AND UNLOVABLE."

Your IMG may use these exact words on you, but likely she has her own twists on the phrases, which have the power to push your specific buttons. Which is why right now, right here, we are going to expose your IMG's Big Fat Lies. Together we will make a list of the insane, crazy, so-not-true-even-if-they-feel-true-in-the-moment thoughts your IMG tortures you with. Because when you can start seeing the sabotaging self-talk running through your head for what it is—untrue BS your IMG is spewing at you in her ineffective and destructive attempts to protect you—then you can separate yourself from your thoughts and gain tremendous power and perspective.

Here's how this Big Fat Lie excavation will go: we will take you through three scenarios, and for each one we want you to put yourself into that situation and imagine what your Inner Mean Girl would say to you in that moment. We want you to speak these words out loud as if you were handing your IMG a microphone and then write them down in your Inner Wisdom journal. We have included some of the common Big Fat Lies we've seen from other women's Inner Mean Girls to get you started.

As you go through this process, write and say as many things as you can remember—let the words flow out of your mouth and onto the page. And if nothing comes, like your IMG has put up a blockade, we've put together a few resources that will help you shine a spotlight on the sabotaging self-talk. The goal here is to let your IMG rant, in full force, without censoring anything. This is important. As the words come out of your mouth and your mind, you become more aware of what is happening inside of you than if you just think them—remember, this is about exposing the scare tactics your IMG is using to bully and manipulate you. Women tell us that when they speak these words out loud so they can actually hear the words they've been silently saying to sabotage and criticize themselves, something powerful happens within them. And that is what we are after here: juicy inner transformation that creates powerful outer shifts.

Scenario 1: When things don't go so well.

Think of the last time something didn't work out or go your way, a time you were disappointed or you failed. This could have been a time when you made a mistake, messed something up, presented something at work that flopped, didn't get something you wanted, or tried something that didn't work.

Common Big Fat Lies:

"THINGS NEVER WORK OUT FOR YOU."
"YOU'RE SUCH A LOSER."
"YOU DON'T DESERVE GOOD THINGS."
"WHY DO YOU EVEN BOTHER TRYING? YOU ALWAYS FAIL."

Close your eyes and take yourself back to that time. Imagine yourself in that situation that didn't go well. What words or thoughts began running through your mind? Allow yourself to remember the moment fully, feeling how crappy it felt, and start speaking out loud what you imagine your thoughts about yourself, the situation, and other people were at the time. Imagine giving your IMG the microphone and let her rant out loud so you can hear and feel the negative self-talk. Then write down what you remember. If speaking out loud is too hard for you, just go right to your journal and write what judgments or stories you were telling yourself.

Scenario 2: When things are going great.

Next, look at what your Inner Mean Girl says to you when your life is feeling really good and on the upswing. You got a promotion or had a fabulous first date or released some weight that wasn't feeling good on your body. Close your eyes and remember a situation like this, including the weeks and days after the initial win. Often IMGs try to steal your joy after the fact, making you nervous it's all going to fall apart or not allowing you to celebrate or receive what's occurred. Get those Big Fat Lies out by letting your IMG speak through you and then write the lies down, pulling them out of the darkness and into the light so they can be transformed.

Common Big Fat Lies:

"YOU DON'T DESERVE IT."
"IT WON'T LAST."
"THEY'RE GOING TO FIGURE OUT THAT YOU ARE A FRAUD."
"WHAT ABOUT THE NEXT TWENTY-FIVE POUNDS? YOU STILL HAVE SUCH A LONG WAY TO GO!"
"THE OTHER SHOE IS GOING TO DROP!"

Scenario 3: Choose one of your top three trigger points.

Using the work you completed in the last investigation area, choose one of your Inner Mean Girl's trigger points. Take yourself back to the last time your IMG attacked in this specific area of your life. What was the negative self-talk she moved through your mind that kept you triggered? Write and say everything that comes to mind.

Some common Big Fat Lies:

"YOU'RE THE WORST MOM IN THE ENTIRE WORLD!"
"YOU'RE NEVER GOING TO GET AHEAD IN YOUR CAREER."
"YOU WILL NEVER FIND TRUE LOVE."

Whew! Good work on your Big Fat Lie excavation! In addition to everything you've uncovered, there are bound to be other Big Fat Lies that your IMG loves to use on you, and now that we've uncorked the bottle, so to speak, more will start flowing out of your subconscious brain into your conscious awareness. If you want to unearth more Big Fat Lies and expand this collection, or if you feel stuck and can't get clear on your IMG's lies, here are three others sources that can help you:

♥ **Reread the archetype descriptions in step one.** Refer back to your primary archetypes, read the list of Big Fat Lies for each, and write down any that apply to you.

♥ **Start a Big Fat Lie list.** Get a small notepad or create a list in your phone, and every time you feel like crap about yourself, feel stressed out, afraid, or confused, stop, close your eyes, and ask yourself *What Big Fat Lie is my IMG bullying or beating me up with right now?* Give voice to the internal bullying by saying the words out loud and then add the lie to your list.

♥ **Check out the free Inner Wisdom Kit (innerwisdomkit.com).** You'll find a list of the fifty-nine biggest lies women tell themselves, taken from Amy's book, *Big Fat Lies Women Tell Themselves*, and a Big Fat Lie worksheet that can help you get unstuck.

Inner Wisdom Reflection: Find Your Inner Mean Girl's Five Favorite Big Fat Lies

If you really did let your IMG rant, chances are you may have a stack of Big Fat Lies. Now what? There is great power in labeling these toxic words as lies your Inner Mean Girl uses to scare and manipulate you into thinking they are truths about you, because naming ultimately takes the sting and power out of the words. Your next step is to take a pause to identify your Inner Mean Girl's playlist—her five favorite Big Fat Lies, the ones that decimate or detour you the fastest.

♥ Take a look through the list you created and look for the common themes. Group together and circle Big Fat Lies that seem similar.

♥ Rewrite them in the simplest way possible, using words that ring most true to you. Remember, IMGs have a very young emotional maturity, so they speak in terms a seven-year-old could understand.

For example, you might have a grouping of lies about money:

"YOU'LL NEVER GET AHEAD ON YOUR BILLS." "YOU SUCK AT MONEY MANAGEMENT." "YOUR BROTHER IS SO WEALTHY— WHAT'S YOUR PROBLEM?"

You might then simplify and capture the essence with:

"YOU'RE DESTINED TO BE BROKE." "YOU ARE A LOSER AND A FAILURE." "YOU'LL NEVER BE AS GOOD AS YOUR BROTHER."

♥ Narrow this list down to the top five Big Fat Lies and voilà! You have your Inner Mean Girl's Big Fat Lie playlist.

Investigation Area 3: What does your Inner Mean Girl pressure you into doing?

You've noticed what triggers your IMG and what Big Fat Lies she bullies and beats you up with. Now let's get crystal clear on what your IMG drives you to do, the actions and choices you make under her command. When she is running the show, you do not act in your best interest. Instead, you do things that take you out of and away from love, happiness, and freedom. You act in ways that are actually against what your heart and soul really desire, even if you think you are acting in ways that serve you.

The insights you are about to gain from this investigation are some of the most powerful you can gather, as it is the beginning of connecting the dots among your actions, your feelings, and your deep, underlying motivations for why you do what you do. Read through the following list of Inner Mean Girl actions, or what we call toxic habits, and check all that apply to you. Be honest. No one is looking. Remember, this is about shining the light on your IMG, not on shaming or judging you.

Inner Mean Girl Toxic Habits

What does your Inner Mean Girl drive you to do (check all that apply)?

Act like a Victim	You feel sorry for yourself.	
Be Arrogant	You think of yourself as better than others.	
Blame	You make others, or yourself, wrong.	
Bully	You steamroll over people you think are in your way, or you push to make things happen.	

Change Who You Are/ Become a Chameleon	You adopt an image to fit the situation or the relationship and sell out your true self.	
Be Codependent	You try to fix others; you allow your emotions to be overcome by others' emotions.	
Collude	You make others wrong and try to get people on your side to prove others are wrong instead of you.	
Complain	You whine and make everything hard; things are bad more than they are good.	
Create Drama and Cause Chaos	You have turmoil in your life and relationships; life isn't peaceful or harmonious.	
Do What Others Expect	You please others even if it means disappointing yourself.	
Disappear	You get small and quiet and fade into the background.	
Feign Confusion	You say things like "I am confused," "I don't understand," or "I don't know," to avoid conflict or expressing hard emotions, when if you looked deeper, you'd have a lot to say.	
Forget about Yourself	You put yourself last on the list and fail to get what you need.	
Get Anxious	You worry and obsess over things you can't control.	
Give and Do More	You often give and do more than you need to or more than you really can afford to offer without sacrificing yourself.	
Gossip	You talk about others in a way that you wouldn't if they were in the room.	
Isolate	You check out, numb out, or detach.	

EXPOSE YOUR INNER MEAN GIRL'S TRICKS AND TRIGGERS

Judge	You criticize others and/or yourself.	
Lash Out	You explode or get inappropriately angry or frustrated.	
Overthink	You let your mind obsessively create stories, scenarios, and plans.	
Overindulge	You overeat, overdrink, overspend, over-everything.	
Obsess on the Future or the Past	You focus your mind on what was or what will be instead of what is right now.	
Overfocus	You put all your energy and time into one part of your life—work, kids, project—and neglect the other parts.	
Procrastinate or Never Try	You avoid moving into action.	
Quit	You give up, run away, and take your ball and go home.	
Search for Data	You ask everyone for an opinion, obsessively search for answers.	
Stay Busy	You keep yourself preoccupied with tasks, to dos, other people's schedules, work.	
Stop Doing Things That Make You Happy	You only work or do things because they produce an outcome or out of obligation, instead of just for joy or fun.	
Try to Control Everything	You try to make everything perfect, control all outcomes, over-manage, and overburden yourself.	
Withhold Love and Attention	You keep and block love and affection from yourself or others.	

Work Harder, More, Longer than Needed	You give way more effort and work way harder than you need to, because you've convinced yourself you have to.	

So, wow, right? Look at all the crazy things that your Inner Mean Girl drives you to do. It is pretty obvious that any of the actions you checked are not driving you in the direction you really want to be going.

You are beginning to get an idea of how many of your thoughts and actions are triggered by your Inner Mean Girl, which means you can more easily notice when she is pulling the strings. Starting today, right now, we want you to start calling her out. We mean it. When you get triggered, when a Big Fat Lie runs through your mind, and when you are aware that you are engaged in one of these toxic habits, take command. Stop right in your tracks and say out loud or to yourself, "I see you. You are my Inner Mean Girl pushing me to do something that is not the best choice for me. And I am not letting you bully me anymore!"

We know talking to your Inner Mean Girl may feel weird, but hey, you have a mean girl living inside you! And just like any relationship, the more you talk, the closer you become, and the closer you become, the more the other person trusts you, and we want your IMG to start trusting you. Because once you can get her to trust you, she'll stop believing she has to work so hard to protect you, and you'll have the power to motivate yourself with things like compassion instead of criticism. We've witnessed thousands of women and girls open up this dialogue within themselves, and while most felt a little funny at first, the results have been pretty spectacular, and that's what counts.

Investigation Area 4:
What is your Inner Mean Girl costing you?

Now that you are aware of what's happening, you must take a stand for yourself, just like you would for someone you love. How? Become fearlessly honest and feel what the self-sabotage, self-bullying, and self-abuse is costing you, and then take a bold action to make a different choice. Because if you won't stand for yourself and what you need and desire, no one else can.

Until you really, truly see what these actions and choices are costing you, it's easy to keep your unhealthy habits going and act as if living this way is no big deal. But when you see the consequence to your happiness, your health, your relationships, your bank account, and so on, something inside you clicks, and just like you wouldn't be able to stop yourself from reaching out to help a friend who was sabotaging and bullying herself, you will be compelled and inspired to start making the changes that are good for you, one bold baby step at a time.

IT'S CHRISTINE HERE, and I remember when I realized that my Doing Addict, Get on It Gloria, was wreaking havoc on my emotional health, inner peace, and happiness. She had my mind so busy with all that I had to do that it took me an hour every night to slow my mind down enough to fall asleep. My body was so full of caffeine, diet pop, and chocolate to keep the adrenaline pumping that I didn't even realize I wasn't happy in my career or my unsustainable lifestyle. I was working all the time, and when I wasn't working, I was feeling guilty about not working or overindulging in pleasure to make up for the lack of it the other 360 days of the year. I was squeezing my happiness in between all the work. I wasn't painting, writing, reading, gardening, or doing the traveling for fun I loved. And based on how my clothes were fitting, I was pretty sure I had even gained about ten pounds from the stress. I had told myself that I had to work hard to pay my mortgage, reach my goals, and have the lifestyle I wanted. But that wasn't true. I had just fallen for a trifecta of Gloria's Big Fat Lies:

"YOU HAVE SO MUCH TO DO."
"SUCCESSFUL PEOPLE HAVE TO WORK HARD."
"YOU MUST FINISH THE WORK BEFORE YOU CAN PLAY OR REST."

When I took a step back to see how much all this work-hard, work-before-you-play-or-rest mentality was costing me—my happiness, my body, my emotional peace—I got pissed off. I was not a workhorse or a machine. I was a woman with a body that needed to be loved and a soul that needed to be nourished. I was a woman who wanted to enjoy her life, not run herself through it. At first I didn't know how I was going to change these deeply ingrained patterns or how I was going to get Gloria out of my head and bed (this IMG was so persistent that it was like she climbed into my bed every night with that big to-do list and then was there waiting for me in the morning with the same to-do list, telling me to get to work the minute I awoke). So from a place of deep self-love, I decided to take a stand for myself that day, and I said, "No more! No more to working so hard. No more to having to wait to play or rest until all the work is done." I wanted to have the space to rest and play as well as do great work in the world. Telling Gloria and myself those words gave me a place to start.

Let's see what your Inner Mean Girl is costing you by taking a magnifying glass to different areas of your life where IMGs generally cause the most damage. We call these Inner Mean Girl hot spots, and there are seven, which are listed in the chart on the next page.

As you look at each of these seven areas of your life, ask yourself, *Where am I currently experiencing the most struggle and stress? Where am I holding back? Where am I caught in the same patterns and self-sabotaging choices?* These are your Inner Mean Girl hot spots.

If your IMG has by chance convinced you that are a hot mess in all seven, breathe and call her out! That is just not true. She's just trying to freak you out and keep you paralyzed with fear and overwhelm so you won't move forward (remember, she wants to keep her job!). The truth is that we can all use more goodness in these different areas, but what we are looking for are the places your self-sabotage is costing you the most right now. Just choose one or two areas, max, to focus on.

Then, for each current Inner Mean Girl hot spot, with total honesty (remember, no one is looking but you), in order to really see what this is costing you, finish the five powerful investigative statements following the chart:

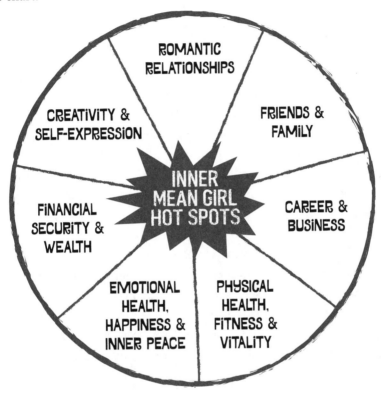

"My Inner Mean Girl is costing me . . . "
"She is keeping me stuck in . . . "
"The truth is . . . "
"I am sick and tired of . . . "
"I really desire . . . "

For example:

My Career. *My Inner Mean Girl is costing me* in my career big time. *She is keeping me stuck in* a job I hate. *The truth is* that I am afraid to make this big change, and I am totally settling in my job. *I am sick and tired of* going to a job that drains my energy. *I really desire* a way to use my gifts and take care of myself financially. I desire both!

My Physical Health, Fitness, and Vitality. *My Inner Mean Girl is costing me* my health. *She is keeping me stuck in* unhealthy eating patterns where I diet, lose weight, and then binge like crazy. *The truth is* that I feel fat and disgusted by my body and ashamed that I can't control myself. *I am sick and tired of* battling with my weight. *I really desire* to have a body that is happy and feels good to me and to be able to enjoy eating food again without fear of gaining ten pounds.

My Finances and Wealth. *My Inner Mean Girl is costing me* in money and financial abundance. *She is keeping me stuck in* credit card debt that never seems to go down, and I can never get ahead no matter how much money I make. *The truth is* that I am in debt and living beyond my means, and I don't know what to do. *I am sick and tired of* always feeling stressed about money. *I really desire* to be at ease with money and be free of the burden of debt.

Give yourself full permission to see the high price you are paying as a result of the self-sabotage and bullying. To get the best results with your IMG hot spots, write them out in your Inner Wisdom journal just like we illustrated for you above. And we've got a double-dog, self-love dare if you want to amp up the intensity. Sometimes we have to feel how much we are hurting ourselves or keeping ourselves from what we truly desire to fire us up on the inside so much that we finally take a stand to make changes. Try this. Have an honesty hearing with yourself. Sit in front of a mirror, look into your eyes, and then using the five hot spot statements we gave you, say the truth out loud and hear and feel the cost to you.

So, how does it feel when you really see the truth of what this self-sabotage and negative thinking is costing you? Aren't you just totally sick and tired of being bullied and manipulated by your Inner Mean Girl? We are fired up for you! It's okay to get mad, just as long as you channel the anger in a way that empowers you, fuels you, and inspires you to make the changes you truly desire.

Take a Stand for Yourself

We'd like you to take a stand for yourself, right here and right now, to stop tolerating what you are sick and tired of and to start making your desires really, truly matter to you—we won't let you settle for less anymore. Taking a stand is a powerful self-empowerment superpower tool we use often in our own lives and at Inner Mean Girl Reform School. It's like putting a stake in the ground, standing tall, and proclaiming to yourself (and the world) that you are doing this thing, no matter what, because you are 100 percent committed to standing up for and staying true to yourself. Taking a stand creates a deeper level of commitment to the person who needs your devotion the most: you.

Look back at your Inner Mean Girl hot spots and change the word *desire* to *choose* in "I really desire . . ." So instead of "I really *desire* to be at ease with money and debt-free," shift it to "I *choose* to be at ease with money and be free of the burden of debt." The *I choose* statement is your stand. You can desire something all day long, but if you don't choose it, all you have is an intention without a commitment. Choosing makes you commit. Write out this self-empowering stand statement and put it somewhere you will see it or refer to it easily and often, so you can remember your commitment to yourself.

Just making the choice is the stand, and the first step. You don't need to know *how* you will deliver on that stand yet or how it will work itself out. Your job is to just believe you *can* receive what your heart and soul desires and then stay present to cocreate that reality with your Inner Wisdom and the Universe. Your Inner Mean Girl may get a bit ornery about this stand, but have no fear, we have a few Inner Mean Girl Deactivators that will take care of her.

Superpower Challenge:
Deactivate Your Inner Mean Girl
When She Attacks

Now that you're getting to know your Inner Mean Girl on a deeper level and putting together clues about her full profile, it's time to start practicing how you can put your IMG in her place in your day-to-day life. You see now that you've begun to shine a light in her direction—you know what triggers her, what Big Fat Lies she uses, what actions she's behind, and what she's been costing you—she's feeling exposed. Inner Mean Girls don't like to feel vulnerable. In fact, right about now is when we see women freak out a little. They begin to feel like their IMGs start getting louder and more aggressive, which isn't actually the case. If this happens to you, take a breath and realize that she's not getting stronger—you are just seeing things you didn't have awareness of before.

To help you navigate your newly exposed IMG, you will need tools to deactivate her in the moments she attacks and flares up—we call these the Inner Mean Girl Deactivators. Often when your Inner Mean Girl shows up and begins to launch an attack, you can feel helpless to combat her overbearing ways. In those times, we want you to pull out one of the Inner Mean Girl Deactivators and see how it works. To stop an Inner Mean Girl attack, you have to take action. You can't just think about this stuff and keep it swirling around or stored in your head—because that is where your IMG wields most of her power, on those old neural pathways in your brain. You actually have to use and experiment with the tools we give you in your daily life, in tangible ways. Think of it like conducting a mad science experiment in which you are the scientist experimenting with how to change your Inner Mean Girl into a lovable being whom you can love and who will love you back. Following you'll find our top three Inner Mean Girl Deactivators, and we've included more for you in the Superpower Toolshed on page 252. Your mission for this superpower challenge is to experiment with these deactivators so you can see which ones work best to chill her, and you, out. And remember to have some fun with this—play gives you more power!

Inner Mean Girl Deactivator 1: The Worst Case/Best Case/ Real Case Game

Let's say your Inner Mean Girl is filling your head with loads of garbage, freaking you out with worry that something bad is going to happen or that you just can't do it, or convincing you that you have no control over the situation and are going to be screwed. She's running scenarios through your head like a mad slideshow and making you feel anxious, angry, or just plain fearful. This is the time to take control of you mind and play the Worst Case/Best Case/Real Case Game by asking yourself a series of questions that take you from the worst possible outcome, up to the best possibility, to land somewhere in the middle of true reality. Here's how:

1. Ask, "What is the worst thing that could happen?" Answer honestly.

2. Now ask, "And *then* what is the *worst* thing that could happen?" Keep asking and answering this same question until you get to the

bottom of the bottom of the very worst thing—it's usually something like death, becoming homeless, being alone forever, etc.

3. **Once you've hit bottom, it's time to come up. Ask yourself, "What is the *best* thing that could happen?"** Answer that and then add on, "What other great things could happen?" and let yourself fully imagine the possibilities.

4. **Last, ask, "What is *likely* to happen?"** And answer that as honestly as you can. By this time, your Inner Mean Girl has been disarmed, you've calmed down, and you can see that what's likely to happen isn't so scary after all.

Inner Mean Girl Deactivator 2: Dance Break

Sometimes the only way to get the Inner Mean Girl out of your mind is to literally shake your body to cause a pattern interruption in the neural pathways that are going berserk. When your IMG has you in her grips, you have to get out of your head and into your body, which of course will feel like the last thing you want to do, but empower yourself and do it anyway. Get up off your butt and move your body. Shake it. Snake it. Jump it. Do some kind of body movement that moves the energy in a different direction, that busts the lid off the self-sabotage dumpster your IMG is trying to stick you into. For extra gusto, pair a song with your movement. One of our students sings the song "Get on Up" as she rises to her feet, pushing her hands in the air. Works every time. Another one just likes to get up and shout whatever sounds come out of her mouth to release the energy. The key is that when you really don't feel like moving it, you push through and keep moving it until you feel her grip and your crazy mind or inner fear loosen. And then slow down, breathe, put a soft smile on your face, and feel how your IMG is quieter. Dance breaks are powerful Inner Mean Girl Deactivators!

Inner Mean Girl Deactivator 3: The Love-Line

Sometimes you need a friend to do what you can't do for yourself. If your Inner Mean Girl has really got you and you just can't shake her, it's time to throw out a Love-Line. A Love-Line is just like a lifeline—you pick up the phone and call a friend and ask for love and support. We've found that being direct, naming the attack, and then asking specifically for what you need is the best way to go. Here's a script of sentence starters to use when you dial up to get assistance to stop the IMG attack:

> **"Hi, <insert supportive friends name>!"**
> **"I'm having an Inner Mean Girl attack."**
> **"My Inner Mean Girl is telling me . . ."**
> **"Can you help me? I just need you to tell me . . ."**

Be specific with your friend about what you need to hear from her. As she speaks the words to you, your job is to listen and receive them fully. Breathing deeply while she speaks to you will help the IMG grip loosen—breath is one of your most powerful IMG deactivators because it connects you to your body. If your IMG still has a death grip on you after your friend loves on you, you can add one other question. Ask your friend for her intuitive hit on what you need to hear. Since your Inner Wisdom is clearly being gagged by your IMG, you can call on your friend's Inner Wisdom to deliver the message yours can't get through.

IT'S AMY HERE, and I have to tell you that the Love-Line is one of my husband's and my favorite superpower tools. When I'm in the midst of an IMG attack, I call Rob and tell him I'm under siege and then I have my Inner Wisdom tell him exactly what to say. Rob loves this because sometimes he's at a loss for the right words. When I ask him for what I want to hear, it creates a win-win.

TRANSFORMATION TALE: I Had My Inner Mean Girl Arrested for Attacking Me
by bestselling author and artist SARK

The Inner Mean Girl attack happened while I was on a book tour, minutes after completing a wildly successful TV show appearance. Instead of celebrating and feeling great about myself for wowing the producers and inspiring the audience and viewers, I found myself sitting in my rental car in a parking lot crying, listening to all the ways I wasn't good enough. As if a gang of IMGs had piled into the front and backseat of my car, all I could hear were words like:

"YOU FORGOT TO PERSONALLY THANK THE PRODUCER."
"YOUR JACKET DIDN'T LOOK VERY GOOD."
"YOU DIDN'T LEAVE THEM A COPY OF THE BOOK."
"YOU SHOULD HAVE DONE YOUR HAIR DIFFERENTLY."

The fact that both the host and producer profusely thanked me, that so many viewers called in that the phone lines were full, that my bookstore appearances were sold out meant nothing to these inner critics. The fact that I liked both my hair and my jacket felt meaningless compared to hearing their harsh opinions of me, running inside of my head.

These parts of us are relentless in their recitations of fear and doom. They literally cannot function differently without our help and supervision.

I created an inner critic care and transformation system for just this purpose. Part of that care system includes close communion with what I call the Inner Wise Self, just like what Amy and Christine call your Inner Wisdom. This is the part of you that's unconditionally loving and wise—if you have the courage and wisdom to hear it.

After several minutes of being embroiled in this self-bullying episode, I finally remembered my connection to my Inner Wise Self and asked it what to do, while saying to myself quite skeptically, "All right, Inner Wise Self, what do you have for me that will help with this?" I secretly doubted that it could do anything since I felt so bad.

My Inner Wise Self said, "Go ask him for help."

I looked over and noticed the him she spoke about was a police officer just getting out of his squad car. I know now that this part of me never guides me to something truly scary. I'm actually a rather shy introvert, so this guidance felt particularly uncomfortable.

I've learned over the years to follow what my Inner Wise Self says—even if it's odd or kind of scary. I have also learned to act in the moment and not overthink the suggestion.

So I approached the police officer and asked if he had time to hear an unusual request. He smiled and replied: "Depends on what it is!"

I felt inspired by his response and explained that I was just starting my book tour and had appeared on TV and was attacked by a squad of inner critics afterward. I then asked if he could arrest them and take them to jail and keep them there until after my book tour. This idea just leaped into my head when I started talking with him. I've learned that my Inner Wise Self *always* delivers what I need, in the moment that I need it.

He laughed and said, "Sure I can. I know about those inner critics. My wife and I deal with them too—we'll have to get your book. What's the title?"

He opened the squad car door, and we escorted all the Inner Mean Girls in. He then asked what the book was about, and I told him it was about being *Glad No Matter What* and that there are processes in it for listening to our Inner Wise Selves, which is what I'd just done by asking him to help me deactivate my IMGs.

He said he'd be getting the book and wished me well. I watched the squad car drive off and felt such relief that the Inner Mean Girls had a place to be while I connected with people and facilitated transformation and change.

I now know that our Inner Wise Selves are made to be in charge of our lives and of our Inner Mean Girls. I've separated from my IMGs and put my Inner Wise Self fully in charge now. While there are still attacks and uprisings, I now have the skills and tools to spend much less time feeling bad.

STEP 3

DISCOVER WHAT MOTIVATES YOUR INNER MEAN GIRL

You have done such a stellar job of digging into who your Inner Mean Girl is and what her tricks and triggers are that you're now ready to get the bottom of what your Inner Mean Girl has been trying to protect you from all these years. It's time to fully see what is freaking her, and you, out and how this protection is motivating your actions and thoughts in ways that are not serving you any longer. In this step, you will start to connect your habits, choices, and thoughts to the underlying fears that have been running you.

Before we start, there's another piece of essential Inner Mean Girl information you need to know so you are fully equipped to deal with her at this deeper level. You already know that your IMG doesn't want to lose her job because she is afraid that if she doesn't protect you, no one will, and you will get hurt again. But your IMG is also hypervigilant because of two F words that make her crazy—*fear* and *feelings*. Your Inner Mean Girl knows if she lets her guard down and stops keeping your mind and life so busy, you will have to face fears and feelings you've been glossing over, stuffing down, and trying to smooth out for years. Some of these fears and feelings you are conscious of, but about others you are clueless as to how they are lurking under the surface, running you and your life in ways that don't ultimately serve you.

We have noticed that we women don't talk about our underlying fears or feelings enough or as openly as we need to—to each other or ourselves, for that matter. Except for the times we sit in a therapist's chair or in a women's circle, participate in a retreat or group counseling session, we are much more comfortable connecting on the surface level, keeping the appearance that we have it all together and all figured out. Even if we do occasionally dig deep and expose our crazy thoughts and bullying negative self-talk, we stop shy of going as deep as is really required for lasting transformation, which is why you keep getting stuck in the same sabotaging patterns. And here's the loving truth about making change: when you skim the surface of your feelings or fears or stop short of the breakthrough because it feels too hard or scary, you miss the deeper awareness of what is really underneath driving and motivating your toxic habits, sabotaging thoughts, and self-abuse, so you can't make changes that stick. Not because you aren't smart enough, but because:

What you can't be with, runs you.

Can't be with disappointment? You will do anything to avoid feeling let down and disappointed, including overworking to try and meet unattainable goals, or overstaying or denying your needs in relationships to avoid hard feelings. Or the opposite: you'll procrastinate or play small so your goals are so small you can't fail to meet them.

Can't be with conflict? Your Good Girl will run you around, trying to make everyone else happy, over-caring for others and undercaring for yourself. Or your Perfectionist will make you overdo everything, convincing you that you *must* keep things all lined up or else chaos will erupt.

Can't be with sadness or shame? Your Overly Optimistic, Partying Cheerleader will keep you numb by overspending, overeating, over-you-name-it! Or she'll sweep in with her Pollyanna glasses so you don't have to deal with the hard, challenging things in your life, allowing you to keep pretending that it will all be okay, as if some magical force will sweep in to save you, discover you, or take care of you.

You get the picture.

We all have different things we just can't be with, depending on how your Inner Mean Girl came to be—remember, IMGs are unique. But there is one common thing almost all women can't be with, something that drives our actions and thoughts all the time but that we rarely know is the motivation behind the scenes. And that is the feeling of not belonging. It's pretty simple human psychology—every one of us needs to feel loved and safe. For us humans, that love and safety comes from being part of a tribe. When we feel like we are part of a tribe, we feel safe and loved, even if that tribe—blood family, work family, friend family, soul family—is totally dysfunctional or ultimately not in support of our highest, healthiest, and happiest expression. Because this is so important to you, your Inner Mean Girl has made it her job to make sure you feel like you belong no matter what, and she uses her particular weapons and Big Fat Lies to do that.

Good Girls will keep you doing the "right" thing or over-giving to others so you don't get ousted from the Good Girl tribe (even if that means sacrificing yourself). Achievement Junkies will surround you with other Achievement Junkies so you feel accepted and like everyone else (even though you are all workaholics). The Worrywart will find other people who also have a doom-and-gloom or fearful outlook on a situation to make you feel supported in your anxiety. Loyalty to the starving artist club, headed by the Martyr, will keep you struggling for money, telling you you're a sellout if you "make it" and have monetary success. And the Head Tripper will do everything she can to make you appear smart and rational so that you can belong to the tribe of responsible realists, who, although fancy themselves as smart and sturdy, often trade freedom and happiness for a false sense of security and so miss experiencing their full potential.

You can see that your Inner Mean Girl works tirelessly to protect you. In some ways your IMG is like a guard dog, completely loyal and devoted, which is kind of endearing, if you think about it. She won't let you out of her sight unless she thinks you are safe. And for a time in your life, before you were a grown woman who could protect herself, it was a good thing that your Inner Mean Girl was around. Her crazy protection measures actually served you in some capacity to keep you safe, loved, and feeling like you belonged. But now those same measures are hurting you, stifling you, and keeping you from the peace, prosperity, happiness, freedom, and love you want and need as a grown woman. If you are going to get your Inner Mean Girl to leave her post, you have to get to the bottom of the feelings and fears she's been guarding you from.

IT'S CHRISTINE HERE, and in the name of us women telling the truth about our fears and feelings, I felt inspired to share with you my personal experience as I went through this step. When I first met my Achievement Junkie, Move the Bar Belinda, I had no idea that my toxic habits of overworking and overdoing were rooted in and motivated by fear. But as I dug deeper, the dots connected for me, and a lightbulb went off! No wonder I could not stop pushing myself so hard to achieve more, working myself into exhaustion, and feeling bad if I wasn't working. My Achievement Junkie had been motivating me up the corporate ladder with such intense pressure because she was afraid, I was afraid, of getting stuck in the limiting, small world I grew up in (from the time I was three I can remember wanting to be somewhere else). I couldn't sit with the fear of being stuck or feeling limited or controlled in any way. Being stuck in a job, a relationship, or any place where I wasn't free to be my full self, where settling was the norm, was a death sentence to my soul. So Belinda made it her job to put pressure on me to achieve my way out by working hard and always staying focused on the next mountain pass, believing that someday after climbing many mountains we would have "made it," out of the threat of others controlling or limiting us, and we would be able to rest, stop driving and striving so hard (even though after forty years that day of rest and feeling like I had made it never came).

For a time, the pressure did motivate and serve me—I earned honors in school, was the only one of my friends to go to college, was accepted into one of the best MBA schools, flew up the corporate ladder, and catapulted out of the almost-marriage that would have kept me stuck for sure. Thank you, Inner Mean Girl! The problem was that once I was free and clear of getting stuck, she didn't know I didn't need to be motivated by that pressure anymore; I didn't know it either. So she just kept doing her job, and I kept being motivated by the fear of getting stuck or being controlled. For years my cycle was drive hard, push hard, fall into a pile of exhaustion, get sick, and have to put myself back together. Work twelve- to fifteen-hour days, starve myself of fun and rest, and then binge on pleasure and suffer the emotional, physical, and financial hangovers. Until the day I decided to get to the root of the fear and feelings I couldn't be with so I could see with clarity the judgments I had been placing on myself.

Using the same steps you are about to go through, I was able stop the toxic habits, or at least reduce them significantly—I still call myself a recovering Achievement Junkie and have to always be alert during high-stress or high-stretch situations for a relapse. Seeing the fear and naming it was the first step in getting to a place inside myself where I could feel like I had achieved enough. It took the entire seven steps to reform my Achievement Junkie and me, plus a continued commitment to feeling and healing this part of me. What served me most about the step that you are in now is that as I went deeper into myself, I started seeing the connection among the fear, my choices and beliefs, and my Inner Mean Girl's devotion to me. Once aware of her love for me, although twisted in its execution, I saw this was all a grand scheme of self-loving self-preservation. With this new perspective, I no longer needed to reject, deny, or avoid this part of me or see these feelings or fears as weak and inferior, but instead I could begin to love my Achievement Junkie.

Now it's your turn. We'll lead the way, taking you through a series of four inquiries that you will ask directly to your Inner Mean Girl, just like you are having a conversation with her. Put on your fearless journalist hat, grab your Inner Wisdom journal, and like a reporter on a mission, promise yourself that you will keep going until you get to the root of what is driving your IMG so fiercely.

STEP 3

Inquiry 1:
What sparked your Inner Mean Girl into action?

As we talked about in the very first chapter, Inner Mean Girls pop up in all kinds of situations over the course of your life. Most IMGs show up early, before the age of eleven, but there is no statute of limitations on when they can appear. They usually, but not always, can be traced back to an experience in which:

♥ people—relatives, friends, strangers, teachers, kids at school, coworkers—hurt you, let you down, criticized you, rejected you, embarrassed you, betrayed you, or took advantage of you;

♥ you expressed yourself and instead of being received in love, you were met with blame, shame, judgment, or criticism;

♥ big shifts—happy or sad—took place in your life that made you feel unsafe, vulnerable, and out of control;

♥ you felt like there wasn't enough—enough money, enough love, enough of something you needed and wanted—and your survival or emotional or physical safety was compromised;

♥ people who were supposed to protect you and love you unconditionally instead criticized, pressured, or hurt you; or

♥ you felt like you weren't good enough, like you didn't measure up, like you were doing a bad job, or like you were going to get left behind.

Maybe your Inner Mean Girl sparked out of a bully or a gang of outer mean girls at school; perhaps it started with a harsh, abusive, or neglectful adult or sibling that caused a Rejection Queen to build up walls to protect your heart or, just the opposite, bred a Good Girl who dismantled your boundaries altogether; or maybe a Perfectionist was born as a tactic to receive approval from a parent. Our childhoods are full of events, some very traumatic and some just traumatic enough to make us feel unsafe, unloved, vulnerable. We can't protect ourselves as children;

the fear gets into our hearts, bodies, and psyches, and without another option, we create Inner Mean Girls in order to product ourselves.

Inner Mean Girls can also sprout up over time as a result of multiple small incidents, whose effects remain dormant in the background for years. Then something happens as an adult that creates fear in you, and all those little cracks that happened over time activate, and you have an internal earthquake that sparks your IMG into full force. Take, for example, one of our students, whose IMGs didn't fully activate until she was in her late twenties.

Debra had, for twentysomething years, "successfully" kept everything in her life held together and looking perfect, doing what she was supposed to do. She was the consummate student, a dutiful and nice daughter and sister, followed the path her parents approved of, did well in her career, and then, because it was the next logical and correct step to take, she enrolled in medical school. Her first year in, Debra started having panic attacks. She began to develop obsessive-compulsive behaviors like biting her nails and keeping her room spotless to the point you could have thrown a dinner party on her floor. She constantly felt an underlying fear swirling around in her chest, which she kept to herself, of course. She was stressed out, and she didn't know why. Together, we uncovered that Debra had been suppressing her true heart's desires to be an artist and an art teacher and to relocate from the East Coast of the United States, where her family lived, to the West Coast, where her soul yearned to be.

> WE CREATE INNER MEAN GIRLS IN ORDER TO PROTECT OURSELVES.

Every time Debra had suppressed her desires, it was a like a small crack formed inside of her, letting just a little more fear in. Over the years, these cracks and fears grew until Debra hit a pressure point that she and her Inner Mean Girls could no longer cover up and smile through. Starting medical school and the thought of becoming a doctor instead of the artist she was born to be sparked her Inner Mean Girls into full force. All the fear that had been dammed up came gushing out in the form of anxiety, OCD, and stress in a way that Debra just couldn't ignore anymore. And thank goodness! Debra left medical school right away, and over the course of a few years, with the support of us, a strong circle of women, a reformed Inner Mean Girl, and a much stronger Inner Wisdom, she moved to California, got a job working in the arts, and had her first art show on Self-Love Day, February 13. (Yes, the day before Valentine's Day is the international day of self-love, which Christine founded and which is celebrated all over the world now. Put it on your calendar!)

Inner Wisdom Reflection: Find Your Inner Mean Girl Sparks

Grab your Inner Wisdom journal and get ready to start taking some notes—you've got a big question for your Inner Mean Girl: "What experiences sparked fear and other feelings inside of me that led me to believe I needed protection?" Use the four spark starters below to ignite your conscious awareness. These are short sentences that will help stimulate your memory and open up your writing. Jot the five Inner Mean Girl spark starters in your journal and then just start writing whatever comes—don't overthink, just write. Do not skip this step, even if your IMG tries to convince you that you don't need it. It can take you less than fifteen minutes (feel free to set a timer), so you don't have to spend hours trying to remember every single time you were afraid. We are looking for the big sparks here.

Inner Mean Girl Spark Starters

1. **Times I Felt Bad about Myself or I Was Hurt by Someone Else.**
   Times when I felt ashamed, embarrassed, afraid, disappointed,

scared; when I didn't feel good about myself. Times when someone let me down, criticized, rejected, betrayed, bullied, abused, publicly embarrassed me, or withheld love from me, or met my excitement with disapproval.

2. **Times I Couldn't Control Something.** Times when sudden or major changes took place in my surroundings or life that I couldn't control or change. These could be happy things or challenging things: parents' divorce, death of a loved one, falling in love for the first time, health challenges, birth of a baby.

3. **Times I Didn't Feel Safe or Like There Was Enough.** Times when my basic physical needs weren't met or were threatened because there wasn't enough money, shelter, clothing, food, etc.

4. **Times I Didn't Listen to or Trust Myself or Times I Didn't Protect Myself.** Times when I didn't trust my intuition and as a result made choices that were dishonoring to me.

For a free, guided meditation to help you find your Inner Mean Girl sparks go to **innerwisdomkit.com**. Once you've finished, take a look back through all the information you gathered and choose up to three "hot" sparks, these are the ones that are ready for you to work with. To find the hottest sparks, do a hot/cold temperature scan, with 10 being "burning to be transformed" and 1 being "frozen tundra," as in it doesn't trigger or bother you anymore or it just isn't ready for you to work with. Circle the three highest numbers and then write the sparks out on a new piece of paper in your journal.

Special Note: Please be gentle with yourself as you uncover these. Some of these experiences may have quite a sting and may stir up emotion for you, and that is okay. Remember, this is a journey to open up space for your feelings to emerge. But if a memory surfaces that feels too big to handle on your own, please reach out for help from a trained, licensed therapist, healer, coach, or professional you trust.

Inquiry 2: What feelings are you and your Inner Mean Girl avoiding?

How were you feeling during those times when your IMG sparked into action? We know this question is tricky because most of us, quite frankly, are not very good at accessing and expressing our true emotions. Many women come from a long line of "feeling stuffers"—women who have been conditioned to hide their emotions and keep their feelings private—so growing up we never observed or learned to openly express. Add to that all the negative cultural conditioning we've received as women regarding sharing and expressing our feelings, and it's no wonder we shy away from fully exposing our truth to others or to ourselves for that matter. We have all unfortunately been affected by cultural beliefs, which are really Big Fat Lies, like:

"NEVER LET THEM SEE YOU CRY."
"IT'S BETTER TO BE RATIONAL AND PRACTICAL THAN EMOTIONAL."
"SHOWING YOUR FEELINGS IS WEAK."
"SHOWING YOUR FEELINGS IS UNSAFE."
"WOMEN ARE JUST TOO EMOTIONAL."
"IF YOU WANT TO BE TAKEN SERIOUSLY, YOU CAN'T BE EMOTIONAL."

We've been made to feel bad, less than, or weak for our tenderness as women. As a result, we've developed some destructive habits, like being ashamed of our emotions, doing everything we can to shove them down and keep a stiff upper lip or a phony smile, or apologizing at the slightest sign of a tear or anger. It's the twenty-first century, yet we still live in a feeling-phobic, patriarchal society that discounts and demeans natural, feminine qualities. How can it still be totally acceptable for someone at work, at the dinner table, or on television to say, "Oh she is just being emotional. She's a woman. What do you expect?" or ask, "Do you have PMS? Just calm down." Is there any wonder we have learned to avoid our emotions, discount them, and mask them in judgments against ourselves? Of course your IMG has been trying to keep you from feeling; it's been dangerous, even among other women.

As we have talked with women around the world, we have witnessed and can share with you that without a doubt we *all* experience shame, embarrassment, anger, rage, anxiety, sadness—even if we do our very best to stuff them down, numb them out, medicate or meditate the feelings away. Which is so sad, because our ability to expose and share our feelings—to be vulnerable—is where our power lies. Every time we gather women into a circle, whether in person or virtually, and they honestly share and expose their truth—not their mental stories but their experiences—a big shift happens for every woman in the room.

A fully-feeling woman is a powerful feminine force, unstoppable in her courage to stand for anything she loves—including herself. We women are powerful not because of our ability to get things done or do things perfectly but because we dare to unleash

> WE WOMEN ARE POWERFUL NOT BECAUSE OF OUR ABILITY TO GET THINGS DONE OR DO THINGS PERFECTLY BUT BECAUSE WE DARE TO UNLEASH OUR INNATELY FEMININE POWER TO FEEL AND EXPRESS.

our innately feminine power to feel and express. It is not okay any longer to keep our emotions and their full, untamed expression under wraps. It's time to revolt against repression and free yourself to be the complete woman you are, free from guilt, shame, obligation, unrealistic expectations, and criticism. It's time to take back the power of your feelings—not to be trapped in them, suffer in them, or become a victim to them but to use your feelings to create the meaningful, fully expressed reality of your heart and soul.

Inner Wisdom Reflection: Reveal What's Hard for You to Feel

Look back at your hottest Inner Mean Girl sparks, and take a moment to tune in to how you felt when your Inner Mean Girl decided it was her job to protect you. Looking at each spark, ask yourself, "What was I feeling in that moment?" To help you access those feelings, which may be buried rather deep, use the following two sentence starters to help you connect your present-day self to the under the surface, often hard-to-access emotions that your IMG has been guarding for a very long time.

1. "I felt . . ."
2. "I felt like . . ."

Grab your journal and for each of the Inner Mean Girl sparks, free write what comes when you finish the sentences "I felt . . ." and "I felt like . . ." We recommend using both in your inquiry because the word *like* gives you access to your judgmental feelings as well as your emotional feelings, both of which are essential pieces of information. If you get stumped for words that express feelings, do an internet search for *feeling words,* and you'll find lots of helpful lists that you can look at to find the emotion that most reflects your experience.

Here are some real examples from women we have worked with and supported over the years, women who had no idea that these events that happened so long ago had any effect on their choices and realities until they opened themselves up to seeing the link.

> "When I was a little kid, the lights got turned off, my parents' cars got repossessed, and my mother ended up in the hospital a lot. *I felt* **worried and unsafe.** *I felt like* I had to **be the adult,** like I had to **be** the **responsible** one."

> "I couldn't control when my parents got divorced. *I felt* **sad and helpless.** *I felt like* it was **my fault,** that **I was to blame,** and like if I could just **do things better,** our family would have stayed together."

> "I was hurt when my father told me I was ugly and fat. *I felt* **unloved and inferior.** *I felt like* I was a **disappointment** and like **no one would ever love me.**"

After you have revealed what you felt, underline the words that reflect what is hard for you to be with, just like we bolded words here. Notice if the feelings you underlined feel familiar or unrecognizable. Notice the link between your feelings and your IMG. Is your IMG protecting you from those feelings? As you look at what you uncovered, take a breath and pause—we just asked you to dig pretty deep. Participate in an act of self-love and acknowledge the level of commitment, devotion, and honesty you are giving to yourself in this moment.

Inquiry 3: What's your Inner Mean Girl so afraid of anyway?

Now that you've connected the dots between your Inner Mean Girl's sparks and the feelings that are hard for you to be with, you are ready to go a level deeper to expose the fear underneath the feeling. There is something powerful about being able to admit to yourself that you are afraid. We spend so much energy running from our fears, because we haven't been taught how to deal with them or we've been made to feel ashamed or weak for having them. But having fear is a normal part of the human experience; it is what you do with the emotion that makes all the difference.

Our good friend and fear expert Rhonda Britten, bestselling author of *Fearless Living*, teaches that fear is your friend, that it is here to protect you. And she is right. Just like your Inner Mean Girl is here to protect you, so is the fear. In fact, the fear and your IMG are really the same. Think of your IMG just like a Halloween costume to masquerade your deepest fears; the treat is to find the underlying fear that lies beneath the façade.

What Are Your IMG's Biggest Fears?

Fear shows up differently for all of us, yet there are common fears as well. The question is which ones are really running you. We've boiled this all down to seventeen common fears. Of course, most of these will sound familiar to you, but we aren't talking to your intellectual mind here; we are diving deeper. So as you read through each one of these, feel which ones might be lurking beneath the surface in you by noticing how your body responds—your body is like your ultimate truth barometer. Using a scale of 1 to 10 as your temperature gauge, with 10 being hot as fire (totally relates to you) and 5 being no sweat (relates to you sometimes), and 1 being cold as ice (doesn't apply to you), rank each of the fears. Note the top three fears that your IMG fessed up to, the ones that feel the hottest.

FEAR OF	I AM AFRAID THAT . . .	Rate 1-10
Being Abandoned	I am afraid that I will be left alone or that love will be taken away.	
Being Alone	I am afraid to be by myself. I am afraid that I will always be alone.	
Being Embarrased	I am afraid that I will be called out, made fun of, or made to look stupid in front of other people.	
Being Called a Fraud	I am afraid people will find out that I don't know what I am doing, that I am not the person I pretend to be, or that I really am insecure inside.	
Being Betrayed	I am afraid that if I trust people, they will hurt me, steal from me, or take advantage of me.	
Disappointing Others	I am afraid that what I do is not enough and that I will be met with disapproval from people I love or whom I need to support me. I am afraid of appearing selfish if I take care of myself.	
Dying	I am afraid of losing people I love. I am afraid of being irrelevant or not existing. I am afraid of dying.	
Failing	I am afraid of people thinking that I am a failure. I am afraid of failing.	
Getting Stuck	I am afraid that I will be trapped, that my freedom will be taken away, that I will be forced to do things I don't want to do.	
Losing What I Love	I am afraid that the people I love could be taken away from me or that I will be perceived as disloyal to those I love.	

FEAR OF	I AM AFRAID THAT . . .	Rate 1–10
Not Being Enough	I am afraid that I am not worthy, not lovable, not deserving.	
Not Having Enough	I am afraid that I will not have enough money, that I will be poor, that I will be destitute.	
Not Fulfilling My Life Purpose	I am afraid that I will die without having reached my potential.	
Not Being Loved	I am afraid that I will lose love or never receive love.	
Being Rejected	I am afraid that people won't like or love me, that my love won't be returned, or if I put myself out there people will say no or reject me.	
Being Vulnerable	I am afraid that I will be attacked, controlled, or physically hurt. I am afraid of feeling or being seen as weak.	
Not Knowing	I am afraid of what will happen if I don't control the situation or have a plan.	

TRANSFORMATION TALE: My Inner Mean Girl Made Me Tired, Broke, and Afraid to Succeed

by Sam Bennett, bestselling author of *Get It Done: From Procrastination to Creative Genius in 15 Minutes a Day*

My work as an actor, writer, and teacher was always good, but the role at which I truly excelled was being a starving artist. I was great at finding bargains, clipping coupons, shopping secondhand, making do, and doing without. I was chronically broke, and I would often steer conversations toward topics like how hard I worked, how little money I had, and how unfair the whole situation was for an artist who truly cared about her craft and worked so hard for so little reward. I felt secretly virtuous. I juggled a bunch of underpaid part-time jobs, and I was always in at least one show that I didn't get paid for at all, even though rehearsals and performances constituted another full-time job. Each month, I made exactly enough money but not quite, and I was permanently exhausted. This, of course, was an important part of my Inner Mean Girl's strategy: if I was busy enough, the only feeling I had to deal with was tired, and I could ignore all those other pesky feelings like sadness, confusion, and low self-worth.

My gang of IMGs—Martyred Mary, Good Girl Gertrude, and You Don't Deserve It Debra—insisted that I wasn't worth anything, and not knowing any better, I agreed with them, staying on the hamster wheel of my life, working harder and harder for smaller and smaller rewards. So here was the perfect circle of feeling and fear avoidance that my Inner Mean Girls and I had created:

♥ I needed to feel useful, to be constantly working and contributing in order to avoid the feeling that I was not worthy of belonging.
♥ I needed to be exhausted in order to avoid feelings of anger and resentment.
♥ I needed to feel like I was always working harder than everyone else (martyrdom) in order to avoid the judgmental feeling that I wasn't as good as everyone else.

One day I came home to find fifteen messages on my answering machine (yes, answering machine; that's how long ago this was), *all* of which said something like "Sam, I know you're busy, but we need help with the bake sale . . ." or "Sam, could you come early to help set up the chairs . . ." or, "Sam, you're the only one we can trust to write the program notes, so could you . . ."

My mind suddenly flashed on a friend and colleague of mine who'd recently made it big in Hollywood. Would any of these people call her, asking her to volunteer her time to set up the chairs? Nope. Would she even consider spending time on the menial tasks I did all day? Nope. She was a star, and part of what made her a star was the fact that she treated herself like one.

It was like having a bucket of ice water dumped on my head: I suddenly realized that no one was going to treat me with love and respect until I started treating myself with love and respect. And step one meant that I was going to have to start being honest with myself about what I was feeling. I started by simply putting my basic needs ahead of everything else. I started by noticing when I was hungry, tired, or crabby and taking the time to eat, sleep, and exercise. Sounds simple, but it was totally radical for me.

I had spent so many years stuffing my feelings that I wasn't always sure what was going on with me, so I got a giant pad of newsprint and some magic markers and began drawing my feelings each morning. The colors and images kept me honest (I couldn't intellectualize my feelings the way I could when I was journaling) and connecting with them in this way helped me realize that all those feelings I had been avoiding for so long weren't too scary after all. In fact, there were lots of treats and rewards for embracing my emotions.

When I took the time to experience my feelings, I found my self-compassion. When I took the time to honor my emotional needs, I found my heart. When I started to treat my feelings as important signals, I found my self-worth.

Gradually I was able to quit all those low-paying, part-time jobs. I started offering the "Get It Done" workshop, which grew into my full-time business, the Organized Artist Company. And I stopped working for free and learned to feel great about my rates. As I tell my clients, "The work is worth it, I am worth it, and so are you." Now my feelings are my allies—they tell me when I need rest or when something's wrong, and they also allow me to receive a deeper gratitude for all the beauty and joy available to me each day.

Inquiry 4: What job did your Inner Mean Girl give herself, and what does she need to feel safe enough to consider taking a new job?

With all this information now at your disposal, you have the opportunity to see much more clearly what is underneath your self-sabotaging, sacrificing, bullying patterns. Let's just pause for a moment to look at all your IMG has been doing to guard you, keep you from feelings that cause you pain, and allow you to feel a sense of belonging and loyalty. Although warped and twisted and not effective anymore, your IMG was doing the best she could—and so were you. So can you give yourself and your Inner Mean Girl some credit here? Recognize, as you look at all the things she has driven you to do and think, that she was trying to help, and for that give her, and yourself, some compassion and gratitude.

Just by giving yourself a little bit of recognition and love, you become more free to choose to motivate yourself in new ways, ways that support instead of sabotage. When you stop rejecting your Inner Mean Girl and these parts of yourself, your IMG will start to open up to the possibility that she just may be able to give up her death grip and stop her relentless use of fear. We want to plant the seed of possibility with your IMG that there is another way to deal with those fears and feelings, a new way of living that will propel you into the life you want for yourself.

Inner Wisdom Reflection:
Give Your Inner Mean Girl the Pen

Imagine giving your Inner Mean Girl the pen and ask her directly to finish the statements below. These are the final pieces to fully uncovering the roots of your fears and begin seeing what job your IMG has given herself. We are pretty sure that your IMG is now ready to spill the beans. So as if you are giving her your hand so she can write, write these sentence starters in your Inner Wisdom journal and see what she has to tell you. We know you may be tempted to skip this or to do it halfway by just thinking about these answers. Don't shortchange yourself. Take ten minutes here, play the game with us, and see what your IMG has to share.

> "I am trying to protect you from . . ."
> "It's my job to . . ."
> "What I need to feel safe is . . ."

There's so much power in knowing which feelings are hardest for you and what fears are most prevalent. This deeper level of awareness explains why sometimes things happen that make you feel more intensely than the situation actually warrants. Your Inner Mean Girl doesn't differentiate past events from current ones, so when something triggers you, she reconnects you not to just the present situation but also to every time you have been triggered in that way. She sets off a superhighway of neural pathways, sending your body into flight or fight and you down the path of negative thinking and bad choices. This is why you can fly off the handle at seemingly small things or unleash a boatload of emotion on someone that was way more than warranted. You are connecting to years of triggers and stored-up feelings, and your Inner Mean Girl is rushing in to do her job.

So now that you are armed with all this awareness about your Inner Mean Girl, what can you do to get her to loosen her grip? You have to bring the information and ideas we've shared with you into real-life experiences in your day-to-day life; otherwise all this just stays in your mind, where your IMG rules, and you'll continue to get triggered, resulting in bullying and sabotaging yourself. And because we've got your back and we've gone down this path before, we put together a superpower challenge and a story for you that we think you will love.

Superpower Challenge: Buck Your Inner Mean Girl's Fear and Take a Bold Action!

It's time to bring all that you uncovered into your daily life with a superpower challenge meant to support you to step outside your comfort zone! Here it goes. In the next seven days, we dare you to take an action toward something your heart and soul desire or that your Inner Wisdom has been suggesting you take but that your Inner Mean Girl has been preventing you from moving on. Stop and ask yourself this question: "What have I been holding back on doing because of my Inner Mean Girl and her fear?"

Using the three sentence starters below, tell the truth, admit the fear, and then commit to taking a bold action this week—yes, in the next seven days. Say your answers out loud, write the answers in your journal, and if you are really serious about breaking through, share your bold action with a friend to help hold you accountable:

"I have been holding back on . . ."
"Because my Inner Mean Girl has been scared that . . ."
"The bold action I will take this week is . . ."

Remember that bold actions don't need to be huge, although they can be; they can also be small and mighty. Don't make it so big that you can't or won't do it. Baby steps can be just as powerful as big leaps; in fact, we need to know how and when to use both.

When Heidi, one of our workshop participants, took this challenge, her Inner Mean Girl revealed some important and enlightening information. When she gave her IMG the pen, Heidi uncovered that she really wanted to take the bold action of leaving her high-powered, stressful job, but her IMG was terrified of being seen as disloyal and selfish in her boss's eyes. As she communed with her Inner Mean Girl, she realized that she needed to find something other than her boss and company that she could be more loyal to—something that was connected to what was important to her: her family.

You see, Heidi's job was taking way too much time away from her children, and her loyalty to the company was getting in the way of her loyalty to her family. Her IMG liked to be loyal; she just needed the loyalty directed in the right direction—toward Heidi and her family.

> LOVE YOURSELF FIRST BY STAYING TRUE TO WHO YOU ARE, EVEN IF THAT MEANS DISAPPOINTING ANOTHER.

Here is an important self-love rule: love yourself first by staying true to who you are, even if that means disappointing another. Contrary to popular belief and your IMG, doing so will actually generate more love, not less, for you and the people around you. At first other people may not always like the change (change isn't easy even when it's good for us), but in the long-term, the truth is everybody wins when you honor yourself.

So Heidi asked all of the workshop participants to hold her accountable for talking with her boss when she got back home. Everyone rallied behind her on our Facebook group, reminding her to shine her loyalty in the right direction, and she took the bold action of talking with her boss about working part-time from home in order to spend more time with the family. This eliminated her commute, allowing her to take her kids to school and enabling Heidi to have some important down time in the morning for herself. Instead of quitting the job altogether, she found a better solution, one that allowed her to be loyal to herself and her family, while maintaining her loyalty to the company. Her Inner Mean Girl needed Heidi to take incremental steps, so the halfway point worked better than cutting the cord all at once. To Heidi's joyful surprise, her boss agreed to a three-month trial. Everyone won—most of all Heidi and her family.

Just like Heidi, we want to make sure your commitment sticks and your Inner Mean Girl doesn't sabotage you. In order to ensure your success, you need support. This isn't a weakness; it's a fact. We all need support—remember, support prevents sabotage. In this case, we want you to find at least one person who can lovingly hold you accountable to yourself to take this step, someone you can tell about your commitment, who you can report back to and share after you take your bold action. Tell this person straightaway about your bold baby step. Our students tell us being accountable to other women makes all the difference. Love yourself and be willing to share those feelings and fears enough to ask for support.

INSPIRED ACTION

Bring Your Inner Mean Girl to Life—Make Your Inner Mean Girl Exposé

Now that you've conducted your full Inner Mean Girl investigation, it's time to compile your results in your official Inner Mean Girl exposé and bring her to life. We even want you to find out her name and create or find a visual image, drawing, or representation of her—you can't very well have an intimate relationship with someone if you don't know her name and what she looks like, can you? To keep your IMG off your back and move her into a new job, you'll need to be on a first-name basis and have a visual to connect to what she looks and feels like.

Complete your exposé before moving on to the next section. Do *not* let your Inner Mean Girl sabotage you. Your IMG may tell you pesky Big Fat Lies, like:

"YOU DON'T HAVE TIME."
"THIS IS SILLY."
"YOU DON'T NEED THIS."
"YOU CAN COME BACK AND DO IT LATER."
"IT DOESN'T REALLY MATTER IF YOU CREATE AN IMAGE OF ME."

If she is, it's time to take a stand. All of those are lies to subvert you from exposing her. Plus, women tell us they love creating their Inner Mean Girl exposé, naming their IMGs and bringing them to life visually because they get to be creative. And don't freak out if your IMG likes to tell you that you can't draw or that you aren't creative. Every woman is creative; most of us have just forgotten or have an IMG that has squashed that creativity. You don't have to be an accomplished artist to bring your Inner Mean Girl to life. We've done this with girls as young as seven, and if they can do it, so can you. And we won't leave you hanging on this—we've put together some special superpower creative tools and even included some samples from our students. This isn't about making a beautiful painting or perfect drawing—it's about you expressing yourself!

Step 1: Gather up the following six pieces of Inner Mean Girl data from all the powerful investigative work you just did.

Using the template (see the sample on the next page), write this information in the book, or make your own template in your Inner Wisdom journal, writing out each of the following pieces of information. You can also get a copy of the template to download and print from the Inner Wisdom Kit at **innerwisdomkit.com**:

♥ Main Archetype(s)
♥ Top Five Big Fat Lies
♥ Toxic Habits (what she drives you to do)
♥ Triggers
♥ Cost
♥ Purpose (her biggest fears/what she's trying to protect you from feeling or experiencing)

Step 2: Name your Inner Mean Girl.

Ask your Inner Mean Girl what she likes to be called, let her archetype inspire you, or have fun and make it up. This is very empowering for

INNER MEAN GIRL EXPOSÉ

MY NAME IS: _____

My Big Fat Lie Playlist
(Top Five):

♥ _____

♥ _____

♥ _____

♥ _____

♥ _____

My Toxic Habits
(Top Three):

♥ _____

♥ _____

♥ _____

My Triggers
(Top Three):

♥ _____

♥ _____

♥ _____

My Main Archetype(s):

_____

_____

_____

I Am Trying to Protect You From:

_____

_____

I Am Costing You:

_____

_____

women and makes it all the more fun. Some of our students' Inner Mean Girls' names have included: Loyal to a Fault Lucy, Beat It Brenda, Perfectionist Peggy, Bitchy Beatrice, and Anxious Annie. (Alliteration can make the name snappy and easy to remember!)

Step 3: What does your Inner Mean Girl look like? Bring your Inner Mean Girl to life with image.

Remember what we said: don't let your Inner Mean Girl freak you out about creating an image—if a third grader can draw her IMG, you can draw yours. This isn't a contest. Here are three ways you can bring your Inner Mean Girl to life. This is an essential part of the process. Have fun and see what emerges!

- ♥ **Visualize her and draw her.** Grab some crayons, markers, a pencil, or even a Sharpie and let your creativity take over. You don't have to draw anything elaborate. Just close your eyes and imagine what your IMG looks like; let the form emerge on the paper. (As a special treat, we also invited world-recognized transformational artist and founder of the Intentional Creativity Movement, Shiloh Sophia McCloud, to guide you through a creative visualization that allows you to see your Inner Mean Girl more clearly. Go to **innerwisdomkit.com** to receive the free visualization video.)
- ♥ **Find an image of her.** Search the internet or magazines for an image that looks like her. You might think of a famous character in a play or movie and search for that. Or just try typing in phrases like *Mean Girl, Good Girl, Perfectionist,* or whatever type of Inner Mean Girl you have, and see what images the Universe delivers to your virtual doorstep.
- ♥ **Make an Inner Mean Girl puppet or find an Inner Mean Girl doll.** Get yourself a paper bag and a few markers and make a puppet of your Inner Mean Girl. At our Inner Mean Girl Reform School live events

and retreats, women have loved creating their IMG puppets. Your puppet can be as elaborate or as simple as you'd like—just drawing a face on a paper bag works great. If you'd like some inspired instruction, one of our Inner Wisdom coaches, Katherine Torrini, created a video for you that will lead you through this process and show you how to use your new puppet. Go to **innerwisdomkit.com** to watch the video. If a puppet isn't your thing but you dig the idea of having something 3D you can relate to, find a doll or some kind of object that symbolizes your Inner Mean Girl. One of our students bought a voodoo doll online, another grabbed a stuffed witch, and another found a miniature troll in a kid's store. Have fun and treat it like an adventure.

Want to be inspired? We put together a mini Inner Mean Girl Hall of Fame at the end of the book (page 243), so you can view Inner Mean Girl images from women around the world. And if you'd like to see even more, we've given you special VIP access to the complete hall of fame online, which includes sample pictures and exposés from other women. You can access the IMG Hall of Fame at **innerwisdomkit.com**.

Let's Celebrate!

Inner Mean Girls are known for just pushing ahead without stopping to celebrate the milestones, so let's *not* do that. Before you move on to step four, let's pause to acknowledge the work you've done:

- ♥ You've identified your Inner Mean Girl Archetypes, the core weapons she uses, and the Big Fat Lies she tells you.
- ♥ You've begun to notice what she's protecting you from, why she got created in the first place, and what her current job is.
- ♥ You've seen what she is costing you and what triggers her.
- ♥ You've noticed what her biggest fears are, and hopefully you've brought her to life with a name and picture or you've even created a puppet.

♥ You've brought your Inner Mean Girl out from behind the curtain and into the light and are gaining the power to shift yourself out of negative thinking and self-sabotaging patterns.

So pat yourself on the back, give yourself a hug, and recognize your commitment and devotion to yourself. Just notice what happens when you make your relationship with yourself a priority. And then get ready, because you're about to meet your new best friend in the steps ahead—your Inner Wisdom! But tell your Inner Mean Girl not to worry; you are not abandoning her. On the contrary, in the steps that follow, you will continue to get to know her better as well.

PART II

MEET YOUR INNER WISDOM

STEP 4

TURN UP THE VOLUME ON YOUR INNER WISDOM

W have some incredible news. As loud and as nasty as your Inner Mean Girl can be, there is another voice inside of you. A voice more powerful than even the most lethal of Inner Mean Girls . . .

Meet your Inner Wisdom.

Your Inner Wisdom is the voice of truth inside of you. The part of you that knows who you *really* are. The loving presence that loves you unconditionally and as a result can offer compassion and care to you no matter what. This wise, inner guidance system knows exactly what direction will lead to your highest good, and so can tell you the best course of action to take. It's the honest, give-it-to-me-straight voice that, like a trusted friend, tells you the truth even when it's hard to hear—but always tells you with compassion and without judgment.

You may call this part of you your higher self; or inner wise woman; or your intuition. You may have a great connection with this part of you already, you may have none at all, or you may fall somewhere in between. Wherever you are is the perfect starting point for this journey.

One of the biggest differences in how we approach things at Inner Mean Girl Reform School is that we don't just stop with getting to know your Inner Mean Girl. While dealing with that inner, critical voice is helpful, without being connected to something even stronger, the changes don't stick, and the deeper wisdom of your heart and the full expression of your spirit can't manifest. You also need to create a deep relationship with your all-powerful Inner Wisdom.

What Is Your Current Relationship with Your Inner Wisdom?

Over the years, as we have coached, taught, and mentored women, we've discovered a few very important things about a woman's relationship with her Inner Wisdom:

1. **Everyone has Inner Wisdom. We are all born with a solid connection to our inner guidance systems.** (Yes, you too—no exceptions on this one; we promise!)
2. **Most women have an inconsistent relationship with their Inner Wisdoms at best, a nonexistent one at worst.** We women receive a lot of social conditioning growing up that weakens our ability to listen to and trust this inner wise voice. And given our busy, overwhelming lifestyles, time to be quiet and tune in to our Inner Wisdom is often the first to go.
3. **Anyone can relearn how to receive guidance from her Inner Wisdom and reestablish a strong connection and trust, no matter how estranged the relationship has become.** You never lose the connection; the strength of the connection may have weakened over time, but it's still there waiting to be revived.

Take Susan, who was certain she just didn't have an Inner Wisdom. When she got quiet and tried to tune in, she could not hear or find her Inner Wisdom's voice. Most of the time all she could hear and feel was her Inner Mean Girl's rants, and if she finally did gain a moment of respite, her mind would go completely blank—no inner guidance, just radio silence. We asked Susan to remember a time in her life when she did something on a whim. She immediately thought of joining one of our intensive breakthrough group-mentorship programs. She told us that she read our invitation and just knew she had to apply, so she did. During our first conversation with Susan, she knew she had to say yes even though the choice defied logic to her. She wasn't the type of person to join a circle of women and dive deep into self-love and feminine power. Yet, when we asked her why she said yes, she replied, "There was this feeling inside of me, like a strong urge, that just knew I had to say yes, even though another part of me was screaming, 'Are you crazy?'" At the time, she had no idea this was her Inner Wisdom guiding her, overpowering her Inner Mean Girl's rants.

When we pointed out this experience to Susan as proof that her Inner Wisdom existed, a lightbulb went off for her; she finally understood what it felt like inside her body when her Inner Wisdom was talking. This insight sparked Susan's commitment to deepening her relationship with her Inner Wisdom, and over the course of our nine months together, we witnessed Susan develop a strong connection to her Inner Wisdom. She began to notice where her Inner Wisdom lived in her body—for her it was in her belly. As she began to tune in daily, her life began to change in the most miraculous ways: she moved cities and landed her dream job, went on a trip to Europe with a best friend, and began dating. This is the power of tuning in and deepening your connection to your Inner Wisdom.

You might be like Susan, just now becoming reacquainted with this powerful inner force. Or you may have been fostering a deeper relationship with your Inner Wisdom for years now, trusting her guidance in many areas and situations of your life. You may also fall somewhere in between. Wherever you are on the spectrum, you likely can stand to improve your ability to receive guidance from, trust in, and act on your Inner Wisdom's sage direction. Just like any other relationship in your life, there is always room for deeper levels of trust, connection, and communication, and the more love and energy you put in, the more you'll receive.

So, what is your current relationship with your Inner Wisdom? Let's take a moment to get a sense of your current connection.

Inner Wisdom Reflection:
Take an Inner Wisdom Pulse Check

Take a moment right now to close your eyes, put your hand on your heart, and take three deep breaths. Pausing to close your eyes and breathe is like picking up the telephone to call your Inner Wisdom. It's the fastest way to move yourself from your mental mind chatter, where your Inner Mean Girl hangs out, to a deeper place of inner heart and body knowing, where your Inner Wisdom lives. Add to that the gesture of putting your hand on your heart, and it's like pressing the talk button on the phone, physically and emotionally connecting you to your heart and soul wisdom.

With your eyes closed, remember a time in your life when you felt guided by an inner force; it might be when you said yes to a date, left a job, or made a financial decision that others deemed crazy, but you knew deep down was right for you. Then read each of the five stages of Inner Wisdom connection below and mark the one that best describes your current relationship. No need to overthink or analyze it. Just go with what stage resonates with you. (Do yourself a favor and tell the truth. This is about supporting yourself to grow from where you are without judgment.)

Strangers	**You don't remember ever hearing the voice of your Inner Wisdom, and you are pretty convinced you don't have one.** You are not sure what we mean by Inner Wisdom. You can't hear the voice no matter how much you tune in. You think you might be the only woman alive not to have Inner Wisdom.

Estranged	**You can remember a time when you did have a connection to your Inner Wisdom, but that was a long time ago.** You no longer communicate with this intuitive part of you, as you've opted to rely more on what is rational, practical, and comfortable. If you can't prove it or see it, you rarely trust it.
Acquaintances	**You have a connection and can receive guidance when you choose, but you don't always tune in, especially in the areas of your life where you don't like what the guidance says.** You invite in your Inner Wisdom only in specific areas of your life. You don't check in every day; you tend to tune in only when things get stressful or you struggle.
Good Friends	**You receive guidance from this inner force often, but you still find it challenging to trust it and act on it.** You have some kind of daily practice that allows you to tune in to your Inner Wisdom, and you do it most, if not all, days. You receive the input, but you don't always take the counsel. You doubt your inner knowing sometimes and that stops you from taking action led by your Inner Wisdom. In certain areas of your life, you still struggle to tell the difference between your Inner Mean Girl and your Inner Wisdom.

	Best Friends	**The main voice that runs through your mind and guides your life is your Inner Wisdom.** You have a strong daily practice that you rarely, if ever, miss. When you face choices, you know how to tune in to and listen to this voice. You trust your Inner Wisdom always, even when that means making a choice different than conventional wisdom. You can change the voice in your mind quickly, and you can discern between the voices of your Inner Mean Girl and your Inner Wisdom with precision.

Now you know where you and your Inner Wisdom stand. Just like with Susan, admitting where you are will help you see how you can reestablish a stronger connection over time. No matter where you are on the spectrum, the next step is to increase your ability to tell the difference between your Inner Mean Girl and Inner Wisdom, to begin to consciously change the negative self-talk into inner-loving truth, and to gain the strength to not only receive the guidance of your Inner Wisdom but to also follow it, no matter what.

Telling the Difference Between Your Inner Mean Girl and Your Inner Wisdom

Given the pressures you face as a modern-day woman to be, do, and have it all (alongside a media engine that constantly reinforces this message that you don't have enough, do enough, aren't enough yourself), it's no wonder that over time, your mind has become like an Inner Mean Girl radio station that blares Big Fat Lies into your mind.

TURN UP THE VOLUME ON YOUR INNER WISDOM

Your body and your mind are like one big radio tower, constantly emitting different vibrations that inform your thoughts and actions. This broadcasting tower has two channels: 88.9 FEAR, over which your Inner Mean Girl broadcasts her rants and sabotaging thoughts, and 108.0 LOVE, through which your Inner Wisdom's loving and honest truth flows. (We use the number 108 because it is a significant and sacred number in many traditions. There are 108 beads in a mala and the yogic tradition is based on the number 108, for instance.)

In every moment of every day, you have the choice which channel you tune in to. You have a choice as to what station you turn up the volume on—your Inner Wisdom's loving, truthful guidance or your Inner Mean Girl's Big Fat Lies. You have the power to decide which thought runs through your mind and what action you take or what beliefs you make up as a result. It's time for you to become highly sensitive to whose guidance is actually coming through: your Inner Mean Girl or your Inner Wisdom. One of the biggest questions we get asked by women is, "How can I distinguish between the lies of my IMG and the truth of my Inner Wisdom? How do I know which voice is which?"

The answer is so simple it is often overlooked: pay attention to your body. Notice the vibration, feelings, and frequency running through you. Your body never lies. Just like you can't hear a station's sound waves until they reach your radio, you can't detect your Inner Mean Girl's or Inner Wisdom's waves until they hit your nervous system and you feel them in your body. Sometimes your IMG and your Inner Wisdom may send messages with the same words—but the way the message feels, the energy it's delivered with, and the way you feel when you receive it are drastically different.

This is why we call the Inner Mean Girl station the FEAR station. When you are attuned to it, feelings like fear, anxiety, doubt, depression, and isolation course through your mind and body. You feel tense, your stomach is in knots, your chest feels contracted, or you have a lump in your throat. Those feelings drive you into self-sabotage and that awful negative-thinking loop that you just can't seem to break free of. But as you become more aware of the different types of emotions and feelings your Inner Mean Girl and Inner Wisdom cause inside you, you also become more aware of which frequency is running through you. Being able to make this delineation empowers you to deal with situations and people in your everyday life in a very different way, because you gain the power to *act from* your Inner Wisdom instead of *react to* your Inner Mean Girl.

Use Your Body as a Barometer

The best guidance we can give you about how to tell whether you are being led by your Inner Mean Girl's fear or your Inner Wisdom's loving truth is to ask yourself these two questions:

"What is my body feeling?"
"What am I feeling?"

Remember, your body never lies.

Use the handy dandy body and emotional vibe chart on page 128 to help you navigate the difference between the frequencies—feelings and sensations—the two channels emit. When you feel any of the body vibes or emotional vibes in the left-hand column, you will know that your IMG is in control and you either are headed for or are smack-dab in the middle of an Inner Mean Girl attack. Your Inner Wisdom does not broadcast on the frequency of fear and what fear generates. Your Inner Wisdom only broadcasts the feeling vibrations in the right-hand column—even if the news is a tough-love truth—because what she comes from is always love and compassion.

Of course, we would all love to be tuned in to the Inner Wisdom channel all the time, but you wouldn't be reading this book (or be a human being) if that were the case. Our lives are a constant practice of choosing what energy and voice we tune in to, and like with anything, you get better the more you practice. And today you are in luck because we have two superpower tools that are proven to increase your mastery and ability to take back control of your mind, emotions, and choices during high trigger times and tune in to and live from your Inner Wisdom guidance more often.

When Your Inner Mean Girl Refuses to Give Up the Control Tower

If you have the choice as to which thoughts you listen to and let drive you into action, what do you do when your Inner Mean Girl won't leave the control tower? When she has already taken over, and your body is in full fear mode. While you would so love to listen to your Inner Wisdom, no amount of affirmations, meditation, positive thinking, or even processing the situation with friends is going to change the channel. So the next question becomes, how can you hear the voice of your Inner Wisdom when your Inner Mean Girl is talking so loudly? How can you get an SOS through to your Inner Wisdom in those moments?

You have to let your Inner Mean Girl rant.

Yes, let your IMG have the microphone. When you are in the midst of an Inner Mean Girl attack, don't resist her and just tell this part of you to be quiet. She'll only get louder. You have to let this part of you speak, without fear or judgment, giving this part of you that is freaked out permission to fully express until she has had her say.

The permission to vent and just let out the Big Fat Lies releases the fear and energy she's been generating and gives your Inner Wisdom the space to come through—which she always does when you remember to ask her. And get this: you can wake up your Inner Wisdom in just three steps, usually in less than ten minutes.

INNER MEAN GIRL STATION: FEAR	INNER WISDOM STATION: LOVING TRUTH
PHYSICAL VIBE **My body feels...**	**PHYSICAL VIBE** **My body feels...**
♥ Airy and spacey	♥ Calm
♥ Contracted	♥ Expansive
♥ Defended	♥ Expressive
♥ Disconnected	♥ Excited
♥ Fragmented	♥ Grounded
♥ Frenzied	♥ Lovingly embraced
♥ Heavy	♥ Light
♥ Pressured	♥ Open
♥ Spinny	♥ Relaxed
♥ Scrunched up	♥ Relieved
♥ Stressed	♥ Safe
♥ Tense	♥ Solid
♥ Tight	♥ Supported
♥ Ungrounded	♥ Surrendered

INNER MEAN GIRL STATION: FEAR	INNER WISDOM STATION: LOVING TRUTH
EMOTIONAL VIBE I am feeling…	**EMOTIONAL VIBE** I am feeling…
♥ Anxious or worried	♥ Accepted
♥ Avoidant	♥ Balanced anticipation
♥ Burdensome and obligation-ridden	♥ Caring
♥ Confused	♥ Compassionate
♥ Controlling	♥ Connected
♥ Critical	♥ Courageous
♥ Closed down and defensive	♥ Empowered
♥ Dread	♥ Free and expansive
♥ Doubtful	♥ Forgiving
♥ Guilty	♥ Graceful
♥ Judgmental and blaming	♥ Loving
♥ Lonely or isolated	♥ Peaceful
♥ Regretful	♥ Present
♥ Rejected	♥ Open and curious
♥ Skeptical	♥ Safe
♥ Shameful	♥ Trusting
♥ Unsafe	♥ Welcoming and embracing

Superpower Tool:
The Wake-Up Call
Three-Step Process

One of our simplest and most effective tools for turning down the volume on your Inner Mean Girl and turning up the volume on your Inner Wisdom is the Wake-Up Call Three-Step process.

We want you to begin using this tool the moment you feel *any* emotion that doesn't feel good, from annoyance to rage to depression to sadness, because whenever a harmful or hard emotion is present, you can bet your IMG is right there with a megaphone, shouting Big Fat Lies at you. Let's practice right now.

Bring to mind an area or situation in your life where your Inner Mean Girl is getting triggered. It might be a conflict with a coworker, how you feel about your body, a situation with your child, or your bank account balance.

We recommend doing this aloud. You can journal it, but make sure you are also saying the words out loud. It's important to give a platform to the competing forces and their voices inside you so they can be released and so you can sense the difference in how they feel in your body.

Step 1: Tune in to your Inner Mean Girl and let her rant by asking: "What is my Inner Mean Girl saying?"

This first question often feels counterintuitive. "Aren't we trying to tune in to our Inner Wisdom?" you might ask. Indeed we are. But here's the thing: we often cannot hear the voice of our Inner Wisdom unless we allow our Inner Mean Girl to rant first. She needs to have her say, take her turn in the spotlight, and be heard in order for her to back off and allow your Inner Wisdom to take center stage. So again ask yourself, "What is my Inner Mean Girl saying?" And then say her answer out loud, with all the energy she has in saying it to you. Really embody her and let her energy come through you. Say the statements as if she is saying them to you. For example:

"YOU ARE WORTHLESS."
"YOU MIGHT AS WELL JUST GIVE IT UP RIGHT NOW!"
"WHO THE HELL DO YOU THINK YOU ARE?"
"YOU CAN'T SAY NO. PEOPLE WON'T LOVE YOU ANYMORE."

What does your Inner Mean Girl have to say to you about this situation? Let her rant!

Remember, saying the words out loud is extremely helpful. When you actually hear these harsh words spoken, their power lessens, partly because they are so *not* true and partly because you are now hearing for the first time just how awful you've been treating yourself inside and how insane this line of thinking really is. You can also write the words in your journal with fierce, strong handwriting (maybe even in red ink) to express the intense energy of fear behind them. Keep going until your IMG feels complete and heard, almost like you've reached the basement and can go down no further or you've let go of all the hot air inside of a balloon.

Step 2: Tune in to your Inner Wisdom by first closing your eyes, then taking a breath, and then asking: "What does my Inner Wisdom know?"

Once your Inner Mean Girl has had her say, it's time to invite your Inner Wisdom to take center stage. Close your eyes (this is important; having your eyes closed helps you go inside, so keep 'em closed), take a deep breath (it is also essential to breathe, as it clears your mind and makes space for your Inner Wisdom), and then ask yourself, "What does my Inner Wisdom know?" Let the words come to you, and say whatever words come out loud—no judgment or censoring. No pondering, no thinking, just go with what you hear and feel. Allow the voice of truth to come forth in all her glory. Really feel the good energy in your body deepen and expand as she speaks to you. Once she says a little, ask the question again, "What else does my Inner Wisdom know?" Keep talking (or writing) until you feel your Inner Wisdom has had her full say. Asking this question a few times is a really good idea, as there is often more under the surface, and just like with any of us, it can take a little bit to go deep and get it all out. You'll know you've hit the truth when the words kind of roll off your tongue and you feel the vibration of truth in your body.

Step 3: Lock in the loving truth with a physical gesture.

Repeat out loud what your Inner Wisdom told you—this is your loving truth—in as simple and as direct a way as you can. Then ask her for a physical gesture or movement that you can use to lock this truth into your body. It could be tapping on your heart, putting your hand on your belly, doing a little dance, rubbing your fingers together—whatever comes naturally. Trust yourself to find the right gesture for you. This is a Neuro-Linguistic Programming (NLP) technique that allows you to connect your truth with a physical movement, thus locking your truth in your brain and body.

Carmen, one of our students, had a relentless Inner Mean Girl broadcasting anxiety, shame, and self-judgment because of how her body looked. She was about thirty or so pounds overweight (at least in the eyes of her IMG) and had tried diet after diet, but nothing seemed to stick. We know from experience that whenever the source and motivation of your actions is your Inner Mean Girl's criticism and fear, your commitment and the results will be short-lived. But if you allow your Inner Wisdom to guide your way, things turn out differently. Carmen used the Wake-Up Call Three-Step process to finally get to her truth. First she gave voice to her Inner Mean Girl's Big Fat Lies and said, "I am fat, and I'll never get this under control. I'm destined to struggle with my weight my whole life. It's hopeless." Then she closed her eyes and took a few deep breaths, accessing her Inner Wisdom's truth. What she said out loud shocked her: "I've had a lot to deal with, and I've let myself gain weight back; I believe in my power to get back on track. I love myself enough to take care of my body. I know the right foods to eat, and I actually love my walks around the lake. I'm ready to make myself and my self-care a priority again."

Then she locked in her Inner Wisdom's truths with a hand gesture—two hands parallel, fingers pointing forward—to emphasize the simple but mighty statement, "I am getting back on track." Carmen had tears streaming down her face as she locked in her truth. She had never approached weight loss as an act of self-love before; usually it was an act of self-hatred and disgust. She was blown away by the connection to her Inner Wisdom and proceeded to get back on track and slim down.

IT'S AMY HERE. I'm ready to hold your hand through this process—that's what we women do for each other, right? I created a video in which I walk you through the Wake-Up Call Three-Step process. Go to **innerwisdomkit.com**, and we will wake up and hear your Inner Wisdom's truth together, step by step. You'll also find another video that will give you a sense of the power of putting this to use in your daily life. It's a live Inner Mean Girl transformation and Inner Wisdom wake-up in which I take "T," an eighteen-year-old woman, through the Wake-Up Call Three-Step process. This was recorded at a Madly in Love with ME event on February 13, Self-Love Day, and brings everyone watching to tears, showcasing the power of this process.

How Do You Strengthen Your Inner Wisdom to Prevent IMG Attacks?

While the wake-up call process is hands-down the best tool to use in the midst of an Inner Mean Girl attack, we hope you have gotten the message by now that wise women also practice preventative care. Think about it this way: you take care of your physical health by eating nutritious food. The same rationale applies with the thoughts that run through your mind and your feelings. You want to take proactive action when it comes to the vibrations moving through you by starting your day with your mind attuned to the loving truth vibrations of 108.0 LOVE, your Inner Wisdom channel.

Our soul sister Kristine Carlson, the *New York Times* bestselling author of *Don't Sweat the Small Stuff for Women,* who has spent over thirty years cultivating a sense of inner peace even in the midst of the chaos that kids, careers, and life brings, wisely teaches that how you start your day is how you live your day. Start your day connected to love and you will be less susceptible to Inner Mean Girl attacks. Think about it: if you begin your day filling your body and mind with feelings of self-love instead of self-criticism, wouldn't

> **HOW YOU START YOUR DAY iS HOW YOU LIVE YOUR DAY.**

your day go better? If you have a daily morning practice already, you know what we are talking about. All lives led by Inner Wisdom require we make and keep sacred dates with our Inner Wisdom (more on how to do this in the next step). Just remember that these techniques may feel uncomfortable at first, but try them anyway. Your IMG will try to make you feel silly, stupid, or weird for doing things like talking to yourself, but that's only because she knows it works.

So, how would you like to wake up every day attuned to love, calm, and spaciousness and as a result be more able to stay connected to your wise, centered self? We've got a superpower tool that is going to strengthen your Inner Wisdom's broadcasting station so that loving truth can be what you experience and tune in to first thing in the morning more often, keeping things like stress, anxiety, and dread out of your bedroom and head!

Superpower Tool: Love Mantras

Love Mantras are powerful statements that generate the vibration of love in your body and mind and transform the fearful Big Fat Lies of your Inner Mean Girl into the love and truth of your Inner Wisdom. Unlike affirmations—which work mostly on the mental plane and can feel like you are trying to convince yourself of something—Love Mantras work on a vibrational level to shift your inner feelings and emotions (inside your body, mind, and spirit) into a vibration of love. The word *mantra* means "a sacred message, charm, or counsel." Love Mantras are sacred messages that counsel you to listen to and feel love instead of fear. They are like self-love prayers.

You can use Love Mantras first thing in the morning, to jump-start your day with love. A Love Mantra a day keeps the Inner Mean Girl away! You can also pull out a Love Mantra whenever you feel an IMG flare-up, as a way to prevent a full-fledged Inner Mean Girl attack. Kind of like a mint that freshens your breath, a Love Mantra freshens your mind. When you feel the channel in your mind or body switching over to 88.9 FEAR, you can say or chant a Love Mantra to yourself and change the channel to 108.0 LOVE before your IMG gains enough power to launch a full-on attack.

> **A LOVE MANTRA A DAY KEEPS THE INNER MEAN GIRL AWAY!**

The most important thing about a Love Mantra is that it rings true for you; it touches your heart and soul, which means that each one needs to be personalized. So let's create a set of your own personal Love Mantras by looking back at the Big Fat Lies your Inner Mean Girl revealed to you during your investigative reporting in step three, starting on page 92.

If you didn't create your list of Big Fat Lies, do it now. And if you do have your Big Fat Lies playlist, great! Let's transform the hurtful lies into loving truths.

Just like the example here shows, taken from one of our Inner Mean Girl Reform School students, let's get the rants from your IMG's mouth and the loving truths from the Inner Wisdom's heart out where you can see them side by side.

INNER MEAN GIRL BIG FAT LIE	INNER WISDOM LOVING TRUTH
I THINK YOU'RE OLD AND UGLY.	I AM STRONG AND BEAUTIFUL, AND MY AGE IS IRRELEVANT.
NO ONE WILL EVER LOVE YOU BECAUSE YOU ARE TOO FAT.	THE PERFECT MATE LOVES ME EXACTLY AS I AM.
YOU ARE FALLING BEHIND, FAILING, AND YOU SHOULD JUST GIVE IT ALL UP NOW. IT'S NEVER GOING TO HAPPEN FOR YOU.	I AM EXACTLY WHERE I'M MEANT TO BE.
YOU ARE A LONER—IT'S NO WONDER NONE OF YOUR FRIENDS CONTACT YOU.	MY SOUL FAMILY IS COMING TO ME—IT JUST TAKES TIME.
YOU'LL NEVER BE A LEADER. OTHERS HAVE IT ALL TOGETHER.	I INSPIRE GREATNESS IN OTHERS JUST BY BEING ME.

Grab your journal and make a chart like you see above. On the left-hand side, list your top five Big Fat Lies. On the right-hand side, next to each of your Inner Mean Girl's Big Fat Lies, ask your Inner Wisdom what she knows to be true and add her loving truth next to the Big Fat Lie. Remember that loving truth doesn't mean sweetening things up and trying to pretend that something false is true. Loving truth is about motivating yourself through the power of self-compassion, acceptance, and empowerment. It may feel aspirational, but it won't feel fake. Tune in by closing your eyes, taking a deep breath, and allowing your Inner Wisdom to respond to each of these lies. Go one by one. Note that at first the words might not come out in their final mantra form, and that's okay—just write what your Inner Wisdom tells you. We will give you some tips on creating short but powerful mantras that ring true to your soul.

Once you have your Inner Wisdom loving truths where you can read them, turning them into Love Mantras is a snap. Get a fresh sheet of paper, grab markers and crayons in bright colors—your Inner Mean Girl tends to live in a black-and-white or gray world, but your Inner Wisdom lives in full-on Technicolor and knows that color opens your heart—and use these tips below to choose the most compelling words to create your powerful Love Mantras.

Love Mantra Tips

♥ **Love Mantras are in present, active tense.** "I am beautiful," not "I will be beautiful." You claim it as if it is so, because it is! You are simply catching up to your Inner Wisdom's truth.

♥ **Love Mantras work best in the positive tense, without *no* or *not*.** The brain doesn't register negatives,[1] so when you say something like "I will not beat myself up any longer," the brain hears, "I beat myself up longer." Ouch! What you want to say instead is, "I choose to be compassionate with myself no matter what."

♥ **Use just enough words and the right words for you so that the mantra packs power.** You want to be able to say the mantra easily, so that you can feel its powerful vibration and truth in your body and repeat it quickly when you need it. When mantras are too long or use complicated words, they lose power. Use simple but powerful words. For example:

> I am beautiful at any age.
> I am lovable just as I am.
> I'm always at the right place at the right time.
> I am already successful.

♥ **Collect evidence to reinforce your Love Mantras.** Your brain is always collecting evidence to support your beliefs and prove you're right, whether those beliefs are empowering or victimizing. This part of your brain is called the Reticular Activation System, a complex part of your brain that has many functions, but for our purposes you can use it to consciously gather proof that supports you to see how your Love Mantras are true. When your IMG tries to find evidence to the contrary, take control, and redirect your brain to find evidence of how beautiful, successful, and lovable you are! (More about your Reticular Activation System can be found in our Superpower Toolshed on page 252.)

TRANSFORMATION TALE: My Inner Wisdom's Crazy-Seeming Advice Saved My Life
by Lissa Rankin, MD, *New York Times* bestselling author of
Mind Over Medicine

Back in 2007, I was a miserable doctor, feeling trapped in a conventional medical job in a busy OB/GYN practice that required me to sell out my integrity, my health, my relationships, and my self-care in a variety of ways. I was taking seven medications for a handful of "chronic" health conditions my doctors insisted would need to be medicated for the rest of my life. I was already twice divorced, but I felt unhappy with my third husband because I had no time to spend with my newborn daughter and felt the burden of paying all our numerous bills. I was also buried in grief and anxiety: I'd lost my beloved father and my dog, and then my brother was hospitalized with liver failure—all within two weeks after I'd given birth by C-section during what I came to call my Perfect Storm. I was a hot mess with no clue what it meant to listen to the guidance of my Inner Wisdom.

But after being driven to my knees with signs from the Universe demonstrating to me that I was out of alignment with the Divine assignment of my life, I prayed for guidance. Just when I was feeling more trapped and despairing than I'd ever felt in my life, I heard a gentle whisper, a loving voice that appeared in the middle of a dark, sleepless night of the soul. It said, "Darling, they're about to break you. You have to quit your job."

I held my breath.

Then another voice—louder, vicious, biting—the one of my over-rational and over-responsible Head Tripper, Invincible Superwoman Inner Mean Girl, said, "What are you talking about? You can't do that! You have a newborn baby. Your husband doesn't have a job. You have a mortgage. Plus, you spent twelve years sacrificing everything so you could be a doctor. You'd be stupid and reckless if you left your job. How would you pay the bills? You'd wind up living under some freeway overpass. And what would everybody think? They'd put you in an institution. Doctors don't just quit their jobs, especially when they have medical school debt and grown-up responsibilities. Don't be silly. You have a great job. You have a terrific husband. You live in a gorgeous house. You should just suck it up and be grateful for what you have. Now stop your belly-aching and go back to sleep."

But the loving truth of my Inner Wisdom was insistent. "You don't have to do it now, sweetheart. But the time is coming for you to quit your job, so get ready. And don't worry. It all will be okay, and you will not be alone."

But how could I quit my job? My husband wasn't working, and I still had medical school debt to pay off. I'd have to sell my house. My husband surely would divorce me. And how could I possibly afford the $120,000 malpractice tail I'd have to pay for the privilege of quitting my job? We'd have to move someplace cheaper. Quitting my job would require a total life overhaul. It was too much to even consider.

My Inner Wisdom continued with her sage guidance. "You don't have to do anything yet. Just make peace with the truth."

So that's what I did. Making peace with the truth was the first step and the hardest part. It was so much easier to just pretend I was stumbling around in the darkness because there was not enough light. But once the truth was illuminated, I couldn't unsee what my Inner Wisdom had spotlighted.

I went back to sleep that night, and a year and a half later I finally mustered up the moxie to leave my clinical practice as a doctor. I embarked upon a wild, precious, magical journey I never could have dreamed possible. The only way I have survived the trials and triumphs of that journey is by steadfastly following the guidance of my Inner Wisdom, even when I didn't like what I heard.

Back then I didn't know I could trust the little voice I heard inside, which I later learned was my Inner Wisdom, which I lovingly call my Inner Pilot Light. I thought it was the voice of my inner crazy person. I now know it's not. So let me reassure you, just in case you lack faith. We have access to this inner guide. If you hear that quiet voice within you, listen up—because that's your soul speaking. And it always speaks truth you can trust.

Superpower Challenge: Take Control of Your Body's Broadcasting Station

Are you ready for a superpower challenge that's going to up-level your self-awareness, make you acutely aware of how your body feels and what emotions arise throughout the day, all day, every day, and thereby empower you to get to your Inner Wisdom's loving truth no matter what? Great! Remember how we told you that your body is your barometer for discerning who is in charge? Well, the other part that you need to know in order to put this to use in your daily life is that you actually have to *pause* and get present in order to check the barometer and change the channel in your mind and body.

So instead of pushing through, stuffing down, or sloughing off your feelings, when you feel something out of sorts or start feeling stress, anxiety, controlling, or anything that resembles the vibrations in fear, we are challenging you to stop and trace the feeling back. We want you to get comfortable hitting the internal pause button that will allow you to access your Inner Wisdom's truth.

This practice is going to pay off big time! Instead of being a victim to the feeling of anxiety or judgment or crazy talk running through your mind, you will become aware that your Inner Mean Girl is giving you a tainted view of the situation. You'll see that she has been triggered, and you will feel empowered to choose whether you let her flare up and go into a full-fledged IMG attack or you take action to change the channel and find your loving truth. Your mission is to practice taking control of your internal broadcasting station by committing to and taking the three actions as outlined in the next few pages for the next seven days. It's one thing to read about this, another to act. But you are ready, and your Inner Wisdom is waiting— and really, you can do anything for one week. Here's how:

STEP 4

1: Start your day attuned to Love.

Start your day with your Love Mantras, and you will find it easier to return to the loving truth of your Inner Wisdom throughout the day. Here are two different ideas for starting your morning with your Love Mantras:

Self-Love Soak: Do Before You Get Out of Bed.

When you first awake, open your eyes to register you are waking and then close your eyes. Wrap your arms around yourself as if you are giving yourself a hug. Repeat the words of your Love Mantras over and over again, saying them like you would say them to someone you love, until you can feel the vibration of love come into your body. Almost like you are wrapping yourself in a blanket of love. At first you may feel nothing. This is common. Sometimes it can take time to get past the protection layers of your Inner Mean Girl to feel the vibration of the mantra reach your heart. But eventually everyone does break through. Remember, self-love sometimes requires crazy, daring acts, so tell your IMG and her skepticism to take a hike and just try it. You would welcome loving words from another person, so welcome them from yourself—it's all the same thing. Consider writing the Love Mantras down on a piece of paper and putting them next to your bed so you can easily remember them. Trust in the process, and keep going until you have the breakthrough of actually feeling love from yourself.

Self-Love Chant: Do Before You Leave the House.

Just like you play a song you love to fill you with joy, play your mantras in the morning. Set a timer for three minutes, take a few breaths, put your hand on your heart, and chant your Love Mantras. Be serious, be silly, be lyrical, whatever you need to do to feel the vibe of love in your body, your broadcasting tower. Again, this might feel uncomfortable, but way less unpleasant than any Inner Mean Girl attack. You can even record the Love Mantras onto your phone and play them back. Plus no one is looking; lighten up, have some fun, and change your vibe!

2: Be more aware of who is broadcasting throughout the day.

Use your body barometer to become more aware of the difference between your Inner Wisdom's broadcasts and your Inner Mean Girl's broadcasts. When you start to feel any of the vibes of 88.9 FEAR, literally stop and ask yourself, "Who is in control of my *mind* right now? Who is in control of my *body* right now? Who is running my *emotions* and *feelings*?" Remember to pay attention to your emotions and your body: they hold the key to knowing who is at the control station. As you learn to tell the difference between these two forces, remember you can reference the physical and emotional vibe chart on page 128. Then use your superpower tools to change the channel.

3: Practice turning down the volume on your Inner Mean Girl and turning up the volume on your Inner Wisdom in the moment.

When you find yourself in the midst of an Inner Mean Girl attack or you can sense a flare-up, use the Wake-Up Call Three Step process on page 130 to get reconnected to the truth and guidance of your Inner Wisdom or use one of your Love Mantras. Use either tool until you feel your vibration shift from fear to loving truth. If you are having an impossible time accessing your Inner Wisdom, first try one of the IMG Deactivators (listed on pages 81–83 or in the Superpower Toolshed in the back of the book).

By using these three actions *each* day, you will gain mastery in key skills in reforming your Inner Mean Girl. You'll be better able to tell the difference between your Inner Mean Girl and Inner Wisdom, you'll be better able to deal with any Inner Mean Girl attacks, and you'll be more able to live a life led by your Inner Wisdom.

Now that we've helped you see the difference between these two forces in an even deeper way, it's time to dive into creating the best relationship of your life—the one with yourself and your divine Inner Wisdom.

STEP 5

MAKE YOUR INNER WISDOM YOUR MOST TRUSTED ALLY

There is no question that following your Inner Wisdom's guidance over your Inner Mean Girl's is the way to go. However, following through on what your Inner Wisdom directs you to do, or truly believing what she tells you, can be difficult. Sure, when it comes to the simple and low-risk things in life—like choosing a new route to take to work or deciding what to eat—you might be willing to follow a hunch.

But when the bigger things in life show up, moments when you stretch yourself or face decisions that feel risky or uncertain or when your Inner Wisdom opposes conventional wisdom or what seems rational, you may find it challenging to completely trust her guidance—and yourself. When the guidance is to defy what you have been trained to believe or what seems normal among your friends and family, this truthful source can soon be doubted and diminished, which is when your Inner Mean Girl moves in for the attack, making you feel doubtful, uncertain, confused, and overwhelmed. The result: you sabotage yourself or you get stuck in the negative-thinking loop and can't find your way out.

An Inner Wisdom–led life is one in which you invite your Inner Wisdom to be your most trusted ally, in all parts of your life— where you both *listen to* and *act* according to her sage guidance, no matter what.

We've found that most women trust their intuitions and Inner Wisdoms in some parts of their lives but not all. You can likely recall instances when you trusted and acted on your inner guidance and reaped the rewards and also when you ignored it completely and suffered some consequences. And now, we want to challenge you to invite your Inner Wisdom to be your go-to girl in *all* parts of your life—relationships, money, health, career, business, home, spirituality, creative expression—every single place you make choices for yourself and the things and people you love. And to do so, you've got to invite your Inner Wisdom into your life to take a bigger role, and you need to deepen your trust in her guidance.

Why Is Your Inner Wisdom's Guidance So Hard to Follow Sometimes?

You were born trusting yourself, programmed with neural pathways that supported you to follow the internal guidance system we call your Inner Wisdom. So, what happened? Where did this trust go? Well, there are a few big reasons you may have learned to doubt or question your own inner knowing—the very thing you were given to keep you safe and on the right path.

First, sometimes what your intuition guides you to do requires you to take a leap of faith, which can feel scary. And you know what happens when fear gets triggered: your Inner Mean Girl moves into action, trying to keep you safe, loved, and feeling like you belong. Second, we live in a time and culture that value rational thinking and practicality over intuition. Most likely, the systems you've been indoctrinated in through your schooling, your career, even your medical care, taught you to believe that if you can't see it or prove it, it's not real. And since you can't see your Inner Wisdom or prove your intuition, how can you trust it's real? And if you can't trust it's real, how can you follow its guidance?

MAKE YOUR INNER WISDOM YOUR MOST TRUSTED ALLY

You see, even though you were born with a deep sense of self-trust, you still need guidance and training on how to keep that trust alive in a world that is so full of fear and inside of a culture that discounts and dismisses intuition. Unless you have sought out training, you simply did not receive what you need to wield your intuitive superpowers on this planet. Think about it: While you learned arithmetic and biology in school, did you get a class in how to receive guidance from your Inner Wisdom? Were you taught the different ways to tune in to your intuition?

The bottom line is that a woman's intuition isn't honored, celebrated, or valued in our mainstream culture as the powerful force it is. A woman's intuition is either masked with more masculine words like *gut feeling* or is totally discounted as "woo-woo," "touchy-feely," or "being overly sensitive." So of course it can feel very unsafe to share your intuition or follow your Inner Wisdom's guidance. You may even feel ashamed of this part of you, or like you have to keep it under wraps, or only share it with certain people. But if you keep hiding, being ashamed of, or discounting this powerful, brilliant, intuitive part of you, your Inner Mean Girl will always win.

Now, we aren't suggesting you start running up to everyone you know, sharing everything your Inner Wisdom tells you. We also are not saying that the rational is always bad and intuition always good—the dominance of either does not serve the individual or the collective. The most powerful place to live from is the integration of both your intuition and your rational thought. And that requires some training in and reclaiming of your intuitive powers.

What we are inviting you to consider is taking a stand to never again discount your Inner Wisdom for any reason. We invite you to be the wise woman you are, choosing to lead a life where your intuition is your most trusted ally, where you trust what you see, know, and feel—and that you do so without apology, reclaiming the power of a woman's intuition for yourself and every girl and woman you love.

Inner Wisdom Reflection: Why Trust Your Inner Wisdom?

One thing we know about making the shift to living a life led by Inner Wisdom is that it takes dedication and commitment. Just like in any relationship, to make it through the rough and risky spots, you have to be connected to a big *why*—as in, *why* does this matter to you? Why are you willing to go against the grain, face your fear, step into the unknown, and follow that inner feeling inside of you, no matter what? Take a moment now and look at the places in your life where you already trust your Inner Wisdom. These are places where you've taken risks or gone against the grain of conventional wisdom or other people's opinions to follow the guidance of your Inner Wisdom, and it's worked out. Think of at least one or two situations.

♥ What action did your Inner Wisdom guide you to take?
♥ What was the benefit of trusting your Inner Wisdom? What rewards did you reap?

Now, remember a situation in your life when you didn't trust your Inner Wisdom, when you had a feeling, a knowing, a sense, maybe even a direct internal order, and you didn't follow your inner guidance. (If none come to mind, look at your Inner Mean Girl hot spots or trigger areas—you'll find one there for sure.) Thinking of this situation:

♥ What action did your Inner Wisdom guide you to take? What did you do instead?
♥ What was the consequence?
♥ What is the truth about why you didn't listen? What was the underlying fear?

Don't be hard on yourself for the ways in which you haven't listened in the past. You were doing the best you could at the time with the information, skill, and trust levels you had. And now you are getting more knowledge and mastery. Wherever you are in your relationship with your Inner Wisdom, whether you are estranged and making reintroductions or you have been best friends for a while, deepening your trust in your Inner Wisdom is both a daily practice and a lifelong process. There are always deeper levels of trust to experience with your Inner Wisdom; you are never done strengthening that bond. As you grow and stretch, as you face new challenges and situations, the stakes get bigger; your happiness, success, and inner peace depend on the strength and depth of the connection to this source of inner truth.

Which is why it is essential that you strengthen your ability to both *listen to* and *act on* your Inner Wisdom's guidance *every day* as a conscious daily practice, not as an afterthought or only during the times in which you struggle. The time to strengthen your trust in your Inner Wisdom isn't during the highest-stress times. You've got to be consistently connecting with your Inner Wisdom daily, through what we like to refer to as sacred dates—time dedicated to you tuning in to yourself and your access to divine wisdom. These sacred dates, when kept over time, not only set you up to move through your day-to-day with grace, they ensure that when challenging choices or situations arise, you have the power to cut through stress and fear to gain access to your deeper wisdom. Maintaining this daily practice is the single most important thing you can do to

> IT IS ESSENTIAL THAT YOU STRENGTHEN YOUR ABILITY TO BOTH *LISTEN TO* AND *ACT ON* YOUR INNER WISDOM'S GUIDANCE *EVERY DAY* AS A CONSCIOUS DAILY PRACTICE.

create a nurturing relationship with your Inner Wisdom, which is there to guide you to your happiest, most successful, healthiest life. Later in this chapter, we will show you how to integrate these sacred dates into your life, no matter how busy you are. But first, we need to check in to see how your particular Inner Wisdom likes to operate and communicate.

How Does Your Inner Wisdom Prefer to Communicate with You?

Just like people communicate differently, so do Inner Wisdoms. And the more you understand how your Inner Wisdom prefers to communicate, the more successful your interactions will be. One of the biggest hurdles we see women have in their efforts to connect with their Inner Wisdoms is they don't know how their intuitions come through. So either they can't quite tune in to their Inner Wisdom channels or the reception is just too fuzzy to get the message.

The good news is that, for the most part, your Inner Wisdom broadcasts on only four channels. While we all have access to each of these four channels of intuition, one or two of the channels will be naturally stronger for you than the others. Your first mission is to find which channel holds the strongest frequency and strengthen that first, and then as your relationship continues, strengthen the others. Over time, we have found that even in the areas we are strongest, there is always a deeper level of mastery to be obtained in listening to and trusting the guidance on each channel.

As you read about each channel, think about current or past situations in your life to see if this may be a strong channel for you.

1. **The Sound Channel.** This frequency is auditory. You hear things. Nope, you're not crazy, but you will hear what can seem like voices and words in your head, as if someone is talking to you or in some

cases even shouting at you. If your Inner Wisdom uses this channel, you will hear words or you will find it natural to have conversations or journal with this inner force. Part of mastering this channel is increasing your capacity to dialogue with this wise voice to receive guidance and to listen to what you receive with discernment but without doubt.

IT'S AMY HERE, and I will never forget the day my Inner Wisdom literally spoke to me, like she was right there sitting on my shoulder while I was on my second date with my now husband. Her message came through loud and clear in the words, "Here he is." I remember telling my dear friend the next night, "I know it sounds crazy, but I think I'm going to marry Rob." And I did. It was one of the best choices of my life, and my Inner Wisdom knew all along. Thankfully, I listened.

2. **The Seeing Channel.** This frequency is visual. You may see pictures or movies play in your head, or images or symbols may pop up in your field of vision. Metaphors that paint vivid pictures may sprout up easily for you. You may tend to daydream and/or have vivid night dreams, or when you meditate or slow down, you receive images or stories that seem like a movie screen playing in your mind. When this channel is strong, the information and guidance is something you see with your eyes or with what's called your third eye, which sees the inner and spiritual world.

For example, maybe you're standing on a street corner, and you look up and see a billboard that speaks to you and answers a question you've been having. Or as you drive to work, you have an image flash through your mind to take a different route than usual, and you find out later there was a major traffic jam on your typical route. Part of mastering the seeing channel is increasing your ability to visualize, see the patterns and symbols in things, and use pictures, images, symbols, and metaphors to tap into your intuition.

We remember a friend who had a dream the night after she began dating a new man. In the dream she had visions of him being cruel and unkind in bizarre ways. She awoke feeling shaken up by the images, but laughed it off as "just a silly dream." Unfortunately, she did not heed the warning that her Inner Wisdom was trying to communicate to her and use these signs to stop and tune in to what was really going on in this relationship. Instead, she married this man, had two children with him, and ended up filing for divorce before the kids got out of diapers, faced with the reality of being a single mom. A decade later, her life has been plagued with having to coparent with a man who is in complete opposition to what she values. He is an incredible source of stress for her and her children. The message broadcasting on the station was clear, but she couldn't trust it nor slow down long enough to listen to what it was trying to say. The conventional wisdom that said, "He's a smart guy. Look, he's an investment banker, went to good schools, and isn't it time you got married anyway?" won out. It's amazing how our Inner Wisdom can communicate warning flags to us to try to set us on the right path. Now, if we would just listen!

3. **The Feeling Channel.** This frequency is sensation and emotion, and it most often uses your body to communicate with you—your stomach tingles, hands get hot, throat gets tight. Some people get what is called "truth chills," which means that when they hear someone speak truth, they feel shivers or tingles run through their body. You may relate to yourself as a kinesthetic or empathic person who, when you describe intuitive hits you receive, references how your body feels or how you feel inside.

   We have a client who told us that the day she interviewed for a new job, her stomach hurt really bad; it was in knots. Not the kind of nervous butterflies that most of us get when going on a job interview, but the kind of stomachache where your Inner Wisdom is begging for you to listen. The job ended up not working out in a big way, but she didn't know it was her Inner Wisdom trying to get through, so she didn't know to stop and say, "Oh, that's my body talking to me. What am I feeling? Let me stop and check in with my Inner Wisdom and get what's going on here." Feelings in your body—especially when they are uncomfortable—are a huge red flag from your Inner Wisdom to stop and feel.

We find that women who are especially empathic and sensitive to other people's feelings to the point where they can often feel what someone else is feeling have this as one of their main channels. While having empathy is healthy, helpful, and a beautiful thing, over-empathizing to the point where you feel other people's pain or feelings is not. In fact, plugging into other people's feelings messes up your own Inner Wisdom frequency. Part of mastering this channel is learning how to use your empathic powers to tap in to the bigger field of information or in to what another person may be experiencing but not plugging so deeply in that you lose your sense of self and center.

4. **The Knowing Channel.** This frequency is a deep inner sense of knowing. You just know because you know, period. You have no proof; you don't know why you know this, but you know the truth. No words come, no pictures, and no sensation in your body. The truth is just there, like turning on a light switch, or having a divine *kerplunk* inside you. You just know that your Inner Wisdom said so, and you can't explain it, and frankly, when you trust this channel, you don't have to. Mastering the knowing channel in some ways can be the most challenging because there isn't a feeling, image, story, or statement that gives you something you can call proof to yourself or others. You have to be able to stand in your own conviction to say, "I just know," and believe it.

IT'S CHRISTINE HERE, and I can remember facing a pretty big career choice in my late twenties. I had been accepted into graduate school, and I wanted a job that would support me through that process. It was clear that my current job wasn't it, so I put my feelers out there and was offered two very different positions. One with a startup dot-com promising me all kinds of stock options and opportunity for growth—it was sexy, alluring, and exciting. The other offer was at a health insurance company—lower salary, no options, but they would pay for part of my school. Now, you should know that this was during the big dot-com boom, when everyone was taking jobs that had anything to do with options and the internet. Except me. I knew that the less sexy, less potentially lucrative job was the one I was to take. It made no sense in my mind, and my friends thought I was crazy, but in the end, when the dot-com boom busted, I had a stable job that paid 80 percent of my tuition, and it turned out to be a very low-stress job. I was able to do the job quite easily, which gave me more time for my studies and gave me the space to go through a stressful life-altering experience—the ending of my engagement and fifteen-year relationship and the biggest spiritual wake-up call of my life—which when I took the job, I had no idea was going to occur. Trusting my inner knowing set me up to have the financial and emotional support and the mental space I needed to do my spiritual work and reconstruct my entire life. Now that is my Inner Wisdom having my back!

Inner Wisdom Reflection: Rank Your Inner Wisdom's Preferred Channels

Take a moment to rank the order in which you think your Inner Wisdom likes to communicate with you. Rank these in order from most used to least developed, with 1 being your number one connection point and 4 being the least developed and used channel. If you don't know exactly, that's okay. Just go with your intuition!

Sound Channel
Seeing Channel
Feeling Channel
Knowing Channel

Your top two are the channels you want to direct energy toward, heighten your awareness of, and strengthen your mastery in. Regarding the two that are least used, if you are already very strong in your top two, pay attention to these other channels more so you can increase your mastery of all channels. If your top two channels are weak or new to you, just focus on those two channels.

How Do I Strengthen My Ability to Trust my Intuition?

Now that you're welcoming your Inner Wisdom into your life even more and you know how she likes to communicate with you, it's all about building your trust muscles. Just like when you go to the gym to build biceps, your trust in your intuition grows the more you work your emotional and spiritual muscles.

We've included three Inner Wisdom Strengtheners to use in your day-to-day life to build up your trust in this wise, although sometimes seemingly wacky, ally. Just like you did with the IMG Deactivators, we want you to experiment with these in your daily life and consciously observe what occurs. Choose one that really inspires you or try out all three, whatever you choose—just practice them so we can find what works for your Inner Wisdom!

Inner Wisdom Strengthener 1: Acknowledge Serendipities— Avoid Skepticism

Notice the signs and coincidences that show up in your life, and instead of pushing them away or disregarding them as just luck, receive them as the magic they are, and say, "Yes, I see you. Thank you, Universe!" Skepticism kills intuition. Of course, there is a difference between being discerning and being skeptical. Yes, be discerning in your decisions— we aren't suggesting you become gullible or make decisions based on wishful thinking. But definitely drop the skepticism; it's a buzzkill and an Inner Wisdom stopper. Your Inner Wisdom loves when you acknowledge and celebrate things without rational explanation but that ring true in your intuitive power center. Stop sloughing off signs and saying things like "That is just crazy" when something magical appears. Instead say, "Wow, that was magical!"

Inner Wisdom Strengthener 2: Share Your Inner Wisdom Publicly

Come out of the closet as the highly intuitive woman you are. Stop masking your intuitive hits with rational reasoning. And definitely stop holding back from sharing your intuitions because you are afraid of what someone will say. Here are a few tips to experiment with: when sharing your Inner Wisdom with others, preface your remarks using intuition preambles. These are sentence starters that call intuition forth and make it easier for you to speak your inner knowings, without self-judgment, and are often better received by the person you share with (people love receiving intuitive hits way more than being given advice). For example:

"My intuition [or my Inner Wisdom] is telling me . . ."
"I am not sure where this is coming from, but my intuition is
   saying . . ."
"This is totally a feeling, and . . ."

To keep your Inner Mean Girl from flaring up in the event someone cannot receive your beautiful intuitive gift (which may happen and
should not be taken personally), always speak your intuition without
attachment. Sharing your intuition should never be about being right,
having the other person validate your thoughts, or matching up your
intuition's messages to some preconceived vision in your mind. Intuition
must be given freely.

Inner Wisdom Strengthener 3: Tune in to Other People's Inner Wisdom, Wisely

Sometimes, it's really hard to trust your Inner Wisdom, especially when
she's encouraging you to take a risk. This is when you need to reach out
for an Inner Wisdom Love-Line and ask a trusted friend to help you
cut through the fear your Inner Mean Girl is causing and get to the
loving truth. Now this is where it gets tricky and where most women
screw themselves up. In these sensitive situations, where you are having
difficulty trusting, your IMG is going to try and get you to reach out
to someone who will back up her story. She will have you calling your
mother, sister, friend, whoever will reflect back to you the fear she wants
you to feel. Don't do this!

Remember: in times of high stress or uncertainty, only reach out to
people who can listen without their own stuff getting riled up—people
who can hold space, be calm, and reflect back to you the truth of what
your Inner Wisdom is saying. If you have these kinds of people in your

life, the ones who will not let their IMGs rile up your IMG but instead call your Inner Wisdom forth, you already know who they are. Put those people on your speed dial. If you don't have these people in your life, find some pronto—whether they are new friends, current friends, or family who could be truly supportive or professionals—like coaches, therapists, spiritual guides, astrologists, or one of our favorites, EFT practioners. (EFT stands for Emotional Freedom Technique and is also known as tapping. We have been using it for years ourselves and in our workshops and programs as a way to calm down Inner Mean Girl fear and get connected to Inner Wisdom.) Visit **innerwisdomkit.com** for a free interview with EFT master, Kate Winch.

TRANSFORMATION TALE: The Silence that Healed My Inner Mean Girl

by Marci Shimoff, *New York Times* bestselling author of
Happy forNo Reason and *Chicken Soup for the Woman's Soul*

I was a wreck. For the first forty years of my life, I had been driven by my Inner Mean Girl terrible trio—the Achievement Junkie, the Doing Addict, and the Comparison Queen. The combination of these three meanies had sucked the joy out of my life and run me into the ground.

Sure, they had accomplished a lot in the process of trying to keep me feeling safe. They had pushed me until I'd achieved a great amount of outward success. I was a well-paid, top-rated trainer for Fortune 500 companies. I considered myself a road warrior—starting every morning at 5:30 AM, speaking in three-inch heels for nine hours a day, and living on planes and out of suitcases.

While it sounds flashy, I felt empty, unhappy, and fried. No amount of recognition, achievement, or success filled the inner void I was experiencing.

Then one day, my dear friend Janet came to me and said, "Marci, you're burned out. You need a break. Why don't you come with me on a seven-day silent meditation retreat?" I looked at her in disbelief and said, "Are you crazy? I'm a speaker. I haven't been silent for more than two hours in my life. I couldn't possibly stay silent for seven days!" But Janet was persuasive, and she was clear that it was time for me to give my Achievement Junkie, Doing Addict, and Comparison Queen a time-out. Deep inside, I knew she was right.

So off I went. The first three days of silence were hell. My Inner Mean Girl wouldn't let me settle down. She kept reminding me that I was wasting my time and being indulgent.

But on the fourth day of silence, something huge shifted. In the middle of a meditation, a lightbulb flashed on in my head. I saw the words *Chicken Soup for the Woman's Soul*, and I knew it was a book I was supposed to write. Jack Canfield, the originator of *Chicken Soup for the Soul*, was my mentor, and I knew that he hadn't thought of creating a series or doing any specialty Chicken Soup books. This inspiration would not only be my ticket out of the road warrior life but it could also touch many people's lives.

My Inner Wisdom had taken over.

There was only one problem with this scene—I still had three more days of silence. I'd just had the great epiphany of my career, and I couldn't tell anyone. But as soon as the silence was over, I ran to the closest pay phone (yes, in those ancient days) and called Jack. He loved the idea and within a month I was working on the book. A year and a half later, it was published and instantly became a number one *New York Times* bestseller. The entire process was filled with meaning and joy, and I went on to write six more *Chicken Soup for the Soul* books that have sold more than fifteen million copies in thirty-three languages.

That silent retreat—when I gave my Inner Mean Girl a vacation—was the turning point for me to live a life that's now guided by my Inner Wisdom.

Eight years later, while on another silent retreat, that lightbulb flashed on in my head once again, and I saw the title *Happy for No Reason*, which also went on to become a *New York Times* bestseller.

I'm certain I wouldn't have the success *and* happiness that I now enjoy if I hadn't given my Inner Mean Girl a vacation. These days, I know that regular silence—not just on a long retreat but every day—is the key to me accessing my Inner Wisdom.

While the terrible trio still show up sometimes and offer their two cents, I know how to turn to the silence that leads me to my Inner Wisdom. And when my Inner Wisdom takes over, my Inner Mean Girl doesn't have a chance.

Why We Resist a Daily Practice

Just like a friend and trusted ally, the more quality time you spend with your Inner Wisdom, the more she will communicate and give you good counsel. You know this intuitively. You want to slow down, rest, replenish, unplug from the daily grind, tap in to your Inner Wisdom daily, but it's sooooo darn hard to stay committed and consistent. It's not that you want to start your day by checking your phone before you pee (yes, we know). You don't want to run out of the house downing a coffee as your prescription for a morning jump start. You don't wish to go to sleep thinking, "Oh I can't wait to wake up tomorrow and start my day in a frenzy, to tackle my to-do list, to have stress and anxiety greet me before my feet even hit the floor." The idea of meditating, taking long walks, journaling, having space to be with yourself before starting your day attending to everyone and everything on your plate sounds good, but in reality it's hard to pull off consistently.

But here's the thing: the only person who you will be with until your last breath is you. Treat yourself with compassion and respect by making sacred dates so you can get back in touch with all that you truly care about and love. It's a practice that strengthens your connection to this inner wise voice, and from our experience with students and women from all over the world, sacred dates are one of your most powerful superpower tools for disempowering your Inner Mean Girl. Which of course is why your IMG loves to tell you that it's impossible for you to commit to or do your daily practice or why deepening your existing one isn't essential. These are all Big Fat Lies to keep your Inner Wisdom from gaining the upper hand. But your Inner Wisdom also has something to say about all this too.

> **The reason you fail to create space for yourself consistently is not because of anything out there—the kids, a job, a partner, your physical surroundings, traveling; the resistance is all inside of you.**

Here are just a few underlying reasons why many women, and perhaps you, keep sabotaging themselves out of the space needed every day to connect to Inner Wisdom:

♥ **You don't value *being* as much as you value *doing*.** You don't really believe deep down that being still and tuning in to your Inner Wisdom is as productive and worthwhile as giving to others, accomplishing a goal, or checking off something from your to-do list. You may think you do, but take a careful look at how you spend your time and the choices you make; internally there may still be parts of you that don't totally trust that being still and tuning inward before you move into action will pay off more than just constantly being in motion in a futile attempt to get everything done.

♥ **You fear slowing down.** If your mind, body, and life were not so busy, if taking a pause was a part of your daily life, you'd be forced to acknowledge your feelings and face the truth of your life, which would require making choices and changes you'd perhaps rather not deal with. Nobel Prize–winning author Alice Walker, in her book *We Are the Ones We've Been Waiting For*, says it all:

> Wisdom requests a pause. If we cannot give ourselves such a pause, the Universe will likely give it to us. In the form of illness, in the form of a massive Mercury in retrograde, in the form of our car breaking down, our roof starting to leak, our garden starting to dry up. Our government collapsing. And we find ourselves required to stop, to sit down, to reflect . . . I am here today to encourage you not to fear it . . . Some of the most courageous people on earth are scared of it, as I have been myself. . . . It is the pause that gives us clarity . . . It is our time of gathering the vision together, of reminding ourselves of what we want for ourselves…The pause, so brief—if only in retrospect— gives us a wonderful intuitive knowing. . . .[1]

♥ **You think you need to find "time" for yourself, but time can't be found or made.** We always crack up when women tell us, "Oh yes, I need to make time to do my daily practice," as if they are going to go into the kitchen and whip up some time. You cannot make time; time is finite. There are only twenty-four hours in a day, seven days in a week. But we do have a secret for you: while you can't make more time, you can create more space.

THE MOST IMPORTANT RELATIONSHIP YOU HAVE IN YOUR LIFE IS THE ONE WITH YOURSELF; CHERISH IT AND HONOR IT WITH ALL OF YOUR HEART—MAKE IT SACRED.

If you approach connecting to your Inner Wisdom as something to do only when you have the time, you will lose every time. You don't need time. You just need the commitment to create space, which can only come if you make your relationship with yourself and your Inner Wisdom sacred. The most important relationship you have in your life is the one with yourself; cherish it and honor it with all of your heart—make it sacred. When you make something sacred, you don't abuse it, forget about it, or prioritize other things over it—you stay true to it no matter what. You make sure that there is space in your life even during the busyness, because it's that important to you, and you value it so deeply.

Commit to Your Inner Wisdom Sacred Dates

Consider this a wake-up call to treat your connection with your Inner Wisdom as sacred as you would a beloved, every day for the rest of your life. To value the pauses your Inner Wisdom requires is one of the most sacred acts you can take for yourself. Try saying these words out loud (don't be shy or too cool for school—just experiment here with us for a moment):

> "My relationship with my Inner Wisdom is sacred."
> "The space I create for myself and my Inner Wisdom is sacred."

There is something really powerful about saying the word *sacred* out loud and applying it to yourself. It's like it conjures up some innate self-love mojo within you. When something becomes sacred to you, you guard it, protect it, and stand up for it without apology and with the same fierceness as a mother protecting her cubs. And isn't it time for you to protect the space you need for yourself and your Inner Wisdom, every day? We think so, because woman to woman, here's the truth: creating and taking space for yourself is not selfish; it's smart.

We invite you to join us in a revolution of feminine power to take charge of how we are valued as women, how we value ourselves and our time and energy, including making sure we get what we need and not just give everything away—even if what we are giving to is good. We challenge you, dare you, to take a stand with us to proclaim that being, listening, connecting with your Inner Wisdom and moving with the harmony of the natural world are as valuable, if not more so, than the doing. Being more and doing less gets more of the valuable and important stuff taken care of instead of wasting your energy trying to do everything or getting distracted by what matters least. It is the sacred space and the inner stillness that give you access to greater peace, clarity, and wisdom, so you can make choices for yourself and those you love with more grace and ease, and ultimately create the life you really want.

IT'S CHRISTINE HERE. I have been keeping sacred dates daily for well over a decade. I don't leave the house without connecting with my Inner Wisdom because I learned the hard way that my life goes better when I connect in the morning and worse when I don't. I can remember the day I made the choice to never again leave my house without tuning in to my Inner Wisdom. I was living in San Francisco and working at The Gap corporate headquarters, a dream job for me at the time, except on this particular day. In the span of four hours, my Inner Wisdom channel on mute, I received a speeding ticket, got into a huge fight with my guy, and turned a vice president's face bright red in a meeting. Needless to say, the choice to miss my Inner Wisdom date cost me money, stress in my relationship, and a good talking to by my boss the next day. Oy vey! Never again. I've kept my promise to connect into my Inner Wisdom before starting my day every day since then. Just like those commercials say, "Never leave home without it!"

> **CREATING AND TAKING SPACE FOR YOURSELF IS NOT SELFISH; IT'S SMART.**

The Golden Rules for Creating Your Inner Wisdom Sacred Date

It is essential that you create a sacred daily practice and daily date with your Inner Wisdom. We have very few rules at Inner Mean Girl Reform School, but this is one of them. There are two golden rules your Inner Wisdom requires from your sacred dates:

1. **Intention of Connection.** Sacred dates must have the intention of a deeper emotional, spiritual, and physical connection with yourself and your divine wisdom. The goal cannot be to work out, burn calories, or lose weight, although they may be added side benefits. Exercise done just for physical sake, while healthy and awesome, does not count as sacred dates with your Inner Wisdom.

2. **Daily Dates Occur in the Morning.** While you may have more than one time of day you commune, the base commitment level starts with a daily morning practice, which you can build on. Even if it's three minutes a morning with a longer date in the evening, you either begin your day with your Inner Wisdom or you don't. Having a daily morning practice creates sacred space with your Inner Wisdom and is not optional if you want to live an Inner Wisdom–led life in which you are making choices in alignment with your heart and soul. If you don't choose to start your day with your Inner Wisdom, your Inner Mean Girl will make the choice for you. How's that for motivation?

IT'S AMY HERE, and I've got to out myself. For years I resisted having a daily morning practice. I always felt that it was a good idea—I even coached my clients to do it—but I never really committed to it. I was the type of woman who let herself believe I just didn't have the time—new business owner, new mom, not a morning person; there was always something my Inner Mean Girl told me to make it seem *hard*. And I just wasn't sure it would really make a big difference. I convinced myself that my runs and hikes, which were mostly about exercise at the time, were enough. And for a while, being a woman who has the innate skill to multitask, I managed. I handled the business, I handled my relationships, and I was relatively happy, but I realized soon after my first child was born that I could not handle it all. I couldn't be the mom and wife I wanted to be and have the transformational impact I wanted to have in the world without being crabby, feeling worry and anxiety, and generally feeling the pressure of the world on my shoulders.

Honestly, I came to my morning practice out of sheer breakdown and exasperation. I was desperate. And like many of the things we surrender to when at our wits' end, the breakdown became one of my biggest breakthroughs, and I've never looked back. It was the day I made the choice and absolute commitment to live an Inner Wisdom–led life. I still do my runs and hikes, which my Inner Wisdom always joins me for, but I never start a day without tuning in to my Inner Wisdom: some days twenty minutes listening to a meditation track and some days with just three minutes of breathing while hearing my baby coo in the background. As a mom and wife, keeping this commitment consistently has meant educating my family and setting boundaries, but guess what? As I've treated my Inner Wisdom time as sacred, so have they. And I've even caught my oldest daughter learning by example and imitating me, asking to listen to a meditation when she wants to calm down.

There are many kinds of sacred dates. Meditation is just one kind of sacred date, and there are many types of meditation, from sitting in complete stillness to taking a guided visualization to listening to sound meditations created to shift your brain waves. If meditation isn't your thing or if you want to shake things up, you can experiment by writing to your Inner Wisdom, presenting questions to her and receiving answers, like your own personal download from the Divine. Cool, huh? And if you want to shake it up even more, you can make your sacred date one of dance, yoga, or tai chi.

If you are already keeping your daily morning sacred dates (again, kudos—this is such a gift of self-love, and so smart!), and you're ready to go deeper and reap even more benefit, you can begin creating space for weekly dates, monthly dates that correlate with the moon cycles, even sacred retreats throughout the year that span a full day or more. There are so many kinds of sacred dates, in fact, that we created an Inner Wisdom sacred date guide for you on page 255, so that you can get new ideas for how to strengthen your connection and commitment to your Inner Wisdom.

We invite you to up-level your connection with your Inner Wisdom, to up-level the consistency and depth of your daily practice and the ways in which you create sacred space for yourself to commune with your Inner Wisdom. We challenge you to trust the guidance you receive, always. Remember, your Inner Wisdom needs you to both listen to and act on her guidance, and when you feel shaky or confused, lean in and get support. You don't have to do it alone.

Superpower Challenge: Show Your Inner Wisdom You Trust and Value Her

Time to strengthen your Inner Wisdom commitment. We dare you to take an action in the next seven days that your Inner Wisdom has been whispering for you to take. What has your Inner Wisdom been hinting at? Make a phone call? Send an email? Ask out that special someone? Consider leaving your job? You know what we're talking about because your Inner Wisdom has been talking to you! And now it's time to listen.

Tune in to what your Inner Wisdom has been telling you to do by finishing these prompts in your journal, and then take action in the next seven days.

"My Inner Wisdom has been whispering to me to . . ."
"I have been scared to take action because my Inner Mean
Girl is telling me . . ."

"But my Inner Wisdom knows that . . ."
"And my Inner Wisdom says I can start with this baby step
of . . ."
"All I need to do in the next seven days is . . ."
"I'm 100 percent committed to . . ."

Over the next seven days, every morning, commit to a daily sacred date with your Inner Wisdom where you ask for guidance she may have for you about this action. Take a look at the Inner Wisdom sacred dates in the back of the book on page 255 or try some of the mediation tracks included in our Inner Wisdom Kit at **innerwisdomkit.com** and choose a practice that inspires and excites you. Promise to keep this sacred date with yourself and your Inner Wisdom no matter what. To set yourself up for success, be honest about what you need in order to keep this sacred date every day and follow through on your action (tell your family, share with a friend, tell yourself it's okay to take care of yourself first, put a sticky note on the bathroom mirror). Take whatever action you need to receive that support.

INSPIRED ACTION

Create a Self-Love Altar— Claim Sacred Space for Yourself

As you complete this section of the book, which has been all about creating a stronger relationship with and connection to your Inner Wisdom, it's time to commit to living a life led by your Inner Wisdom— for real, not just in theory. As women, when we come to these turning points in our lives, one of the most powerful tools you have is to create a sacred ritual. A sacred ritual doesn't have to be a big production; it is simply a ceremony you create and partake in to honor the commitment you are making to yourself. This specific sacred ritual is a physical manifestation of the emotional and spiritual shifts you are making inside. It's a testimony of love for yourself. We humans need physical evidence and things we can touch and see to believe the changes we feel inside are happening on the outside.

To complete this part of the process, your inspired action is to make a sacred self-love altar for you and your Inner Wisdom in your home and then commit to sacred dates with her every morning; or if you are already connecting every morning, expand your time with her to include additional weekly, monthly, or semiannual dates. This self-love altar will be the place you can go to connect with her, a special place just for the two of you. Having this space in your home will remind you of your Inner Wisdom and your commitment to treat this relationship as primary and holy in your life.

Making a sacred altar can be as elaborate or as simple as you like, as public or as secret as you want. This doesn't have to be some big project; in fact, start small and simple right now by following these instructions, and then if you want, you can add on later. Don't delay; get started now. We've made this so simple, you can do it immediately. And if you already have an altar in your home, make another one or add to it in honor of your Inner Wisdom. Or create one in your office or in your garden outside. A girl can never have too many sacred self-love altars!

Four Simple Steps to Creating Your Sacred Space and Committing to Yourself

1. **Choose a space in your home that can be just yours.** This can be a nightstand, a bookshelf, a table, the top of a dresser, or even a hat box that you put a scarf over. Something flat that will allow you to put just a few sacred objects on it—objects that no one else has to know are sacred if you don't want them to. Your bedroom or closet is a great place for an altar, because it tends to be a more private, or a special room that is mostly for you, but anywhere in your home will do just perfect. Don't be shy about claiming space in your home, no matter who else lives with you.

2. **Choose three items to place on your altar that feel sacred, remind you of your fullest self, or just feel beautiful.** Ideas include photos of you, a crystal or a stone or something from nature, a candle, special jewelry, a flower, a stuffed animal, a chalice filled with rose petals or something meaningful, inspiring words, a special card or picture that opens your heart, a written mantra you want to remember, spiritual items with special meaning to you. With a meaningful or beautiful scarf or cloth as the base, this place is fast becoming your sacred altar.

3. **Consecrate your altar by committing to your Inner Wisdom–led life.** You'll want some natural element for this—like fire (a candle or incense) or water (a glass of tap or sparkling) or wind (a feather)

MY COMMITMENTS TO LIVE AN INNER WISDOM-LED LIFE

I choose to live an Inner Wisdom-led life.

I promise to connect with my
Inner Wisdom daily.

I promise to keep my relationship with myself
and my Inner Wisdom sacred.

I choose to listen to and act on my
Inner Wisdom's guidance, always—

even when the direction is scary, different,
and outside my comfort zone,

I choose to live an Inner Wisdom-led life,

I choose to live an Inner Wisdom-led life,

I choose to live an Inner Wisdom-led life.

or earth (just a handful of sand or dirt, or a stone). Don't get fancy—just grab what you have. Stand in front of this beautiful simple altar you have created, ignite whatever element you've chosen (i.e., light the candle, sprinkle some water or earth on the altar), and say the words on the previous page out loud. For extra superpower, make sure to say, "I choose to live an Inner Wisdom–led life" three times slowly, pausing and breathing in between each one so you can really *feel* the words and the energy of self-love and commitment behind them. The repetition, pausing, and breathing helps you lock into your promises to keep your commitment to living an Inner Wisdom–led life.

4. **Keep your sacred morning dates with your Inner Wisdom every-day, no matter what.** Use this altar as a reminder to keep the promise of sacred dates with your Inner Wisdom every morning. And when you travel, pack one piece of the altar to bring with you and set it up wherever you are. Your Inner Wisdom loves to take trips with you!

Want Some Sacred Altar Inspiration?

To inspire you to create your awesome altar, we set up a gallery of self-love altars made by our Inner Mean Girl Reform School students and other women we love. Check out the gallery at **innerwisdomkit.com**.

PART III

MAKE SHIFT HAPPEN

STEP 6

GiVE UP SELF-BULLYiNG FOR GOOD

Before we dive in, we want to acknowledge the incredible work you've done. It's too easy to get so focused on what's next that you forget to recognize what's already occurred, which is one way your Inner Mean Girl gets the upper hand. But when you pause to acknowledge the shifts happening inside and see the resulting shifts outside (in your life), your Inner Wisdom gains power and your connection to her grows stronger. Celebration and self-acknowledgment prevent self-bullying.

In the past five steps, you've increased your awareness of the two forces inside of you—your Inner Wisdom and your Inner Mean Girl— and created deeper relationships with both. You've learned how to turn down the volume on your IMG's Big Fat Lies and turn up the volume on your Inner Wisdom's sage guidance. We applaud your commitment to yourself! In fact, let's just pause here so you can acknowledge yourself.

♥ **What new awareness do you have about yourself today that you didn't have before starting this journey?** What truths have you been able to see and admit? Name and acknowledge at least two insights.

♥ **What actions have you taken to stand up for yourself and change self-bullying habits into self-loving ones?** What specific self-sabotaging actions and negative-thinking patterns have you made different choices about? Name and acknowledge at least two breakthroughs.

STEP 6

Now that we've celebrated, it's time to take your self-love adventure one step further by introducing you to one of the most potent Inner Mean Girl remedies and anti-self-bullying tactics on the planet: compassion.

As you face any challenge or situation in life, you always have two choices about how to motivate yourself—criticism or compassion. If you are like most women, you likely motivate yourself more often by criticism than compassion. Answer these questions as a quick pulse check to find out:

♥ Are you more likely to *criticize yourself* for what you haven't done or more likely to *acknowledge yourself* for what you have achieved?
♥ Are you more likely to *get down on yourself* when things get hard or more likely to *give yourself a break*?
♥ When things are going great, are you more likely to *tell yourself you don't deserve it* or more likely to actually *celebrate and receive the goodness*?
♥ Are you more likely to *be impatient, to put pressure on yourself*, to think you should be further along or better than you are? Or are you more likely to *be gentle, kind, and patient with yourself*?

It's okay—be honest.

We think we'd all agree that the compassionate choices are the better options. Yet most of us seem to default to using judgment, pressure, and criticism as a way to motivate ourselves rather than offering ourselves the compassion we would easily offer to a child, best friend, or beloved in the same situation. In all the work we have done with women around the world, almost all agree that they want to be more compassionate with themselves, but almost all also say that they find it extremely hard to do in everyday life. We women know how to be a best friend or good mother and offer compassion unconditionally to someone else, but when we are going through a hard time or struggling, we just can't seem to do it for ourselves. In fact, it seems the more we struggle, the harder we are on ourselves, when the correlation should be the more we struggle, the more compassionate we are with ourselves. Think about how that might be true in your own life.

You have been operating—consciously and subconsciously—under the mistaken understanding that pressure and judgment will motivate you to produce the best results, when in reality the opposite is true. We actually achieve more, and feel better about what we accomplish and how we are living our lives, when we motivate ourselves with loving truth and compassion. Your Inner Mean Girl has convinced you otherwise because she knows just how powerful compassion is at deactivating her toxic habits. Compassion is like kryptonite to your Inner Mean Girl. Compassion holds the superpower to instantly transform fear, loneliness, shame, blame, and stress into love and can stop an IMG attack in a snap. Compassion is one of your most effective tools for changing your neural pathways.

> WE ACTUALLY ACHIEVE MORE, AND FEEL BETTER ABOUT WHAT WE ACCOMPLISH AND HOW WE ARE LIVING OUR LIVES, WHEN WE MOTIVATE OURSELVES WITH LOVING TRUTH AND COMPASSION.

And we have some great news for you! You were born knowing how to be compassionate to yourself. Being kind, gentle, patient, and understanding with yourself is actually your natural state. Think about it: when you were learning to walk as a baby and you fell down, you didn't berate yourself and say, "You loser, get up! You're falling behind all the other toddlers!" No, you let yourself move at your own pace and just got up and started again. It never occurred to you to criticize, push, or judge yourself, until you experienced the judgmental thoughts and critical energy from other people, which then made you question your natural loving, supportive, and compassionate ways. What this tells us about you and how you are wired is awesome. You don't have to *learn* how to be compassionate with yourself, you need to *remember* to be compassionate. Think about it. Beneath all the critical and judgmental neural pathways that have been running all these years lie deeper, *original* pathways programmed for compassion. Compassion runs deep inside you—you just need to tap back into it. Compassion is your birthright. With some attention and intention, you can reconnect your brain, heart, and body to your original operating mode where you naturally choose to support yourself instead of bully yourself. This will not take years. You can start experiencing changes right now.

What Is Self-Compassion?

Ultimately, self-compassion is just compassion directed toward one's self. But for such an important aspect of life and such a powerful tool, we think it warrants a more full definition. Here's how we define self-compassion:

> *self-compassion* (n): the choice to open your heart and offer yourself kindness, gentleness, forgiveness, understanding, and patience—whenever you need it, without cause or condition.

Sounds good, right? Positive? Something you would teach your kids or tell your friends to do? So if it sounds so good, why is it so hard to do?

Well, for one thing, most of us don't think about compassion in terms of ourselves. As women, we are taught to give compassion to others. Giving compassion to others is heralded in our society—just think about our biggest spiritual teachers of compassion, modern and ancient: the Dalai Lama, Mother Teresa, Gandhi, Buddha, Jesus and Mary, and more. Compassion is at the heart of almost every spiritual tradition. But we are taught through most of our religious and educational systems only to direct the compassion out there—to others. If you were to dig deeper to the roots of what these spiritual teachers actually taught, you'd find that they were big fans of compassion directed at the self, knowing that compassion for others starts in our capacity for giving compassion to ourselves. For example, in the Buddhist tradition, when doing a specific meditation for loving-kindness, you always begin with sending loving-kindness to yourself before moving onto others. And as one contemporary spiritual teacher, Pema Chödrön, an American Buddhist nun, stated so clearly: "To the degree that we have compassion for ourselves, we will also have compassion for others. Having compassion starts and ends with having compassion for all those unwanted parts of ourselves, all those imperfections that we don't even want to look at."[1]

Your Inner Mean Girl mistakenly tells you that being compassionate with yourself is selfish and self-indulgent.

Your Inner Wisdom knows that the more compassionate you are with yourself, the more compassionate you will be with others.

Just think of a time in your life when you were being hard on yourself, feeling a lot of pressure, pushing yourself—were you more or less patient and kind with others? Let's be honest now. A lack of compassion toward yourself makes you crabbier, more controlling, and more critical of others. Your fuse is shorter, your tolerance thinner, and your capacity to understand lower. Compare that to times when you felt supported, loved, and cared for, when you felt spaciousness in your process—the increased love on the inside makes more love on the outside.

This is why spiritual teachers have always taught both compassion and self-compassion. Compassion is a both/and equation, not an either/or. Compassion is also something that you automatically just deserve, just because you are you. You don't have to do anything to deserve compassion—there's no scale that says what kind of situation deserves compassion and what doesn't. All day, every day, you deserve to meet yourself and be met by others with understanding, kindness, gentleness, and patience.

What other Big Fat Lies about self-compassion might be hanging out in your consciousness? And what do you say about rewiring them so that we can clear the pathway between your head and heart and wire you up for motivation by compassion?

We've listed here some of the most common misunderstandings about compassion and self-compassion, Big Fat Lies that make it hard for you to choose self-love over self-bullying. Then we've provided you with the original loving truths that you were born knowing, truths based on ageless spiritual wisdom. Read each Big Fat Lie and ask your Inner Wisdom if you have been mistakenly running on that misperception. If your answer is yes, mark it and notice how this misunderstanding may be contributing to your inner and outer realities. While you may not have been affected by all of these misunderstandings, it's important to know which ones have crossed your internal wiring and then set yourself straight.

INNER MEAN GIRL BIG FAT LIE. Your judgment and criticism of others has nothing to do with your judgment and criticism of yourself.

INNER WISDOM TRUTH. Whenever you point the finger at someone else, you are really judging yourself.

When you cannot be compassionate with all the parts of yourself—the good, the bad, the scared, the brave, the weak, the strong, the shamed, and the celebrated—your IMG finds that fault in others, acts out, and judges and resents those people. But really the person you can't be with is you.

This is why we see so many outer mean girls on the playground, in the conference room, and at PTA meetings. Believe us when we say that when a woman acts like a mean girl to others, she has an even harsher Inner Mean Girl. A bully, no matter how old, is masterful at self-bullying.

We really saw how powerful using self-compassion can be to stop the Inner Mean Girl from becoming an outer mean girl when one of our students, Nancy, taught a group of women in prison about their Inner Mean Girls and self-compassion. She helped each of the women personify and name her IMG and understand that her IMG was just trying to protect her. The next day Nancy came to work, and the prison guards stopped her, asking, "What did you teach these women? The women stopped fighting! The moment they would get all riled up with each other, they would stop and say, 'I am not going to fight with you—that's just my Inner Mean Girl talking.'" They saw the link between the Inner Mean Girls and their actions, applied compassion, and as a result the violent energy evaporated and the prisoners made a different choice.

If it's possible to stop violence among women in prison by exposing the Inner Mean Girl and applying self-compassion, imagine what compassion can do for your own life. We dare you, the next time you find yourself on the receiving end of an outer mean girl attack, to use compassion.

Superpower Tool: The Outer Mean Girl Deactivator

Before reacting from your IMG, so you end up in a mean girl battle with another woman, experiment with this Inner Mean Girl deactivator by taking these three steps to diffuse the situation with compassion:

1. **Feel your Inner Mean Girl's presence and play out internally how she would like to have you react to protect yourself.** Stop and be totally present with what's happening in your body before responding, so you can feel your IMG. Notice the trigger and the intensity in your body, notice what Big Fat Lies are present, and clearly play out in your mind how your IMG would respond if you let her.

2. **See the other person's IMG (or Inner Bully, if he's a man) not as a threat but as the fearful little one inside.** Instead of reacting right away in your own knee-jerk, fearful response, slow everything down

by observing what's occurring. Challenge yourself to look beyond the woman or man to see the part that is acting from fear, stress, judgment, etc., goading you to react in the same fashion. And just like the prison inmates did, refuse to play that mean girl game, if for no other reason than because of your love for yourself.

3. **Respond from compassion, for you both, instead of criticism, combat, or fear.** Soothe both your IMG and hers with kindness. This doesn't mean being a doormat, stuffing your feelings, or sacrificing your needs—that's not compassion; that's self-sabotage.

INNER MEAN GIRL BIG FAT LIE. Being compassionate means you have to suppress your feelings so you don't hurt others. To be compassionate means sacrificing yourself for another or sugarcoating things so everyone feels better.

INNER WISDOM TRUTH. Being compassionate means being truthful and loving and doesn't require self-sacrifice. Being compassionate requires you come from love for yourself and others, even as you draw a boundary, say no, or stand up for yourself and speak your truth.

Compassion does not mean being submissive, letting people step on your boundaries, putting up with toxic relationships, or allowing people to treat you poorly; that is being a doormat. Compassion does not mean putting yourself into situations or relationships that harm or drain you.

Women are prone to think that we need to make everyone feel better or make the hard stuff seem easier. Compassion is not about putting frosting on everything to make the bitter stuff taste better and make everyone smile as if everything is okay. Neither you nor others are best served if you ignore the truth and the hurt. We all know that when we repress that crap down and ignore our emotions, it just surfaces in other, passive-aggressive ways or in big bursts that make bigger messes later. The best course of action is to apply compassion and admit it does hurt and allow others to live their own experiences. While not easy, as it requires us to be vulnerable (which IMGs hate), learning how to be compassionate toward ourselves and others while still getting our needs met is a lesson and skill all of us women would be better served to master in this lifetime, and then teach our children to do the same.

Women also get into trouble because we believe we are being good, compassionate women by putting up with hurtful behavior from friends or family in the name of love. In reality, when you find yourself in these kinds of situations, it's really your Inner Mean Girl motivating you to look the other way or "be the bigger person" as a cover-up for your own fear of losing love or looking like the bad, unforgiving, uncompassionate, intolerant one. You never win in these situations; you just end up in the land of resentment because you have let others step all over you again. Sure, occasionally when someone you care about is having a hard time and she is not being her most evolved, loving self, you may cut her some slack as an act of compassion because, like we said, we all deserve compassion. But giving people free passes over and over again is not empowering, no matter who that person is—even if she is your mother or child. Condoning acts of disrespect is self-sacrificing, and that is something no one who is self-loving can afford.

To speak compassionately—to others and yourself—is to speak loving truth. Sometimes that truth is difficult to say and difficult for the other person to hear, but when it comes from love, it's all good. Authentic compassion is all about where you are coming from and how you hold the person in your energy field. Do you hold her in a negative energy, like contempt, anger, or resentment, or can you hold her in a neutral to positive field based on detachment from outcome or unconditional love? Responding with compassion instead of reacting from fear and protection is all a matter of the field of energy you create from your heart; from there, the words and actions flow.

INNER MEAN GIRL BIG FAT LIE. Being compassionate is about saying the right words to make others feel good.

INNER WISDOM TRUTH. Being compassionate is something you feel first and then emit through words and actions that transmit a loving energy that touches another person's heart. Love does the work for you.

Compassion is something you feel and then offer. It's not passive; it's active. You first make the choice to open up your heart as a witness to another and to yourself and as a result, emanate waves of kindness, understanding, and forgiveness that offer the power to touch, heal, and transform.

While you may say nice words to someone, it's not the words that matter or that create the powerful impact of compassion; it's the energy behind the words that matters, which comes from your heart authentically listening, understanding, and then choosing to emit those feelings. When you are in the compassion-giving vibe, it really does feel like you open the door of your heart and allow kindness and loving truth to stream out. This is why whenever someone has said nice words to you that sound compassionate but lack sincere kindness and understanding behind them, the sentiment feels empty, placating, and even passive-aggressive.

This is also why the Wake-Up Call Three Step process works so well, because as you switch from the Inner Mean Girl fear rant to your Inner Wisdom loving truth, the energy changes. Even if the words are exactly the same, the energy from your Inner Wisdom is filled with loving truth and compassion. So next time you find yourself in a situation where you have the choice to respond from compassion or from fear, pause to feel the energy in your body, choose to open the door to your heart, and let the loving truth flow out. You, and anyone else involved, will feel the difference. Compassion is something you have to feel in order for it to be real.

INNER MEAN GIRL BIG FAT LIE. If you give yourself too much compassion, you will become a slacker, never reach your goals, or become too soft.

INNER WISDOM TRUTH. Compassionate people are fueled by love and radiate positive energy. As a result, they achieve more of what matters and have a more positive impact in the world.

Let's get real. You can trust yourself and let go right now of any irrational IMG fear that if you become compassionate with yourself, you will lose your edge, fall behind, or fail. We meet so many women who fear the feminine way of being—surrendering control, doing less, living in spaciousness, being compassionate and collaborative instead of calculating and competitive. Their IMGs have done a number on them, telling them if they pause and refuel, spend time in reflection, stop pushing themselves so hard to get ahead, or let go of timelines and the detailed plans they have for their lives, they'll become couch potatoes who never get anything done or who don't get what they want because they didn't work and push hard enough.

> COMPASSION IS SOMETHING YOU HAVE TO FEEL IN ORDER FOR IT TO BE REAL.

The truth is if you give yourself true compassion, you won't condone sabotaging behaviors. You won't achieve less; you'll actually achieve more of what matters to you and makes you happy, and you will enjoy the process a heck of a lot more. If you are kind, gentle, and truthful with yourself, and if you love yourself instead of cajoling, pushing, or guilting your way forward, you will stop creating undue stress and pressure and start creating more spaciousness. You will be able to feel that you are enough, that you have done enough, and that you have enough.

Remember, self-compassion is knowing that you are doing the best you can, you've always done the best you can, and you are a human being who is always learning and growing. So with compassion, when you fail, fall down, or get stuck, or just need a break, you lend yourself a helping hand connected to a loving heart.

> **INNER MEAN GIRL BIG FAT LIE.** The hardest people to forgive are other people.

> **INNER WISDOM TRUTH.** The hardest person to forgive is you. What you can't forgive in someone else is a sign of a bigger, hairier, scarier ball of resentment, anger, blame, and shame you have toward yourself.

Most of us carry around emotional and energetic sacks of anger, frustration, and resentment toward other people for the ways in which we have been wronged, hurt, or not seen. And for any of us who have been wronged, hurt, or unappreciated, which is all of us to some degree, we know that forgiving that person, while it could alleviate lots of pain and suffering, is hard to do. If you have ever forgiven someone, you know what a weight it can lift off your heart, mind, even your body. But there is one person who is harder to forgive than anyone whom we rarely focus on when we think of forgiveness—that person is you.

IT'S CHRISTINE HERE. When my fiancé broke up with me on the way to our engagement party after also admitting he had cheated on me (ouch), I was hurt and angry, of course. But within a year I was able to forgive him for cheating on me and breaking up with me the way he had, because I was able to see he didn't have the emotional skills to do it any other way (me either at that time). But it took me five years to forgive myself for staying in a relationship that I knew wasn't the right one for me; five years to forgive myself for not listening to my Inner Wisdom, who had been telling me for a long time to leave; five years to forgive myself for the truth that I almost gave up the life I really wanted because I was afraid of losing his love. But the crazy thing was that it never occurred to me that I needed to forgive myself until I realized that underneath my anger at him was so much more anger at myself. And until I was able to release that self-directed anger, my heart would never be able to be fully open to myself or anyone else.

Inner Wisdom Reflection: What's Your Lack of Compassion Costing You?

Take a look at the Big Fat Lies about compassion that might be influencing you, or think about something in your life that's happening right now or occurred in the recent past in which you were hard on yourself instead of kind to yourself. Specifically notice how you have been trying to motivate yourself through criticism, comparison, self-judgment, pressure, pushing, setting unrealistic expectations, and perfectionism, instead of understanding, patience, kindness, and gentleness. Journal or pause and reflect on these questions, and be as specific as possible in your answers:

- ♥ **How does your lack of self-compassion show up?** Are you being über-critical, expecting too much from yourself, pushing yourself too hard, putting loads of pressure on yourself?
- ♥ **What's this self-compassion deficit costing you?** Notice the negative impact in your relationships, health, money, and happiness.
- ♥ **If you were to apply compassion instead of bullying yourself, how would you act differently toward yourself?** Consider both your

day-to-day life and situations when you struggle. What act or thought could you change immediately to be good to yourself?

We love what Kristin Neff, author of *Self-Compassion: The Proven Power of Being Kind to Yourself*, has researched and proven about the effects of self-compassion. She accurately stated,

> Instead of mercilessly judging and criticizing yourself for various inadequacies or shortcomings, self-compassion means you are kind and understanding when confronted with personal failings—after all, who ever said you were supposed to be perfect? You may try to change in ways that allow you to be more healthy and happy, but this is done because you care about yourself, not because you are worthless or unacceptable as you are. Perhaps most importantly, having compassion for yourself means that you honor and accept your humanness.[2]

Here's a great example of this in action. One of our Inner Mean Girl Reform School students, Anya, was being extra hard on herself about her career. She was really struggling with leaving a job she didn't love, and with taking the bold step to move across the country even though she didn't have a new job yet. For years she thought about moving to California but out of fear had been settling for her life in the Midwest. Single but living in suburbia at the young age of forty, her vibrant, colorful heart and soul were dying in a job that felt like a desert every day. She had worked with coaches, done tons of self-awareness work, but still could not move. Her Inner Mean Girl was all over her, telling her, "You are a loser. You are never going to make this move. You don't have the courage. You've done all this work on yourself, and, look, you are *still* here. Nothing's changed. Just give up! You'll be stuck in a job and city you hate forever." On the outside, of course you would never have known this self-bullying was going on. To her friends, family, and coworkers, Anya was a success-ful, independent woman who had "made it," but on the inside Anya felt more like she was faking it, living someone else's life other than her own.

Not a smack of compassion anywhere in those words or in Anya's harsh judgments about herself—thank you, IMG! This required an inter-vention using some of our best compassion activator superpower tools. First we had Anya see and be with her Inner Mean Girl and her inner judgments, looking them square in the eye and feeling the cost of this lack of self-compassion in her heart. When Anya saw how critical, harsh, and horrible she was being with her-self, a remarkable thing happened. Like a mother who was defending her baby cub or a girl who was defending her best friend from a bully on the playground, a self-love fire exploded in Anya, empowering her to say, "No more! That's it. I give up this self-bullying. I choose self-compassion."

> YOUR INNER WISDOM IS A TRUTH TELLER WHO USES LOVE AND COMPASSION TO MOTIVATE YOU FORWARD, INSTEAD OF GUILT AND SHAME.

With this fierce stand in hand, we then had Anya turn to her Inner Wisdom, who didn't coddle her and say, "Oh, Anya, it's okay. It's so hard. I know. So scary. There, there. You don't have to move. Just stay here where it's safe." No way! Her Inner Wisdom (and yours) is a truth teller who uses love and compassion to motivate you forward, instead of guilt and shame.

Anya's Inner Wisdom said to her, "Anya, yes this feels scary, and it's a big move for you, but you are ready for this. Just keep putting one foot in front of the other. You are on the right path. You are going to be just fine. And it's okay to go as fast as the slowest part of you can go." Boom! Compassion.

With the boost of compassion to motivate her, instead of freezing up because of the judgment and criticism of her Inner Mean Girl, Anya was able to continue to take the small steps that eventually led to the big bold steps. For Anya, that meant starting a "freedom fund", a savings account specifically for amassing money for when she was ready to move. It meant starting to be herself at work now, not waiting for some perfect new job someday—free self-expression! And most important, because she was choosing compassion instead of criticism, Anya began enjoying her life in the moment instead of putting her happiness on hold for the day she finally moved.

Compassion makes you more present in your life now, and when you are more present, you are happier, and when you are happier, you are motivated to just go for what your heart desires. This is the truth. And it's about time we women start believing it and proving it to be true by how we live our lives. All you have to do is decide to set down the bullying bat and open your arms and heart to yourself.

Superpower Challenge: Give Up Self-Bullying and Choose Self-Compassion for Good!

It's time to give up your self-sabotaging ways for good by making a promise to yourself that you will never regret: to give up self-bullying and to choose to motivate and meet yourself with self-compassion—and then keeping this vow every day for the rest of your life. When you make a promise to yourself, and really mean it, the promise gives you the power to stay true to how you want to be with yourself no matter what.

Promises pack superpower. They are like self-love anchors that keep you connected and committed to your heart and soul, so that in the moments when you are about to do something hurtful to yourself—like negative self-talk—you have the power to make a different choice. Or in the cases when you do something stupid or sabotaging, the promise will help you find the self-love rope you use to wrap and embrace yourself with compassion instead of hang yourself with criticism.

Your mission in this superpower challenge is to take the self-love promise to give up self-bullying for good with full gusto and complete dedication. Then, because we are setting realistic expectations, let's be honest: your old negative self-talk and self-sabotaging neural pathways will still get activated, and you will be tempted to bully yourself using the same old toxic habits. You may even go into a full-on IMG attack. That's okay—the promise and the compassion activators we are about to share with you have the superpower to pull you back from the depths of the Inner Mean Girl shadow. The goal isn't to never again have your IMG show up and try to bully you. Even reformed, in times of stress and uncertainty when the stakes feel really high, she can resurface. The point is that you will be so aware and so prepared, your IMG won't be able to take you out or sabotage your happiness, success, or ultimate inner peace.

To take a vow and have it stick, you need to feel that self-love fire inside as you take a stand for this being you love so much, which in this case is you! Just like you feel love for someone you make marriage vows with, you want to express that deep love here for yourself. We've written the vows for you, in the words we find the simplest and in an order we find most powerful to make them easy to remember, and in a way that ends it all with a punch! Read through them to get a sense of what we are inviting you to commit to.

To get the full effect and impact you will need to involve your body, mind, and heart. This is the perfect time for a simple yet powerful sacred ritual, don't you agree? Play along with us: put your hand on your heart and say the entire set of vows out loud clearly, slowly, and with fierce love for yourself. Pause between each one to let the feeling sink in. And for extra power, we double-dog dare you to take the vows in front of a mirror, so you can look yourself in the eyes.

After you take the vows, it's a great idea to lock them in by writing the vows in your Inner Wisdom journal or creating a piece of art with

THE VOWS OF SELF-COMPASSION

(A SUREFIRE REMEDY FOR GIVING UP SELF-BULLYING!)

I give up being hard on myself.
*I promise to be **gentle** with myself.*

I give up bullying myself.
*I promise to be **nice** to myself.*

I give up talking negatively to myself.
*I promise to be **kind** to myself.*

I give up putting pressure on myself.
*I promise to be **patient** with myself.*

I give up judging myself.
*I promise to be **understanding** with myself.*

*I promise to be **compassionate** with myself.*
*I promise to **love** myself.*

them and then signing your name to it to seal the deal. You may even want to put a sticky note with this commitment on your bathroom mirror or car dashboard. Better yet, put these words on your self-love altar as a sacred reminder.

Then (this is very important), the next time the negative self-talk starts or you are tempted to push yourself hard or you feel yourself about to self-sabotage, remember your self-compassion vow! Say with gusto to yourself, your IMG, and your Inner Wisdom, "I gave up bullying myself. I promised to be compassionate with myself." Or whatever vows ring out the most for you. Keep saying how you gave up the bullying and promised compassion until the neural pathway stops looping the criticism, judgment, and pressure through your body and mind. Saying the vow with oomph in this way breaks the pattern and empowers you to find a new way of being that is much more compassionate. Experiment and have fun!

And for those moments when you need to call in extra reinforcements—like you cannot feel the compassion no matter what you do—we've included three of our favorite compassion activators. These are simple superpower tools you can use to generate within minutes IMG kryptonite, aka self-compassion. Experiment with these too and make some self-love!

Compassion Activator: The Love Stream

Write yourself a love letter oozing with compassion. You know how good you feel when you receive a loving email or letter from a friend? How your heart opens up and you feel all warm inside? Well, you can do the same thing for yourself. But instead of just writing a letter, you open your heart so it can stream love to you. Here's how this works. Grab your journal, computer, or a piece of paper. Close your eyes and imagine yourself tuning in to your Inner Wisdom's channel of loving truth and ask, "What loving truths do I really truly need to hear right now?"

Keeping your eyes closed (yes, closed!), open the love stream and start writing—in other words, open up your heart and in a stream of consciousness write whatever comes, as if it's just flowing out of you. And usually because you are writing so fast and with your eyes closed, the handwriting will be messy or the typing full of typos, but you can go back and make it pretty later. When love streaming, your job is to flow compassionate statements about yourself, starting your sentences with the word *you*. They are like your own personal Self-Compassion Love Mantras. For example:

"You have done so much already."
"You have positively impacted the lives of so many people."
"Chill out—you are doing great. Look how far you have come!"

If you can't get into the flow right away, use these primers to get started, putting your name in front of each one as if your best friend, or Inner Wisdom, in this case, was actually streaming love right at you:

"<Your Name>, you really are . . ."
"<Your Name>, you have . . ."
"<Your Name>, you can feel so good about . . ."
"<Your Name>, you are doing the best you can with . . ."

Compassion Activator: The Love Boosts

Consume shots of love that open your heart. Just like you can take a shot of espresso to wake yourself up, you can take a shot of love to wake up your compassion simply by using your five senses and consuming anything that opens your heart. We call these love boosts! In the moments you are being hard on yourself, instead of wallowing in your misery or sticking around for your self-bullying session, get out into the world and find evidence of love and take it in, maybe even by taking a photo of it to capture the essence. You can:

- ♥ **See love.** Find pictures of anything that opens your heart up: your kids, animals, music, photos, flowers, anything that makes you feel loved. Or take a walk and look at things that open your heart.
- ♥ **Touch love.** Ask for a hug. Pet a puppy. If you can't find a human or an animal to hug, buy yourself some fresh flowers—flowers are instant heart openers! Plus, you get the benefit of smelling the roses, literally.
- ♥ **Hear love.** Put on music that opens your heart and let it move you, physically and/or emotionally. Some of our favorites include India Arie, Nadine Risha, and Karen Drucker; their music just oozes self-love.

Compassion Activator: The Compassion-Making Love Mantras

Pour on the kind words until you feel the love open your heart, so you can give yourself a break! You've already experienced the power of taking the self-compassion vow, and you've also experienced the power of Love Mantras when you transformed your Big Fat Lies into loving truths. We happen to have three superpower Love Mantras that have the specific power to generate the energy of compassion for you to use in the moment to remind you of your vow and deactivate your IMG. You will love them:

> **"I am doing the best I can, and it's enough."**
> **"I'm learning, and that is okay."**
> **"It is okay to go as fast as the slowest part of me can go."**

To activate the mantra power, close your eyes, take a deep breath, and put your hand on your heart. This allows you to feel a greater connection with your heart's energy, the home of compassion in your body. Repeat one or all of these mantras until you feel what we call a compassion click, an opening of your heart to yourself. When you experience the click, it's like a switch goes off, and the hard and harsh feelings of judgment and criticism transform to a warm, soothing energy. Your heart will feel like it literally softens, and the love and compassion will flow in.

Go ahead and try it here, just for a minute or two. Think of something that you are being hard on yourself about or feeling stress over. Close your eyes, take a breath, put your hand on your heart, and repeat one of the self-compassion Love Mantras until you feel your heart open and compassion flow in. You can either use the second-person pronoun *you* and imagine your best friend saying the words to you or you can use the first-person pronoun *I* and give love to yourself.

Sometimes you will find it challenging to let the love in, and in that case, you will want to enlist the help of a friend. Well, we happen to be friends with one of the Love Mantra queens, singer-songwriter Karen Drucker, who specializes in mantras that generate love and compassion. She gave us one of her most powerful self-love songs to share with you called, "I Am Gentle with Myself" which you can download from the Inner Wisdom Kit at **innerwisdomkit.com** and listen to when you need to activate compassion. Karen's music makes self-love happen.

TRANSFORMATION TALE: Compassion Saved My Life
by Christine Hassler, bestselling author of *Expectation Hangovers*

My Inner Mean Girl was born in the fourth grade when a group of my so-called friends, who turned out to be a gang of outer mean girls, formed the I Hate Christine Club. And I was the Christine they hated. So at the tender age of eight I decided that something must be dreadfully wrong with me to make me so unlikable, and, as a result, I became much harder on myself than anyone else ever could be. I became addicted to over-achieving to compensate for where I felt "not enough." Getting less than an A on anything was unacceptable to me. I placed a tremendous amount of expectation on myself to be wildly successful and relentlessly pushed myself to some imagined future that I believed would finally make me feel worthy.

My Inner Mean Girl was a pro at using criticism, perfectionism, and comparison to motivate me to accomplish things. By twenty-six, I had a big-time movie producer boyfriend, designer clothes, a perfect size-two figure, and an extremely successful career as a literary agent in Hollywood that came with a six-figure salary. From the outside, my life looked great. I was well on my way to "having it all." There was just one problem: I was absolutely miserable. Each time I reached a goal, instead of celebrating and feeling like I had made it, my IMG would just set the bar higher.

Where was the happiness I thought all my goals would deliver? Daily I tried to talk myself into liking my job. I felt obligated to stay because this was what I thought I wanted and had worked so hard for, but I hated my job so much that it was making me sick. To save myself from a total meltdown, I quit. But things didn't get better—they got worse—and I had a series of what I call expectation hangovers. I went thousands of dollars into debt, was diagnosed with an "unknown autoimmune disorder," and got dumped by my fiancé. Nothing turned out like I expected despite my meticulous planning and perfect overachieving.

And my Inner Mean Girl was right there to constantly remind me that I was failing to live up to her expectations. One pivotal night I found myself lying on my bathroom floor, contemplating how I could end my life. I felt so incredibly hopeless and lost.

And then something happened. Seemingly out of nowhere, a wave of compassion flooded over me. Time stopped. My pain was replaced with comfort. I had an inner knowing that everything was happening for a reason. The feeling of peace and love that came with this compassion only lasted for an instant (my mind came in to try and figure it out); however, the impact will last a lifetime.

For the first time since I was eight, I allowed myself to cry without any judgment or analysis. Instead of hearing the harsh voice of my IMG say, "What's wrong with you? Stop crying. Get over it!" I heard the voice of compassion say, "It's okay. Let it out. You're doing great. I'm here." I felt comforted and loved. My emotions felt safe and free to be expressed.

And in that moment I realized that in addition to the Inner Mean Girl inside of me, I also had a part that could hold the space of compassion for me through my struggles and learning, just like an unconditionally loving and nurturing parent who could give me permission and encouragement to express my feelings fully.

Before compassion, I motivated myself to be better by believing I was fundamentally flawed. But through the eyes of compassionate love toward myself, I saw a sweet young girl who faced challenges; I was able to wrap her up in a lavender blanket of compassion and allow her to feel and express the feelings she previously suppressed in order to survive.

Compassion has taught me that there is nothing wrong with me, that I am lovable just as I am. Compassion has gently guided me away from the voice of my Inner Mean Girl and toward the voice of my Inner Wisdom. Compassion is a judgment-free zone. There is no opinion, analysis, pity, or criticism because there is nothing wrong with me or what I am going through. I am simply with my suffering, disappointments, and fear. From that place of acceptance, I am able to move from my very strong mind into the infinite sea of love in my heart. Compassion continues to be the key to getting through all expectation hangovers in my life.

STEP 7

ASSIGN YOUR INNER MEAN GIRL HER NEW JOB

It's time to redeploy your Inner Mean Girl so she can serve you and assist you in your personal breakthroughs. You and your IMG are ready to use her talents in service to you instead of as a force against you. Your IMG now feels seen and heard. She feels your compassion and understanding. She trusts that you can take care of yourself, protect yourself, and make good choices for yourself, with your Inner Wisdom as your go-to guide. All of this had to occur before your Inner Mean Girl would even consider a new job.

So congratulations on making it to this final step where we are about to call a truce in service to your best and happiest life! Yes, your Inner Mean Girl is about to be given a new job. Now that you know these two parts of yourself distinctly, and now that you have promised to employ self-compassion over self-bullying for the rest of your days, the two formerly opposing forces can be put to work in service to you.

The questions we need to ask now are: What is your Inner Mean Girl really good at, and how can you use her talents to serve you?

Choose the Lucky Inner Mean Girl

It's up to you to choose the one Inner Mean Girl you will redeploy and give a new job. If you are one of the women who, like Amy, has one

IMG with multiple personalities, she's the one you'll focus on for the rest of this chapter, but we recommend choosing her most prevalent archetype. If you are like Christine and have an army of Inner Mean Girls who feel like distinct individual forces within you, choose one IMG who is ready to be given a new job. How do you know which one is ready? Look at each Inner Mean Girl archetype you've identified and feel into your body. It's often the one who is standing front and center right now, most obviously in the way, the one whom you have the most awareness of, the one whose toxic habits and cost are the most debilitating. The one whose Big Fat Lies are the loudest. She's just itching for a new job! And remember that you can always ask your Inner Wisdom which IMG is ready. If you are really stuck, do the Wake-Up Call Three-Step process (page 130).

Consider Potential New Jobs

Your Inner Mean Girl's success at her new job starts with you understanding what her skills are and the energy she embodies within you and then transforming that energy to be used for good. From years of doing this work, we know that our students often find it helpful to review potential jobs before sitting down and formally giving their IMG a new gig.

Read through the ideas on the following pages and consider the potential possibilities and new roles for this once nefarious and destructive inner force. As you read through the energy and skill descriptions and the suggestions for the new jobs, notice what resonates with the energy your IMG carries and the skills she possesses. One of the tricks of successfully redeploying your IMG is to pinpoint her specific flavor of energy and then redirect it in supportive and productive ways. She is just like a small child who, if set loose without focus, can wreak havoc, but who, with a little direction, can channel all that pent-up energy in creative, expansive ways.

ACHIEVEMENT JUNKIE

ENERGY AND SKILLS	TRANSFORMED ENERGY AND NEW JOBS
Energy: Harsh, relentless, driven, ambitious, tireless **Skills:** Good at driving you to achieve more, do more, have more, experience more Good at making sure that you don't fall short of your potential Good at keeping you striving for higher levels of excellence	**Energy:** Proud, visionary, bigger than life, motivational, devoted, celebratory, grateful **Jobs:** **Recorder and Reflector of Greatness**—Instead of moving the bar on you every time you reach a goal, she holds a big mirror to you to reflect how much you have already accomplished. She's been keeping notes all along. And every time you have even a minor success, she is writing it down for you to remember. **Vision Holder**—She holds the vision for your highest potential, and she knows that you can't screw up your destiny. So there's no rush—she just keeps holding the vision so you can keep living into it and enjoy the process versus pursuing it relentlessly, missing out on all the celebratory milestones.

COMPARISON QUEEN

ENERGY AND SKILLS	TRANSFORMED ENERGY AND NEW JOBS
Energy: Snide, petty, passive-aggressive, critical and judgmental, superior **Skills:** Good at seeing the beauty, brilliance, and accomplishments of other people Good at finding and focusing on what you don't have but what you want Good at putting others down and making them feel small in an effort to make you feel superior	**Energy:** Excited to go out and find genius, beauty, new things you've not thought of; inspiring, motivational, and ready to give a hand up **Jobs:** **Talent Scout**—She brings you talented and inspiring people to encourage you to your greatness. You can learn from and even partner with these special people. **Motivational Mentor**—She brings you others that you'd be a fabulous mentor for or finds great mentors for you.

DOING ADDiCT

ENERGY AND SKILLS	TRANSFORMED ENERGY AND NEW JOBS
Energy: Busy, can't stop, Energizer Bunny–like, manic, frenzied, overwhelmed, highly active mind **Skills:** Good at remembering everything you have to do all the time and keeping a to-do list a mile long	**Energy:** She is on it, clear, focused, put together, on task, and taking care of what's most important, reprioritizing the rest. **Jobs:** **Super Personal Assistant**—She carries an awesomely big clipboard to hold all your to dos so you don't have to. You just give them to her to keep track of and prioritize. She also holds the list all night long so you don't have to go to sleep with it or wake up with it. **Sacred Space Scheduler and Guardian**—She creates and guards sacred space time for you to rest and replenish. She knows taking this time out will ultimately make you more productive.

DRAMA QUEEN

ENERGY AND SKILLS	TRANSFORMED ENERGY AND NEW JOBS
Energy: Swirling, stirring up trouble, intense **Skills:** Good at creating drama, stirring up energy Good at keeping everything moving Good at creating interesting stories	**Energy:** Creative, generative, eloquent **Jobs:** **Story Spinner**—Since she is so good at spinning stories, she is going to spin good ones for you. Put her to work creating great legends about your life—ones that empower you and inspire you. **Reality TV Writer**—Your Drama Queen is hired! She is now in charge of a wild and wonderful reality TV show whose ratings depend on the drama. She puts her dramatic skills to work on this imaginary show and leaves you and your life alone.

FIXER/RESCUER

ENERGY AND SKILLS	TRANSFORMED ENERGY AND NEW JOBS
Energy: Nosy, know-it-all, codependent, pushy **Skills:** Good at seeing what is wrong with other people Good at coming up with solutions for any problem Good at focusing on one thing or person	**Energy:** Compassionate, knowledgeable, wise, considerate **Jobs:** **Personal Therapist**—She turns all her rescue energy on you. You now have your own personal therapist who is finally focused on your own needs and who can find all the best resources for you! And she isn't taking on new clients. **Wise Woman**—She sits with people as a witness, listening without having to fix or give advice. Like the best old grandmother, she just gives love, never opinions, unless she is expressly asked, and even then she only reflects what she sees in the other person.

GOOD GiRL

ENERGY AND SKILLS	TRANSFORMED ENERGY AND NEW JOBS
Energy: Submissive, invisible, inauthentic, self-depriving, people pleasing **Skills:** Good at seeing others' needs Good at understanding what others want you to do Good at being compassionate and empathetic	**Energy:** Abundant, unapologetic about her self-care, grounded, connected to herself and her needs, giving and receiving, compassionionate, kind **Jobs:** **Personal Caretaker and Boundary Setter**—She shines her empathy all over you and is relentless in making sure that you get what you need. Her first question is "What do *you* need?" It's her job to make sure that you get it. And she guarantees that you don't put yourself last or sell yourself out. **Intuitive Informant**—She's good at sensing what's going on with others and seeing their truth. You use these skills to read others and inform you how to support them without going into self-sacrifice.

HEAD TRIPPER

ENERGY AND SKILLS	TRANSFORMED ENERGY AND NEW JOBS
Energy: Heady, cool, downer, wet blanket, allergic to enthusiasm, doubting, skeptical	**Energy:** Focused, aware, alert, eagle-eyed in service to you, discerning
Skills: Good at predicting problems and finding reasons to worry	**Jobs:**
Good at making up elaborate stories	**Inner Wisdom Bodyguard**—She can spot other people who are "wet blankets" on your dreams and keep them away from you. Their skepticism can't touch you!
Good at anticipating what outer critics will say	**Discernment Diva**—She is great at finding the issues you need to be aware of to make smart choices but discards the rest. She knows how to balance the intuitive and the practical.

INVINCIBLE SUPERWOMAN

ENERGY AND SKILLS	TRANSFORMED ENERGY AND NEW JOBS
Energy: Victim, martyr, overwhelmed, burdened, over-responsible, over-committed, alone, world is on her shoulders	**Energy:** Strong, supported, on top of the world instead of the world on top of her, committed to herself and those she loves
Skills: Good at taking more and more on	**Jobs:**
Good at seeing all that has to be done	**Delegator**—Since she is now on top of the world, she no longer has to be the one doing it all—she delegates. With superwoman strength, she passes things off with power and grace.
Good at looking like superhuman feats are simple and no sweat	**Negotiator**—She negotiates on your behalf, telling people that you can't do X but you could do Y, still allowing you to show up strong without being a sucker.

THE MARTYR

ENERGY AND SKILLS	TRANSFORMED ENERGY AND NEW JOBS
Energy: Holier than thou, untouchable, better-than, artistic, eccentric, justice warrior **Skills:** Good at connecting you to spirit, creativity, and a good cause Good at getting by with just enough, not needing extra or excess	**Energy:** In service to people, in service to the Divine, in service to herself, connected with human beings **Jobs:** **Student Teacher**—Since she's been studying so long at all this spiritual stuff, artistic stuff, or social stuff, now she can go out and teach what she's learned—not as a know-it-all but in a way that is inclusive and vulnerable. She realizes that she is learning just like everyone else. **Self-Server**—You are the mission! She serves you and your needs with all her gusto. She asks you, "How can I serve you?" and "What do you need to feel supported?"

STEP 7

OVERLY OPTIMISTIC, PARTYING CHEERLEADER

ENERGY AND SKILLS	TRANSFORMED ENERGY AND NEW JOBS
Energy: Irresponsible, delusional, gluttonous, overly optimistic, crazy positive **Skills:** Good at making things fun Good at seeing the bright side of things Good at cheering people up	**Energy:** Fun, grounded positivity, balanced optimism, centered **Jobs:** **The Fun Mom**—She is the one you can count on to help you stay responsible while having a blast. She gets to take care of you now. **Everyday Joy Finder**—She uses her partying skills to help you and others find joy every single day. She uses gratitude and appreciation with ease and shares love with the world through positive posts on social media, text messages, and phone calls.

PERFECTIONIST

ENERGY AND SKILLS	TRANSFORMED ENERGY AND NEW JOBS
Energy: Hypercritical, obsessive, compulsive, nitpicky, uncompassionate	**Energy:** Diligent, persistent, detailed, orderly, harmonious, stands for excellence
Skills: Good at pointing out everything that isn't perfect, that is out of order in your life	**Jobs:** **Order Creator**—Give her one task that will help your life run smoothly to funnel all of her perfectionist energy to.
Good at finding fault in someone— either you or someone else	**Perfection Holder**—She makes a list of all the things that need to be fixed so things are "perfect"—you tell her to put things on the list, so you don't have to worry about them or keep them in your mind.
Good at seeing what is out of harmony and balance	

REJECTION QUEEN

ENERGY AND SKILLS	TRANSFORMED ENERGY AND NEW JOBS
Energy: Too cool for school, isolated, snobby; or the flip side: hopeless, unlovable, depressing, needy **Skills:** Good at showing you all the ways in which you don't fit or belong Good at attracting bad matches in relationships for you to prove you're unlovable Good at making you loyal to others to keep their love even if they aren't good to you	**Energy:** Cool, different, special, unique, on task, curious, on fire; out to find and keep love, but only good, pure, healthy love and relationships **Jobs:** **Personal Private Investigator—** Put her to work to find the people you should not date or be friends with; she can ferret out the truth about who people are and whether they are in alignment with your highest good. **Trendsetter**—She shows you how to be yourself without needing approval from anyone else. You set your own trends, and people start to follow you, but you don't need them to because you feel like you fit with you—you choose you!

WORRYWART

ENERGY AND SKILLS	TRANSFORMED ENERGY AND NEW JOBS
Energy: Worried, anxious, nervous, tense, apprehensive	**Energy:** Grounded, practical, secure, spacious, calm
Skills: Good at finding danger, spotting potential disaster	**Jobs:**
Good at waiting for the other shoe to drop	**Risk Manager**—She runs ahead to find the potential pitfalls, and she calmly presents them to you and your Inner Wisdom so that you can make better decisions. You don't have to fret, because she has it all under control for you.
Good at creating stories about all the possible things that could happen	
	Inner Child Nurse—She takes care of your inner child like a doting NICU nurse. She rules out all the bad things, soothing you with positive words, and monitors your inner child's well-being so you can heal (and relax!).

Call a Sacred Truce and Give Your Inner Mean Girl Her New Job

Okay, now that you have ideas about what's possible, it's time to get personal and focused on you. In this step, we will guide you through holding a sacred meeting with your Inner Mean Girl, your Inner Wisdom, and you so that you can get them working together in your favor and get your IMG started in her new role. It's like having peace talks and creating a sacred truce between two formerly warring states. You will come to the table with these two forces to renegotiate how you will operate in your life every day and especially in times of struggle, when you are in the process of breaking down to break through. It truly is an inner peace talk.

One of our favorite stories about giving an Inner Mean Girl a new job was shared with us by one of our students, Elizabeth Gibbons, an amazing visionary artist whose IMG, Nasty Nellie, had been running quite the racket on her for years. Nasty Nellie kept Elizabeth from the success, recognition, and self-confidence she desired and deserved. This Inner Mean Girl, a very mean Comparison Queen, had made it her job to make Elizabeth feel inferior and diminish her power by pointing out all the great things other women were doing and then fabricating stories about why she didn't measure up. She did this all so that Elizabeth would play small and not risk really fully putting herself out in the world as the talented artist and wild creative soul she is.

But on her sacred truce day, Elizabeth and her Inner Wisdom took a stand to have a breakthrough. Elizabeth decided, with her Inner Wisdom by her side, that she was ready to release all the psychic and emotional garbage that had been keeping her from expressing herself fully and freely. So she orchestrated a meeting so Nasty Nellie could be redeployed, and her skill for finding lots of garbage to pile on Elizabeth could be redirected in a way that served Elizabeth instead of suffocated her. Elizabeth and her Inner Wisdom decided to bestow the new title of Queen of the

Shovels and Buckets to Nasty Nellie, giving her the job of shoveling out the psychic garbage, instead of shoveling it in.

When Elizabeth did the sacred truce process we are about to share with you, something astonishing happened. As she bestowed this new title on Nasty Nellie and saw why her IMG had been working so hard to keep her from her dreams, she began to cry. Nasty Nellie confessed that she was being mean because it was the only way she felt like she received attention. Nasty Nellie told Elizabeth, "I never get noticed. I am the one who carries the dark side of you, all the anger, the sadness, the regrets, the shame, the guilt. Without dark, you would have no light. I am the contrast that makes your bright lights brighter, yet all you ever want to do is ignore me or send me packing." Elizabeth said that her jaw practically dropped to the floor as she listened to this revelation. All these years, she had been so unwilling to be with the darker sides of herself that Nasty Nellie took it all on, as a way to protect Elizabeth (oh, IMG logic!). So instead of being angry at Nasty Nellie for spending so many years making her life a living hell, Elizabeth opened her heart, let the compassion flow, and experienced a major break-through. It was at this point, when compassion arrived, that her IMG took the new job of Queen of the Shovels and Buckets with excitement.

As the final part of the truce, they agreed to become a circle of love and to work together. This empowered Elizabeth, along with her Inner Wisdom and newly reformed IMG, to say no to rejecting parts of Elizabeth no matter how dark, to say no to isolating herself from the community around her, and to say no to avoiding feelings or hiding from circumstances that were difficult to deal with. They said yes to accepting all parts of Elizabeth—the dark and the light, the holy and the wild—and yes to using all of Elizabeth's essences in service to her artwork. This was the day that Elizabeth's Inner Mean Girl became a queen and Elizabeth came out of hiding as the full-spectrum being, artist, and woman she is. To mark the occasion, Elizabeth even put her full artistic expression to use making a piece of art out of a garden shovel to signify the new self-empowering tool that now helped her instead of hurt her.

Now it's time to call this sacred truce for yourself! We've created a special guided process to help you facilitate this transformation. This process is an essential part of reforming your IMG. It's an adventure of sorts that will guide you to give your Inner Mean Girl a new job. This experience is an active one, which requires your presence and playfulness, and we encourage you to create the space to have this sacred truce and take a stand for your own personal breakthrough. Just walking through the guided process in your mind and going through the motions won't work. You can't just read our instructions; you've got to take the journey. That is why we've written it out fully here and also recorded a version, which you can download at **innerwisdomkit.com.**

The Sacred Truce

Before you begin, create a safe, sacred space for this truce, one where you won't be distracted or feel self-conscious. Create the physical space where you literally have three spaces to sit: one for you, one for your Inner Wisdom, and one for your Inner Mean Girl. This could be at your dining room table or in your living room; you can set up some cushions on the floor near your sacred self-love altar or even do it outside in nature, whatever feels right for you. Just make sure everyone has a designated spot.

Then, you'll need to turn off the outside world so that you can deeply access your inner world. Begin the inner journey by taking a few deep breaths. Close your eyes with your hand on your heart. With each breath in and out, feel and imagine yourself calling this sacred truce. As you feel yourself slowing down and tuning inward, we are going to ask you to take a series of four deep breaths, with your hand still on heart, imagining yourself summoning these two forces within you to the sacred truce table. With the first deep breath, summon your Inner Wisdom to the peace talks and to her seat. With your second deep breath, call in your Inner Mean Girl, who is ready to be reformed, and imagine her taking her seat. With your third breath, call yourself to these peace talks and feel your body at the truce table. With your fourth breath, for good measure, call in some energy from the Divine, breathing and feeling a beautiful circle of light surrounding all three of you so that all of you can feel really safe.

When you open your eyes, imagine that your Inner Wisdom is sitting in her place, with big smiles and a twinkle in her eye, helping you relax even more, reminding you that all is well. Imagine also that your IMG has taken her spot at the table, and she seems patient, willing, eager, and even ready to be redeployed into a new job.

Begin the meeting by saying out loud, talking directly to your IMG and Inner Wisdom, "We have come here with a distinct purpose. We are calling a truce. No more warring between us or fighting for control. It's time for peace. We all want the same thing, to have the best life possible—full of love, grace, abundance, and joy. And we have to stop fighting with each other or that is never going to happen." Pause. Breathe. "Look, each of you at this table has special skills and talents; we must use them for good and in service to my best life, or we will all just continue to suffer. Agree?" Pause. Breathe. Imagine your Inner Mean Girl and your Inner Wisdom nodding heads.

Continue: "The time has come to stand in our full power, and I need for us to band together so that we can create the most amazing life possible, beyond any of our wildest dreams. It's time for us to get on the same page. It's time for us to <insert what you are really desire for yourself>." Pause. Breathe.

Imagine looking over to your Inner Wisdom, who is full of love and compassion, as are you. And then look directly into your Inner Mean Girl's eyes, as if she were sitting right there with you, and say out loud, in your most reassuring voice, "Sweetie, we are safe. Thank you so much for protecting me. I know that you were trying to <insert what you believe she was trying to do for you>. I know that you feel like it isn't safe to stop doing this. But we are here to let you know the time has come to release the role you've had for such a long time. You can let go, and we need you to, because what you are doing is no longer helping me; it's hurting me." Pause. Breathe. Really feel how these IMG actions and thoughts are hurting you.

Remember all the ways in which she has bullied or sabotaged you and see how her acts were ones of self-preservation. Allow yourself to feel compassion toward yourself and your Inner Mean Girl for doing the best you could at the time based on what you knew. And then, from a place of true self-compassion, reassure your Inner Mean Girl that you want her to stay, saying, "We don't want you to go away. We love you. We want to find you a new job, one that you love and that makes our lives better." There is just one more reassurance that she needs before she knows for certain it's safe for her to leave the job that she has done so well for so long. Ask her, "What is one thing you need from me in order to feel safe enough to leave this current job?" Allow the answer to bubble up from deep inside; allow your Inner Wisdom to help you find the answer. Then look your Inner Mean Girl in the eyes and tell her—that scared, smaller part of you— the exact words what she needs to hear to know that it's safe to try something new.

After hearing those words, take a breath, imagine your Inner Mean Girl and your Inner Wisdom taking a breath, and feel a sense of relief coming over you and your IMG—relief that she no longer needs to steal your dreams; keep you doing, doing, and doing; find horrible people for you to date; numb you out; and so on—she doesn't need to do those sabotaging things anymore, and she is actually happy about it!

Now that your Inner Mean Girl has let go, and you are all breathing easier, with curiosity ask your IMG, "<Inner Mean Girl name>, what are you really good at?" Give her the space to answer that question and add on to what you see her skills and talents to be, acknowledging them as skills and talents.

And continue: "Given that you are so good at <her skills>, what job would you like to have now? What could you do that would help us instead of hurt us?" Look to your Inner Wisdom, who joins in solidarity, and brainstorm potential new roles for your reformed Inner Mean Girl. Continue throwing out ideas and thoughts until you feel the rightness of one in your body. Once you have a role for her, ask her, "Would you be willing to take the new job of <insert title>?" And once you find a new potential role that she seems agreeable to, ask her, "How will you use your energy and skills in this new job?" Pause. Breathe. Listen for the answer. If you agree, bestow her with a new title and name.

In true team spirit, ask her, "What do you need from me in order to succeed in your new job?" Ask yourself what words you can say or what transformation tool you can use when she gets scared and goes back to her old ways and habits to protect you. This is essential, because just like anyone new to something, she will have moments when she reverts to old behaviors; you want her permission to know how you can calm her down and take care of both of you to feel safe and loved.

Reassure her that her new job can be on a trial basis. She doesn't need to commit to doing it forever.

Thank your Inner Mean Girl for being so honest and willing. Thank your Inner Wisdom for her guidance. Thank the three of you for coming together in solidarity of self-love to call a truce and start working together as a team.

To complete this ritual truce, take a deep breath and put your hands out to your Inner Mean Girl on one side and your Inner Wisdom on the other, close your eyes, and make a pact and commitment together—a commitment to fully and freely be your most true self, a commitment to allow your Inner Wisdom to lead the way in all your thoughts and choices, a commitment to your IMG's new job. Add any other commitments you need to make. Say the commitments out loud, imagining you are all saying them together.

Seal the deal by bringing each hand to your heart. With the first hand, imagine you are bringing your reformed Inner Mean Girl into your heart. Lifting the other hand, imagine your Inner Wisdom also coming into your heart. With both hands on your heart, feel a golden light wrapping around you, and these two forces within you, creating a circle of love around you, melding and integrating you all together. Take a few deep breaths to really feel the integration in your body and close the truce; feel excited by the new job of your IMG and her transformation; feel deeply connected to the presence of your Inner Wisdom; and feel empowered that your IMG is no longer running the show. You are now stepping more freely into the life you truly desire for yourself.

Superpower Tool: The Inner Mean Girl Wisdom Treaty

Just like warring countries create and sign a treaty after a truce, having a treaty for yourself, your reformed Inner Mean Girl, and your Inner Wisdom is a wise move. Think of it this way: while your IMG may be in total agreement now to try out this new job, the minute something happens that triggers one of your hot spots or activates an old fear-filled neural pathway, your IMG is going to freak out and likely try to revert to her old ways. When you are learning or trying something new and things get a little scary or you feel vulnerable, it's normal to go back to old patterns as a way to cope.

This treaty you are about to create, sign, and commit to is like a living, breathing document you can wave in the face of your IMG when she gets scared and tries to go back to her old job and ways to say, "Hey, remember that we signed this agreement and promised each other that we were going to create inner peace, not inner warfare?" And then you can refer back to what and how you all agreed to operate and get back on track.

To create your personal treaty, get out your Inner Wisdom journal or grab a fresh piece of paper and use the five treaty starters on page 221 to write out this powerful agreement. Making this visual and writing it

THE INNER MEAN GiRL WiSDOM TREATY

♥ Today, on <date>, my Inner Mean Girl, <name and archetype> has willingly relinquished the job of <what she used to do for you>.

♥ She has willingly taken on the new job of <new job title>.

♥ She said yes to this new job on the condition that <what she needed from you to know it was safe to leave her old post>.

♥ She has promised to use her energy and skills of <energy and skills> to help me <focus and benefit of new role>.

♥ In order for her to succeed in this new role, when she gets scared or riled up, I need to say/do <insert the words or the superpower tool you've agreed will help your Inner Mean Girl>.

out activates the intuitive, creative centers in your brain, which are the places that will give you the power to stop old pathways and patterns from sabotaging your breakthrough. It works wonders; trust us—make the treaty. For extra inspiration, we also created an Inner Mean Girl Treaty template you can download and use from the Inner Wisdom Kit, **innerwisdomkit.com.**

Sign your name and your Inner Mean Girl's name, date it, and there you go, signed, sealed, and delivered!

Give Your Inner Mean Girl a Makeover

Now that your Inner Mean Girl has taken her new job and you've made this truce, she deserves a reward, and so do you, something to symbolize her transformation. We recommend an IMG makeover, because what girl doesn't love that?! This could include a new wardrobe, a new hairdo, a facelift, new ways for her to use her old tools, and of course, a new name.

IT'S CHRISTINE HERE. When I redeployed Get on It Gloria, my Doing Addict, she got the works. She was in pretty wacky shape before the new job: crazy red hair, a bad suit, and a brown clipboard she always kept with her with an annoying pen she would *tap tap tap* to remind me of how much I had to do. She had bad shoes; bad thick, wool tights; and bad glasses. When we gave her the new job of Rock Star Assistant, the old name and old getup didn't fit. So first we changed her name to I've Got It Gloria! to signify her new role as the person who could hold all the tasks that I had to get done. That way I didn't have to remember them, hold on to them, and feel pressured by them. Next we got her a new clipboard, a big one that was big enough to hold my ever-increasing number of responsibilities. Whenever I would feel the pressure of having to do something, I would just yell over to Gloria, "Hey, Gloria, put it on the clipboard!" And whoosh. Pressure off of me! This clipboard wasn't some dingy, brown one. Oh no, it was green (for abundance and love) with big, white polka dots (for play and fun!). Finally, we had to get her a new outfit. We burned the gray suit and bad shoes and hose (we didn't want to pass that negative energy on by donating them to Goodwill), and we got her a snazzy, supercool running suit with a fabulous pair of tennis shoes. Hip and functional at the same time, so she didn't have to sweat it, and neither did I!

One of the added side benefits that you should know about when you redeploy your Inner Mean Girl is often real, live people will show up in your life to reflect these new roles—again, your inner transformation showing up as outward manifestation. Pretty cool, huh? My transformation marked the beginning of always having an assistant in real life. Since the transformation, I have had three different real-life assistants, all rock stars and masters at holding all of my to dos so I didn't have to. And just like with Gloria, when something new to do comes along, I send them an email; they keep the master list so I don't have to. As a result, I get more done, have more fun, and sweat it way less.

Let's give your Inner Mean Girl that makeover and provide some extra motivation and also some extra fun for you. Seriously, you've given so much of your energy and time to reach this point let's seal the deal on your IMG's new job. There are three areas to consider in your makeover process. Brainstorm with these in your journal and have fun with these, and then in the superpower challenge we will give you a dare to bring this all to life so you can see the transformation with your own eyes.

Makeover Area 1: Her new name.

What does your IMG want to be called now that she has her new role? If your Inner Mean Girl didn't give you a new name at the sacred truce meeting, what would you like to call her? Something that feels good when you think about having her on your personal support team. She could receive a title, like Elizabeth's IMG, who got elevated to Queen.

You can drop or replace the bully part of her name, or change her name altogether.

Makeover Area 2: Her tools.

How can the tools she used to torment you be transformed to support you? This could be a new, more magical and helpful version of a weapon she used to use, like Get on It Gloria's improved clipboard so that her old skills could be redirected. If your IMG didn't have a tool before or you can't determine how to transform it, consider what tool she would love to use to be helpful instead of hurtful. Use your imagination!

Makeover Area 3: Her new look and feel.

What clothing does she need to do her new job? Imagine taking her on a shopping spree for a complete wardrobe refresh. In her new essence, what is the style and what are the colors that reflect her? And what accessories can you add to keep her fun and bright? Remember to consider getting a new hairdo, makeup and accessories too.

Superpower Challenge: Activate Your Creativity and Bring Your IMG Transformation to Life

One of the pieces of wisdom that we hope we have impressed on you throughout these steps is the power of your creativity—including words, images, and movement. We have learned that to successfully transform, we must go beyond words and thoughts. We need to bring things to life through creative expression and imagery. We would be remiss if we didn't bring this IMG transformation to life without a visual representation of the internal shift, something you can touch and see. Because the visual shift, along with the spiritual, emotional, and intellectual shifts you have experienced, will make your transformation so much more real for you. And will help you be more successful in keeping your IMG working for you in partnership with your Inner Wisdom.

Our challenge to you is for you to activate your creativity and take one action to bring this Inner Mean Girl transformation into physical form, and to do it or begin to do it in the next twenty-four hours. Choose one or more of the four options below and materialize this makeover:

1. **Draw or find a new picture of your reformed IMG.** Bring her new name, wardrobe, and tools to life by drawing her yourself or by finding a new image. Christine did this with her reformed Doing Addict below.

2. **Make her weapon into a magical tool.** Buy an object that represents her former weapon and then use your creativity to transform it. Just like Elizabeth did when she transformed a plain garden shovel into a magical glitter shovel that could remove emotional garbage.

THE OLD GET ON IT GLORIA   THE NEW AND IMPROVED
I'VE GOT IT GLORIA

3. **Draw or paint a big heart over your original Inner Mean Girl.** As you draw the heart, consider that you are blanketing this IMG with love so that she doesn't have to feel scared anymore. Make sure to include her new name on this picture.

4. **Find a sacred object that signifies the sacred truce that was made.** A symbol or metaphor of her new role in your life could be something like a mirror with a heart on it for a reformed Comparison Queen or a feather or a smiley face to lighten up a reformed Worrywart.

TRANSFORMATION TALE: I Took a Stand for Myself to Break Through No Matter What

by Lisa Nichols, *New York Times* bestselling author, speaker, and breakthrough specialist

For the first thirty years of my life, I never questioned what people in authority positions told me to believe about myself. My English teacher told me I was the weakest writer she had ever met; my speech teacher was adamant that I should never speak or teach in public. I just believed what they said about who I was and what I could be. As a result, my mind operated on a self-sabotaging belief system that for years kept me broke emotionally, spiritually, physically, and financially.

Even though I had a deep soul desire to teach, speak, and write, my Inner Mean Girl, having collected evidence of my lack of qualifications for years, would tell me, "Lisa, you are not qualified to inspire people. You are not smart enough. You have no degree. Get real—you were born in South Central Los Angeles, your son's father is in prison, and you got an F in speech!"

So, no matter how much I tried to follow my dreams to inspire, speak, and teach, the self-sabotaging belief system my Inner Mean Girl had constructed in my mind would drive me to give up on myself and sabotage all my hard work. And no matter how hard I tried or worked, I just couldn't break through to success.

Until the day when the burning in my belly—my Inner Wisdom's fire—became bigger than the conversation in my head, and my entire life changed. It happended on one of the lowest and highest days of my life, as most breakthroughs do. For me the breakthrough happened while standing at an ATM, needing twenty dollars to buy diapers for my son. The problem was I only had eleven dollars to my name; too prideful to ask for help, I instead chose to wrap my son in a towel for two days while I waited for my welfare check to come in. It was in this break-down moment, which became my breakthrough mind-set moment, that I realized I had a choice—I could keep letting these sabotaging patterns run my life, or I could press reset and transform my life.

You can guess probably—given that I am a six-time bestselling author and I speak around the world to big companies and huge audiences—that I chose the breakthrough. I looked at my son, Jelani, that day and told him, "Mommy will never be this broke again." In that instant, I made up my mind that I could be more than what other people had told me I could be. I made up my mind to be the person I always knew myself to be. I didn't have the answer or the plan, but taking back command of my mind—from my Inner Mean Girl and all the people of "authority" I had given my power to—I knew that I was done with my old patterns.

Breaking through requires fierce and humbling honesty. I had to look at every single part of my life that was in breakdown—my relationships, finances, parenting, personality, work, everything. I had to open myself up to learn from people I didn't know. Not from traditional academia but from trainers, coaches, people who knew transformation. It wasn't easy, but breakthroughs aren't supposed to be. I didn't have money, so I got a loan for five thousand dollars to pay for my first workshop. And I had to be willing to let the old me die to become who I knew I truly always was—even if that meant my family didn't accept the new me.

It was my Inner Wisdom who told me I could rise above all the doubt and fear. She helped me believe I was qualified to teach. She told me that while I may not be credentialed to teach calculus, given the number of breakdowns and breakthroughs I've had in my life, I was perfectly suited as a breakthrough specialist. And I chose to take that belief on to motivate me forward.

Since my big breakthrough, I've never stopped. I've broken through limiting set points again and again in my finances, business, work, and personal well-being, and my life has continued to be full of more abundance, happiness, and love as a result. You are never done evolving and raising your mind and experience to match the ever-expanding expression that is the Divine, fabulous one-of-a-kind you. And that's a life worth living. It may not always be easy, but it's never boring!

INSPIRED ACTION

Put Your Inner Mean Girl and Inner Wisdom to Work for You—Commit to a Breakthrough

Now that we've reformed and transformed your Inner Mean Girl, given her a full makeover, and put your Inner Wisdom in her rightful place of leadership, we won't let you finish this transformation without having you make a specific breakthrough. We want to make sure that all of the hard work you've done sticks—that you keep the momentum to shift those sabotaging neural pathways and habits into supportive ones. And that you continue to experience the shift from sacrificing and bullying yourself to supporting and loving yourself in real, tangible ways.

The truth is, Inner Mean Girls do better when you give them something to focus on and direct their energy toward, especially when they are learning and you are creating new supportive habits and neural pathways in your brain. Since your IMG is just getting used to her new job, we are going to choose an assignment for her to work on with your Inner Wisdom—a personal breakthrough that you would love to have in any area of your life where you are ready to shift a self-sabotaging habit and pattern. Specifically, here's the assignment:

1. Choose one self-sabotaging pattern or toxic habit that you are ready to break through.

2. Take a stand to support yourself with compassion and loving truth as you break on through to the other side!

3. Send your Inner Mean Girl and Inner Wisdom out on assignment for forty days to create this breakthrough for you.

When you stay committed and devoted to yourself, you can experience significant breakthroughs. The important thing to remember is to start where you are; small changes can yield mighty results. The key is to stay compassionate with yourself as you make your way through your breakthrough.

Step 1: Choose your breakthrough.

Isn't it exciting that you get to have a breakthrough with a sabotaging pattern or toxic habit that is creating stress or unhappiness for you? This could be one of your Inner Mean Girl hot spots that you said you were sick and tired of, or a toxic habit that you can see and feel the consequences of, or just something that you would like to be different. Your mission is to choose the pattern and habit you are ready to break through.

The key is to choose a pattern or habit that is simple, specific, and something that you can be successful with in the short term. Your IMG may try to persuade you to choose either change or a breakthrough that is way too hard. But your Inner Wisdom will choose what is ripe, ready, and reasonable for transformation today. So what pattern or habit are you sick and tired of and ready for a breakthrough in? Use this format to get the words out so that you can get clear:

> "I commit to releasing my self-sabotaging pattern of . . .
> I commit to embracing the self-loving pattern of . . .
> I am creating a <insert your specifics> breakthrough!"

Here are a few examples:

I commit to releasing my self-sabotaging pattern of overworking and exhausting myself. I commit to embracing the self-loving pattern of leaving work by 6:30 PM each day. I am creating a self-care breakthrough!

I commit to releasing my self-sabotaging pattern of mindlessly eating in front of the TV after the kids go to bed. I commit to embracing the self-loving pattern of moving my body while watching my favorite shows. I am creating a body breakthrough!

Step 2: Take a stand and break through.

It's one thing to say you want a breakthrough—it's another thing to take the stand for yourself to have it. You have to be committed and devoted to yourself to experience significant breakthroughs. It's critical to practice preventive care with breakthroughs by being honest and saying YES to the things you need to support you in this breakthrough and saying NO to the things that will sabotage you.

IT'S AMY HERE. I remember vividly the day many years ago that I made the commitment to break through the toxic habit and sabotaging pattern of spending beyond my means and running up credit card debt. I embraced the self-loving habit of getting real about my finances and setting up systems to create true wealth. I was really ready to hand the reigns of my life over to my Inner Wisdom and take a stand to create a positive financial future. But I knew I needed to say yes and no to some specific things, so I made the following declaration to myself and the world. I say no to:

- ♥ Using credit cards
- ♥ Chaos and disorganization with my finances
- ♥ Undercharging for my services

And I say yes to:

- ♥ Creating a monthly spending plan and sticking with it
- ♥ Hiring a bookkeeper to take over my household and business financial organization and meeting with her each month to stay honest
- ♥ Generating more money in my business in ways that are creative and inspiring

Making these declarations gave me support as I went through the breakdown-to-breakthrough process because they gave me permission to stay true to myself—to say no to what needed to be let go of and to say yes to what I needed to support me. It was miraculous to see the financial turnaround that happened for my family and myself after just forty days. My income dramatically increased, I felt peace around money, and we became free of credit card debt within a year.

Now it's your turn to do the same. Write out a list of the all things you need to say yes to and no to in order to support your breakthrough—remember, ask your Inner Wisdom. Choose three yesses and three nos, and make them actionable and specific, not so grandiose that they aren't grounded in physical reality.

Either on a separate piece of paper or using the Breakthrough Stand Promise and Proclamation on the next page as your inspired guide, write out and speak out your stand for yourself.

Step 3: Send your Inner Mean Girl and Inner Wisdom on assignment for forty days.

When it comes to making changes in order to create new routines and patterns in our lives, most of us start out with gusto but run out of steam and give up because it's too hard—or because we get too hard on ourselves. We won't let that happen to you! So now we bestow upon you

MY BREAKTHROUGH STAND

I hereby declare by the power vested in me by myself and my Inner Wisdom that:

I, <your name>, commit to releasing my self-sabotaging pattern of <the old pattern>.

I commit to embracing the self-loving pattern of <the new pattern>.

I am creating a <your specifics> breakthrough!"

I promise to support myself with compassion and loving truth, and therefore:

I say NO! to:

♥

♥

♥

I say YES! to:

♥

♥

♥

the superpower tool known as the Forty-Day Self-Love Practice—do anything for forty days as an act of devotion and commitment to love yourself and you can have a breakthrough, scientists and spiritual teachers agree.

Science says it takes twenty-five to thirty days of conscious, mindful effort for you to create a new neural pathway, new habit, thought pattern, and belief. Yogis, metaphysicians, and others from many spiritual traditions have taught and practiced for thousands of years that if you can stay committed, devoted, and focused for *forty* days, you can break habits and patterns and have powerful personal breakthroughs. It's interesting that while the numbers aren't the same, they're close enough to show that spiritual teachers were perhaps ahead of science in realizing how long it takes to create new patterns. For example, in the Hebrew Bible, the rains fell for forty days and forty nights, and in Christianity, Lent lasts for forty days. Metaphysicians say that the number forty metaphorically means "enough," and here at Inner Mean Girl Reform School, we agree that forty days is enough to break a self-sabotaging pattern or habit. Because while the mind may only take twenty-five to thirty days to break the old neural pathway and habits, it takes an additional ten days for the head, heart, and spirit to align.

Forty-day practices are simple in design but aren't always easy to complete. Your first step is to count today as day one and then count out forty days from now and mark that as the Day Forty Celebration on your calendar. This will create an energetic container for the forty days and remind you to set space to reflect on and celebrate what has shifted for you. Release expectation of how it will happen, surrender to the process, and know that if you just practice two simple touchstones—a daily sacred date and an increased daily awareness for forty days—you will experience some level of breakthrough. Remember, your Inner Wisdom and Inner Mean Girl are working for you! Here is the simple but powerful way to construct your Inner Wisdom and IMG assignment for the next forty days:

*Every Morning: Commit to yourself and
your breakthrough every day.*

As part of your Inner Wisdom sacred morning date, reread your breakthrough stand to yourself. As you progress, reflect on what you are noticing with compassion, not judgment. Do this in your journal or have an internal conference with your Inner Wisdom and Inner Mean Girl. Ask for evidence of what happens when you choose self-love over self-sabotage and self-bullying. Celebrate your progress, notice your insights, and give yourself compassion where you are still learning.

*Day-to-Day: Be aware of the pattern, reflect with
compassion, and experiment with new responses.*

Whenever you notice the self-sabotaging pattern coming up, reflect on how you can do things differently next time. Remember that you are learning! In moments when you are able to stop yourself in the midst of a self-sabotaging pattern, consciously choose to change your response using any of the superpower tools or ideas you've learned over these seven steps. And over the forty days, as you continue reflecting and experimenting with new responses to situations, you will start creating a new neural pathway that supports the new self-loving patterns.

By day forty, you will have started making new grooves in your brain, and you will begin to trust your new ways of being and responding. Your autopilot response will have been broken in at least one profound way, and you will be well on your way to rewiring your brain into supportive and loving patterns. This doesn't mean that your Inner Mean Girl will never try to get you into her toxic habits again, but you will be much better prepared to deal with her (and win!).

You are now well on your way to creating a forty-day breakthrough, loving yourself instead of bullying yourself forward into the life your heart and soul desire.

CONCLUSION

AN INVITATION TO JOIN THE SELF-LOVE REVOLUTION

When we came together to teach the first Inner Mean Girl Reform School class, we had no idea that we were birthing a revolution to free women and girls everywhere from self-bullying. Since that day, we've been joined by thousands of women on six continents in solidarity to give relief to the struggle and wasted energy that occurs as a result of the cruel things we say to ourselves and the immense pressure we put on ourselves to do and be it all perfectly.

It was after teaching our first class that we would see that something epic and empowering was occurring. We both still remember vividly sitting in Amy's office on her blue velvet couch reading the responses from a survey we had sent out to participants of Inner Mean Girl Reform School. One by one, as we read the women's stories of personal transformation and breakthrough, tears streamed down both of our faces as we witnessed the vulnerability, the common themes, and the courageous stands these women had taken for themselves. That's when we knew we had to lead this revolution forward.

Today, even though we may not have personally met you yet, we witness you heart to heart in your stand for living an Inner Wisdom–led life filled with unapologetic self-love. We acknowledge you for your courage to give up negative thinking, to put an end to self-sabotaging patterns, and to do so from a place of absolute compassion, knowing that you don't have to do anything to deserve compassion and love—it's your birthright.

We witness you reclaiming and strengthening your intuitive feminine power, daring to listen to and trust your Inner Wisdom and its guidance above all else. We know that you and every woman and girl in your life will be better off because you have made these choices and because you have committed to continuing the ongoing practice of living from your Inner Wisdom and loving yourself.

In recognition of your commitment to yourself, we invite you to be part of our self-love revolution to put an end to self-bullying, negative self-talk, and putting so much pressure on ourselves. We won't stop until every Inner Mean Girl on the planet has been transformed and every girl and woman has remembered what a powerful, divine force she has inside of her that knows exactly what she needs, who she is, and how she is meant to live her life, regardless of what anyone else has to say.

We know that when women come together, shift happens. We need the support of each other to stay committed to ourselves. We need sisterhood to have the courage to be changemakers within our societal and family systems. And we need love from each other when we fail, fall short, and are just plain tired and need a rest.

There are several ways you can become part of our self-love revolution and also ways that you can receive additional support, sisterhood, and love from us, which we've included on the following page.

We stand shoulder to shoulder and heart to heart with you as we create a world in which every girl and woman is filled with love, compassion, and kindness for herself, confidently following the truth of her Inner Wisdom, loving and trusting herself completely.

With great heart,
Amy and Christine

Four Powerful Ways to Participate

1: Get Support for Your Inner Mean Girl Transformation and Inner Wisdom–Led Life

Inner Mean Girl Reform School offers two interactive programs with support from our coaches to help you to deepen your IMG transformation and strengthen your mastery of living a life that is in alignment with your heart and soul. These programs can be taken from anywhere in the world—all you need is internet access. All participants of these programs become part of our inner tribe and receive special support throughout the year.

This is a comprehensive, interactive program in which we take you step by step through the Inner Mean Girl Reform School transformation process, including recorded teaching sessions, videos, expert interviews, workbooks and more. This course contains additional material and teachings not included in this book and is a full multimedia experience. If you would love to receive accountability, community, and live support, we created this just for you.

Go to **innermeangirlreformschool.com** to find out more.

This is a forty-day practice that guides and supports you to give up your Inner Mean Girl's toxic habits and self-sabotaging patterns. Supported with daily emails, videos, and more, you will receive and put into practice self-love antidotes for common IMG toxic habits—including compari-son, perfectionism, obligation, guilt, and more—creating new supportive habits instead.

Go to **innermeangirlcleanse.com** to find out more.

2: Share the Inner Mean Girl Transformation Process with Others

When many coaches, therapists, teachers, and women who work within systems that serve women and girls experience the power of this trans-formation, they want to share the tools, information, and processes. To find out more about how to share these tools with your communities, clients or the girls and women you love, go to **shareinnermeangirl.com**.

3: Join our Facebook Page

We love creating communities of women around the world who support and lift each other up. Join our Facebook page at **facebook.com/inner meangirl** to celebrate your wins, get support during an Inner Mean Girl attack, and receive inspiration from Amy and Christine.

4: Be a Self-Love Ambassador— Celebrate Self-Love Day, February 13

Every year thousands of women and girls around the world celebrate the international day of self-love on February 13 by hosting self-love parties or circles in their homes or throwing self-love events for their communities. They become ambassadors of self-love, sharing the message and power of loving ourselves in practical and fun ways. All self-love ambassadors receive a self-love kit and more. Participation is free and fun!

SELF LOVE DAY is Feb. 13

Go to **selfloveambassador.com** to find out more and sign up.

ACKNOWLEDGMENTS

This book never would have been created without our students—the women from all around the world who so daringly said yes to Inner Mean Girl Reform School, who participated both virtually and in person in our retreats and online programs, and who shared their hearts and journeys in our intensive inner wisdom circles. Your honesty, your courage, and your deep devotion to yourself inspired us to continue to grow this work and make it available to even more women and girls. You are the fire in our hearts that ignites us to keep growing and going . . . thank you for sharing your stories, your truths, and your love.

This book, and the global movement to transform women's inner critics and empower women to trust and live by their Inner Wisdom, was only possible with the support of a tribe of angels:

To our team: Sarah Mardell, Lucie Mosny, Heather Wells, Tarja Sovay, Noah Martin, Shannon Kaiser, Nikko Bivens, Lea Guthrie, Katherine Torrini, Ariana Pritchett, Melanie Bates, Jennifer Wallace, and Michele PW. Thank you for holding us and this work and for giving your genius so it could flourish.

To our soul sisters and brothers that helped our partnership and work flourish, grow, and transform: Alexis Neely, Carol Allen, Lisa Nichols, Kristine Carlson, Karen Russo, Shiloh Sophia McCloud, Lissa Rankin, Mike Robbins, and Steve Sisgold. Thank you for holding space, sharing your gifts, and reminding us of our truth.

To all who helped birth this book into being: Michele Martin and Steve Harris, our agents. Thank you for being a stand for us and this work. To the team at Beyond Words, especially Emily,

ACKNOWLEDGMENTS

Gretchen, Lindsay, Emmalisa, Jackie, and Whitney, thank you for your clarity, commitment, and collaboration to make this the best book possible.

And to all of the people who have supported Inner Mean Girl Reform School over the years: Claire Zammit, SARK, Arielle Ford, Jennifer Longmore, Maggie Ostara, Christine Hassler, Marci Shimoff, Sam Bennett, Brian Burt, Sarah Jenks, Christy Whitman, Stacey Morgenstern, and Carey Peters. Thank you for your belief in the power of this work.

FROM AMY... My love and thanks to my two glorious daughters, Annabella and Evie Rose, who are my constant source of inspiration and support. Thank you for choosing me to be your mama. Thank you to my husband, Rob, who is my rock. Your goodness takes my breath away. And for my beloved family: my mom and dad; Laura and Todd; Becky and Brian; Kathy and Cardo; Pat and Sue; Max, Ellie, Sam, Brody; Adam and Aubrey; and my tribe of friends, including the Mindful Mamas and my LA family. Thank you for always believing in me. And for all my clients, readers, and students: thank you for being my mirrors, allowing me to teach and coach what I most need to learn.

FROM CHRISTINE... Although I write books primarily for women, the core of my support, the person who has been there for me always, to support me emotionally and spiritually (not to mention make sure I eat and rest when writing!) is my soul partner Noah Martin. Thank you, Noah, for supporting and caring for me so that I could have the strength and focus to bring this work to the world for women and girls.

And for all the souls I've worked with and walked with over the years, thank you for your courage and willingness to choose the path of love (especially self-love) no matter what. And to my spiritual mentors, healers, and soul family who have supported me to transform my own Inner Mean Girls, so I could remember the truth of who I am, and that it's safe to trust love again, thank you. I love you!

THE INNER MEAN GIRL HALL OF FAME

A t the Inner Mean Girl Reform School, we've helped tens of thousands of women reform their Inner Mean Girls. On the pages that follow, we've gathered up real pictures and exposé excerpts of IMGs created by our students, as well as one of Amy's daughters and one of Christine's goddess daughters. Use these images for inspiration as you bring your own IMG(s) to life. They are awesome reminders that you are not alone and that it's okay to laugh at just how ridiculous our Inner Mean Girls can be. Remember to ditch any Inner Comparison Queen Big Fat Lies— let inspiration lead the way.

Want even more inspiration? Check out the full Inner Mean Girl Hall of Fame at **innerwisdomkit.com** and submit your own Inner Mean Girl.

PATTY PESSIMIST

half empty

Archetypes: Comparison Queen and Rejection Queen

Big Fat Lies: "You'll never fit in anywhere/find anyone to love you."

"Why haven't you found anybody/gotten over him?"

"You should be better at being more feminine, being happy/positive, smiling more."

Contributed by: Jennifer

WORRYING WINNY

Archetypes: Worrywart and Head Tripper
Big Fat Lies: "You're going to die in the dark alone."
"Nothing will work out for you."
Contributed by: Kelly

MALICIOUS MOLLY

Archetypes: Good Girl and Perfectionist (with a little Comparison Queen thrown in)

Big Fat Lies: "I think that you are getting chubby."

"Why haven't you worked out today?"

"You'll never attract a man!"

"You should be better at controlling your eating and drinking."

"And another thing: don't forget to make everyone in your life happy."

Contributed by: Amy

MEAN MILICENT

Archetypes: Comparison Queen, Perfectionist, Achievement Junkie, and Good Girl

Big Fat Lies: "Why haven't you become more spiritual *and* achieved financial freedom by now?"
"You're taking too long!"

Contributed by: Shantini

CONCRETE CONNIE

Archetypes: Comparison Queen and Martyr

Big Fat Lies: "I will never change so there's no point in trying."
"Your attempts to change will never stick. Why even bother?"

Contributed by: Tina

STEALTH STELLA

Archetypes: Comparison Queen, Doing Addict, and Good Girl
Big Fat Lies: "You don't measure up to everyone else."
"You are not enough."
"You better be a good girl and not rock the boat or shine too brightly."
Contributed by: Lea

BRUNHILDA BRUTE

Archetypes:	Doing Addict and Perfectionist
Big Fat Lies:	"You might as well give up now."
	"You will never keep your commitment to yourself (to exercise, lose weight, finish IMG Reform School!)"
	"What is your problem?"
	"How could you be so stupid?"
Contributed by:	Jane

VICIOUS VICTORIA

Archetypes: Comparison Queen

Big Fat Lies: "She is so much better than you!" "Be better at this like she is!"

Contributed by: Jane (age 11)

MONSTROUS MINLI

Archetypes: Good Girl and Invincible Superwoman

Big Fat Lies: "Don't be such a baby!" "You're fine." "You can't do it!"

Contributed by: Annabella (age 7)

INSTANT INNER MEAN GIRL DEACTIVATORS AND INNER WISDOM STRENGTHENERS

Throughout the book, we've given you some of our most powerful superpower tools, and we have two additional sets of tools that we think you will find handy in both deactivating your Inner Mean Girl and strengthening your Inner Wisdom:

> **Inner Mean Girl Deactivators:** Use when your IMG strikes to stop the attack, turn down her volume, and get through to your Inner Wisdom.

> **Inner Wisdom Strengtheners:** Use these sacred dates to strengthen your connection to your Inner Wisdom and your ability to communicate with her and trust her guidance.

Inner Mean Girl Deactivators

The "I Surrender" Plunge

Remember the Nestea Plunge commercials back in the day where the person falls back into the swimming pool? Same idea, except you fall backward, arms spread wide open, saying the words *I surrender*. (We recommend having a bed behind you!) Continue to surrender with your arms out to either side of you, saying, "I surrender," until you actually do. If the falling-back thing freaks you out, just put yourself on the ground, with your body in the surrender position (like a cross, with your arms out to the side) and say the words out loud again and again until you feel your IMG's grip release. Tears may come, and that's okay—that is a good sign of release.

The "Strike a Pose" Move

Reset your mentality by changing your physicality. When you're in the midst of a negative thought or heading toward a self-sabotaging Inner Mean Girl attack, pull the halt lever, stop dead in your tracks, and rearrange your physical body into a posture that matches what you'd like to be grooving on. Then, state the words you want to be thinking and watch your brain respond. Try this right now: look down at the floor and crunch your body into a tight ball and say, "I am happy to be alive." Your body and brain don't buy it, do they? Now try looking up toward the sky with your eyes wide open and a big smile and say, "I'm so sad and depressed." Doesn't work either, does it? Finally, say, "I'm happy to be alive," while looking up toward the sky with a big smile and arms wide open. Yes! That is what you want: congruency with your words and physical body shape equals love, peace, and happy-producing mental thoughts.

The Perspective Shift

Transform bad vibrations into good vibrations by changing your perspective and therefore your words. For example, instead of proclaiming, "I feel overwhelmed," try, "Wow, I have so much going on . . . I am so popular!" Or "I am so busy" becomes "It's a really intense time; I am going to make sure I take even better care of myself." Or the next time things feel chaotic or like you are in the midst of a breakdown, instead of judging yourself or going into a pit of despair, notice that a breakthrough is afoot, change your perspective, get curious and excited, and ask yourself, "What breakthrough is on its way?"

We also recommend outlawing the words: *should, must,* and *have to* and replacing them with words like *could, love,* and *choose to.* For example:

"I *should* go visit my mother" ➡	"I *choose* to go visit my mother."
"I *must* finish this." ➡	"I'd *love* to finish this!"
"I *have* to work this weekend." ➡	"I *could* work all weekend, but I *choose* to work Saturday and rest on Sunday."

The Love-Talk Stand

Remember in step six, you made a promise to give up self-bullying and choose compassion instead. Just like giving up smoking, sugar, or soda and telling yourself "I'm a nonsmoker" or "I don't drink soda" when offered, when your Inner Mean Girl offers you the opportunity to think negative thoughts about yourself, your life, or someone else, you decline. How? When you hear a Big Fat Lie begin to take form, stop dead in your tracks, stand tall, take a big deep breath, and from a place of unapologetic self-love say out loud, "Absolutely not. I gave up negative self-talk. We don't do this anymore!" This strong stand is a powerful pattern interrupter, as if you are literally grabbing the control switch from your IMG and taking command. Drawing a strong boundary will begin to calm your IMG down. Just like with a toddler, you need to calmly and lovingly remind her that you are in charge. She'll eventually back down because you stood up for yourself.

The Evidence Collector

The next time you feel an Inner Mean Girl belief creeping in, stop and notice how your brain, using its Reticular Activation System (RAS), is trying to collect evidence to support the IMG story, almost like a scanning gun that your IMG is using to pull all this negative energy in. Imagine pushing your IMG out of the way and giving your Inner Wisdom control of the RAS. Create the story or belief you want to be true and then ask your Inner Wisdom to go out and find evidence to support your empowering belief. For example, if your IMG is telling you how unsupported you are and is showing you all the ways that is true, stop and choose the belief that you are supported and ask your Inner Wisdom to help you find evidence to back this up.

We're sure you've noticed this phenomenon before. Let's say, for example, you bought a brand-new red Prius. You hit the road in your new car feeling snazzy, and you end up seeing a ton of red Priuses on the road. That is your RAS doing its job. You decided that red Priuses were important, because you now own one, and you want to reinforce that your decision to buy one was a good choice; therefore, your brain begins to point these red cars out to you. You can use this part of your brain to deliberately program your mind by choosing the exact messages, stories, and beliefs you wish to reinforce.

Inner Wisdom Strengtheners

What follows is a full spectrum of sacred dates with your Inner Wisdom—with the first few being ideas for your morning practice. This is foundational. Remember that a daily morning practice is required for you to successfully reform your Inner Mean Girl. No exception. Then you get to add on with afternoon hookups and love-filled evenings.

Sacred Morning Dates

These are sacred dates to do before you even leave your bed to make sure you start your day connected to your Inner Wisdom and to self-love.

1. **Take a self-love soak in bed.** Tell yourself what you need to hear most. When you first awake, open your eyes to register you are waking and then close your eyes. Wrap your arms around yourself as if you are giving yourself a hug. Imagine beautiful lavender or pink light wrapping around you like a warm, soft blankie. Ask your Inner Wisdom to tell you what loving words you most need to hear, and then say them to yourself silently or in a whisper, always beginning the sentence with your first name and the self-love statement. It could be, "Christine, you are doing enough." Or, "Amy, you are a great mom." Or you can just say, "Christine, I love you." Or, "Amy, you are loved." Repeat the words over and over again, saying them like you would say to someone you love, until you can feel the vibration of love come into your body. At first you may feel nothing. This is common. Sometimes it can take weeks or months to experience the compassion click when you get past the protection layers of your Inner Mean Girl. But eventually everyone does break through. We suggest faking it till you make it, just imagining what it would feel like to be wrapped in love and receive these love words, until you actually experience it. For extra help, consider getting yourself a pink, lavender, or fuzzy, soft blanket that gives you a physical sensation you love.

2. **Ask your Inner Wisdom for advice, directly.** Sometimes you just need your Inner Wisdom to give you a straight answer to a question you have. You need guidance, clarity, something to direct you on the right path. Your Inner Wisdom can always help, if you ask and if you also accept that her guidance may not be what you want to hear. You'll need to learn to decipher her guidance and learn to trust it.

She appreciates you asking her questions. Three powerful ways to communicate and ask her advice is through:

♥ **Writing or Journaling.** You become the vehicle for which she can guide your pen. Write your question: *Dear Inner Wisdom, <insert your question>.* If you don't have a question, write, *Hi, Inner Wisdom. What do I need to know today?* and pause, close your eyes, put your hand on your heart and take a breath and write what comes. Just let it flow, without judging. Stay out of your mind, which short-circuits your Inner Wisdom's ability to get through. Analyze later. If your handwriting gets messy, that's okay, keep flowing and decipher later.

♥ **Intuitive Drawing.** If no words come, or if your Inner Wisdom uses the seeing channel, spontaneously draw at least six things on one piece of paper in relation to your question and see what emerges. This technique was shared with us by master artist Sue Hoya Sellars, and it's brought forth the most amazing messages, especially if you practice for multiple days in a row. Using symbols and metaphors to communicate can be more powerful than words because they bypass the conscious, limiting mind.

♥ **Use Oracle Cards.** The word *oracle* means "message from the Divine," nothing spooky or weird about it—just a way to open the channels to connect to the Divine wisdom inside of you. Oracle cards are not about asking anything outside of you for information; they are not fortune-telling cards—they merely give words and symbols to the unexpressed divine wisdom inside of you. They can also be called wisdom decks, and they usually have a theme—like fairies, angels, goddesses, spirit animals, etc. Choose one that resonates for you personally. When using your cards, close your eyes, hold the deck in your hands, and ask your question or ask your

Inner Wisdom to give you guidance for the day. Pick a card and use your intuition and the description to decipher the message. Some of our favorite decks for beginners include all of Doreen Virtue's (for those that resonate with fairies or angels) or *Medicine Cards* by Jamie Sams and David Carson (if you are a nature or animal girl). For more advanced oraclers, our faves are the *13 Moon Oracle* by Ariel Spilsbury and *Tarot of the Spirit* by Pamela Eakins.

3. **Embody your Inner Wisdom.** Let her move through you. You don't have to sit still to connect with your Inner Wisdom. You can actually walk or even run when you do it consciously by being present to the steps you take, feeling your feet hit the ground, step by step, and being present to the surroundings around you. Take an inquiry with you to connect with your Inner Wisdom, take a gratitude walk where you express appreciation with each step, or go agenda-free to just be open to what she has to say. No cell phone, no to-do list running in your head, just total presence to what is. If running, walking, or hiking isn't your thing, then dance! Moving your body with music or with breath helps you open up the channels of self-expression. It's as easy as this: choose three songs that really open up your heart, download them onto a portable device, and every morning, dance and sing these songs as your morning practice. Do it in your bedroom or living room, or if you are feeling daring, do it in your driveway or in the park—who cares what others think! Less than ten minutes to pure bliss.

4. **Make a mind movie and watch it.** See the reality your heart desires to create and play it as a reality show every day. Your nonconscious mind responds the same to real and imagined ideas and thoughts, which is why things like vision boards and guided visualizations work and why high-performing athletes will envision winning the big game or meet before the actual day—to train their brains to create

what they want. Yes, even though the conscious brain knows that you are imagining, your subconscious mind responds as if it is true.

Use mental rehearsal to your advantage with your Inner Wisdom (instead of allowing your IMG to use it to imagine worst-case scenarios) and train your brain by seeing in your mind all the positive things you want to happen in your life. Just play a three-minute movie of the reality you choose to create, using your Inner Wisdom's visual and feeling channel. See it and feel it. You can fool your brain into starting to build the neural pathways to expect and respond to things as if you're wealthier, more in shape, more at peace.

5. **Ask your Inner Wisdom for protection, and zip up your energy fields.** Your Inner Wisdom loves helping you keep your energy fields clean and protected, as they help ward off Inner Mean Girl attacks during the day triggered by other people's energy. In less than three minutes, she can get you zipped up every day, with these three energy protectors. Think of it this way: you wouldn't leave the house without clothes on; you also don't want to leave the house energetically naked without your energetic shields on. Use these three energy protection tools, and you'll be ready to go into the world, protected with light and love, for real. You may not be able to see these things, but you will feel the difference.

♥ Ask your Inner Wisdom to place a bouquet of red roses with big thorns and vibrant petals and leaves with strong stems in front of you. This is called a sentry because, like a guard, it protects you from frontal energy assaults from others. Every morning, ask her to replace the flowers (they will usually be dead the next morning from absorbing outside energy).

♥ Ask her to wrap a vine of beautiful flowers around your entire body, any kind you love, surrounding you in a mantle of love for the day.

♥ Imagine a white bubble of light around the entire circumference of your body about a foot out from your physical body. Notice any places that seem dark or weak and ask her to send white light to smooth and secure those spots.

Sacred Afternoon Hookup: Tune in every day at 1:08 PM

Tuning in to your Inner Wisdom during the day is a very effective preventative measure against Inner Mean Girl attacks, increasing the probability that your Inner Wisdom will be the one making your choices. Both of us keep this sacred date with our Inner Wisdom every day, and have for years, and it takes less than thirty seconds. Here's how it goes. Given your Inner Wisdom broadcasts on 108.0 LOVE, what better time to tune in to her than 1:08 PM? At 1:08 PM every day, a peaceful-sounding alarm goes off on our phones. When we hear the sound of the gong or harps on our phones at 1:08 PM, whatever our Inner Wisdom told us that morning, we remember in that moment, reconnecting us to our center and ourselves. And for the times when we don't have something specific going on, we take this as a moment to breathe, connect with ourselves, and surrender to divine wisdom, reminding ourselves that the Universe is indeed conspiring in our favor. As an extra bonus, women around the world do this exact practice. So no matter what time zone you're in, you're likely connecting to a powerful circle of women at 1:08 PM who are tuning in to their Inner Wisdom right when you do. How powerful is that?!

Sacred Date Nights

1. **Make a Love Fest in Bed.** Get into bed and get all comfy, and then ask your Inner Wisdom, "What three wins did I have today?" or, "What are we grateful for?" Then answer yourself out loud, write the answers down, or simply close your eyes, put your hand on your

heart, and ask your Inner Wisdom to show you, tell you, help you feel (use her favorite way to communicate with you).

2. **Soak Together.** In our fast-paced society, it's really easy to become a shower person and reserve baths for special occasions when you "have" time. Stop waiting for time and start taking space for an energy soak in the evening, minimum once a week. This is not just a pampering moment—it's a must for anyone who wants to keep her energy centers clean and clear. An energy soak is a warm bath with good salts. The salt regulates your energy system and clears out your energy fields. We recommend pink Himalayan salt or Epsom salt. There are other good salts out there with scents like lavender and eucalyptus—just make sure the salts are not the commercialized, perfumed versions that end up adding more chemicals to your body. Go to stores that carry natural, organic products. You can also add to the experience by burning incense, lighting candles, and putting calming music on.

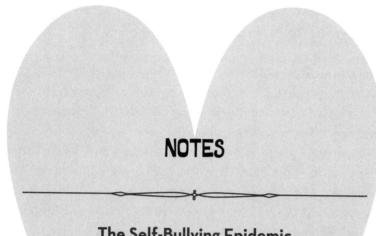

NOTES

The Self-Bullying Epidemic

1. Go Red for Women Editors, "Causes and Prevention of Heart Disease," American Heart Association, accessed July 7, 2014, https://www.goredforwomen.org/about-heart-disease/facts_about_heart_disease_in_women-sub-category/causes-prevention/.

2. "Easy Ways to Take the Edge Off," *ABC News*, April 22, 2009, http://abcnews.go.com/Health/video?id=7392433.

3. Ellen Frank, Danielle Novick, Azadeh Masalehdan, and Ken Duckworth (reviewers), "Women and Depression Fact Sheet," National Alliance on Mental Illness, November 2003, updated October 2009, http://www.nami.org/Template.cfm? Section=Women_and_Depression&Template=/ContentManagement/ContentDisplay.cfm&ContentID=89194.

4. Betsy Stevenson and Justin Wolfers, "Paradox of Declining Female Happiness," *American Economic Journal: Economic Policy 2009* 1, no. 2, (August 2009): 190–225, http://journalistsresource.org/wp-content/uploads/2013/01/WomensHappiness.pdf.

5. "What Are Eating Disorders?" National Eating Disorders Association, 2012, https://www.nationaleatingdisorders.org/sites/default/files/ResourceHandouts/General Statistics.pdf.

6. Oprah, "How Did I Let This Happen Again?" *O, The Oprah Magazine*, January 2009, http://www.oprah.com/spirit/Oprahs-Battle-with-Weight-Gain-O-January-2009-Cover.

7. Robin Madell, "Thriving or Surviving? Work-Life Balance Tips from Ariana Huffington," *U.S. News & World Report*, April 15, 2014, http://money.usnews.com/money/blogs/outside-voices-careers/2014/04/15/thriving-or-surviving-work-life-balance-tips-from-arianna-huffington.

8. "Super Soul Sunday; Elizabeth Gilbert, Part 1," OWN, the Oprah Winfrey Network, October 5, 2014, http://www.oprah.com/own-super-soul-sunday/Full-Episode -Elizabeth-Gilbert-Part-1-Video.

9. Marci Shimoff, *Happy for No Reason: 7 Steps to Being Happy from the Inside Out* (New York: Atria Books, 2008), 83.

Step 2

1. Ervin Laszlo, *The Chaos Point: The World at the Crossroads* (Newburyport, MA: Hampton Roads Publishing Co., Inc., 2006), ix.

Step 4

1. Tami Jackson, "Does the mind hear negative words?" Examiner.com, May, 2013, http:// www.examiner.com/article/does-the-mind-hear-negative-words.

Step 5

1. Alice Walker, *We Are the Ones We Have Been Waiting For: Inner Light in a Time of Darkness* (New York: The New Press, 2006), 300.

Step 6

1. Pema Chödrön, *When Things Fall Apart: Heart Advice for Difficult Times* (Boston: Shambhala, 1997), 99–100.

2. Kristin Neff, "Definition of Self-Compassion," accessed November 11, 2014, www.self -compassion.org/what-is-self-compassion/definition-of-self-compassion.html.

ABOUT THE AUTHORS

CHRISTINE ARYLO is a transformational teacher, internationally recognized speaker, and bestselling author of the official self-love guidebook, *Madly in Love with ME: The Daring Adventure to Becoming Your Own Best Friend*. After earning her MBA from the Kellogg School of Management at Northwestern University and climbing the corporate ladder for fifteen years, working for companies like The Gap, PepsiCo, and Kraft, she chose to devote her life to creating a new reality for women and girls, one based on self-love and true feminine power instead of the relentless pursuit of having to do, be, and have it all.

Christine is the founder of the international self-love movement and Self-Love Day on February 13; the author of the go-to book on love and relationships, *Choosing ME Before WE*; the cofounder with Amy Ahlers of Inner Mean Girl Reform School, the virtual self-love school for women; and the creator of a series of forty-day self-love practices. She also acts as a self-worth advocate and specialist for organizations that serve women and girls and a spiritual mentor for women leaders. Her dedication earned her the affectionate title the Queen of Self-Love.

Christine is often featured in the media—including CBS, ABC, FOX, WGN, and E! and in the *Huffington Post*, as well as at spas and conferences, and on stages around the world, including TEDx. She normally lives in California with her soul partner, Noah, but is known for her love of travel and spiritual adventure and exploration and so can often be found leading transformational conversations and sacred retreats around the world.

Go to **chooseselflove.com** to learn more about the self-love movement and receive the free self-love kit. Or visit **christinearylo.com** to learn more about Christine, her retreats, speaking, and mentorship.

AMY AHLERS, the Wake-Up Call Coach and bestselling author, is on a mission to put a stop to women being so darn hard on themselves. Since 2000, she has been an International Certified Life Coach, and is CEO of Wake-Up Call Coaching, cofounder of Inner Mean Girl Reform School with Christine Arylo, and cofounder of Find Your Calling with Lissa Rankin and Martha Beck. Amy is also the creator of the Mama Truth Circle, helping mamas embrace the whole truth of motherhood, messiness, and magic.

Amy has been a featured expert on lots of TV and radio shows and media outlets such as ABC and FOX. She loves lighting up the stage at events where she wakes people up to the voices of their Inner Wisdoms and helps them cultivate the courage to act on it. Her first book, *Big Fat Lies Women Tell Themselves: Ditch Your Inner Critic and Wake Up Your Inner Superstar* shot up to number one in several categories on Amazon, including Self-Help, Happiness, and Self-Esteem.

A 2010 recipient of the Women Who Dare Award from Girls Inc., she holds a BA from the University of California, earned the Certified Professional CoActive Coach (CPCC) designation from the Coaches Training Institute, and is a Master Coach Equivalent. Amy is known best for her unconditional love, relentless enthusiasm, and kick-ass truth telling. She loves noticing the everyday sacred. Amy resides in the San Francisco Bay Area, where she loves to snuggle with her beloved husband, Rob, and firecracker daughters, Annabella and Evie Rose.

Visit **wakeupcallcoach.com** to find out more about Amy, her celebrated programs, and to receive an inspiring free gift.

Connect with Christine and Amy Online

LIKE US ON FACEBOOK
facebook.com/christine.arylo
facebook.com/amyahlerscoach

CONNECT WITH US ON TWITTER
twitter.com/christinearylo
twitter.com/amyahlers

FOLLOW US ON INSTAGRAM
instagram.com/christinearylo
instagram.com/amyahlerscoach

SUBSCRIBE TO OUR YOUTUBE CHANNELS
youtube.com/user/selflovestation
youtube.com/user/wakeupcallcoaching

Connect with Inner Mean Girl Reform School Online

JOIN THE FACEBOOK COMMUNITY
facebook.com/innermeangirl

VISIT OUR WEBSITE
innermeangirl.com